THE SCAM THAT SHOOK A NATION

THE SCAM THAT SHOOK A NATION

THE NAGARWALA SCANDAL

PRAKASH PATRA | RASHEED KIDWAI

HarperCollins *Publishers* India

First published in India by HarperCollins *Publishers* 2024
4th Floor, Tower A, Building No. 10, DLF Cyber City,
DLF Phase II, Gurugram, Haryana – 122002
www.harpercollins.co.in

2 4 6 8 10 9 7 5 3 1

Copyright © Prakash Patra and Rasheed Kidwai, 2024

P-ISBN: 978-93-5699-862-9
E-ISBN: 978-93-5699-908-4

The views and opinions expressed in this book are the authors' own and the facts are as reported by them, and the publishers are not in any way liable for the same.

Prakash Patra and Rasheed Kidwai assert the moral right to be identified as the authors of this work.

All rights reserved. No part of this publication may be reproduced, stored in a retrieval system, or transmitted, in any form or by any means, electronic, mechanical, photocopying, recording or otherwise, without the prior permission of the publishers.

Typeset in 11.5/15.2 Adobe Garamond at
Manipal Technologies Limited, Manipal

Printed and bound in India by Replika Press Pvt. Ltd.

This book is produced from independently certified FSC® paper to ensure responsible forest management.

To

My parents Bidyutchhaya and Ganeshwar Patra
—Prakash Patra

Cousin and friend late Abdul Ali Kidwai
—Rasheed Kidwai

CONTENTS

Authors' Note   ix

SECTION I: THE PHONE CALL. THE HEIST. THE TRIAL

CHAPTER 1	The Loot	3
CHAPTER 2	The Ordeal	11
CHAPTER 3	Trails and Tales of Taxi-Wallahs	18
CHAPTER 4	Nagarwala's Day Out	27
CHAPTER 5	Nagarwala's Arrest	36
CHAPTER 6	The Interrogation	45
CHAPTER 7	Judgment Delivered	57
CHAPTER 8	Twists and Turns	67
CHAPTER 9	Letters to Indira	81
CHAPTER 10	Death of Investigating Officer Kashyap	90
CHAPTER 11	Mother and Son: Nagarwala's Letters from Hospital	98
CHAPTER 12	Death on His Birthday	108

SECTION II: PROFILES: NAGARWALA AND MALHOTRA

CHAPTER 13	Nagarwala: Performer, Player or a Victim of Circumstances?	117
CHAPTER 14	Malhotra: Sincere, Sound Sense, Inexplicably Naive	136

SECTION III: THE REDDY COMMISSION

CHAPTER 15	The Political Landscape (1966–71)	147
CHAPTER 16	Indira Appears before the Commission	163
CHAPTER 17	The Sanjay Story	178
CHAPTER 18	Odd Characters	187
CHAPTER 19	The Lawyer's Story: Nagarwala's Last Words	199

SECTION IV: WHODUNIT

CHAPTER 20	Prime Minister Morarji Desai Makes an Allegation	209
CHAPTER 21	Was It a CIA Operation?	217

SECTION V: WRAPPING UP

CHAPTER 22	Key Findings: Was It a Botched-Up Probe?	227
CHAPTER 23	Justice Reddy's Conclusions	248
	Bibliography	259

AUTHORS' NOTE

The relations between rhetoric and ethics are disturbing: the ease with which language can be twisted is worrisome, and the fact that our minds accept these perverse games so docilely is no less cause for concern.

—Octavio Paz

The 1970s were a watershed period for Indian politics. The turbulent decade saw the division of Pakistan and a war, a feather in India's political and military cap; the country going nuclear; the loss of political morality; and the emergence of a rainbow coalition of Opposition parties that included opinions aligned to the right. But before all these momentous events took place, something else would leave the nation gasping in collective disbelief in the summer of 1971.

More than half a century later, the Nagarwala affair—the scam that shook the nation—remains as enigmatic as ever—and not only because of the then-mind-boggling sum of Rs 60 lakh that was withdrawn from a public sector bank on a mere verbal command over telephone, purportedly from the highest echelons of the government in power at the Centre. In 1971, the sum of Rs 60 lakh was no joke. (As per https://scripbox.com/plan/inflation-calculator/ the amount would have been Rs 170.62 crore rupees in 2024.)

Readers who take the trouble of going through the labyrinth of twenty-three chapters in this book will perhaps understand why we, as authors, had to make a conscious effort to be politically neutral. At the same time, it was also necessary to document the lackadaisical approach of the entire system.

When one goes through the reams of papers related to the Nagarwala saga, one can see a clear pattern. There is admission of guilt, but the identities of the real culprits remain hazy to many. The commission set up to probe the scam reached its conclusions, but its assumptions are debatable. The investigation process was speedy—in fact too speedy—to allay doubts.

The purpose of presenting this work is simple. The story, the sub-plot, the sequence of events, the characters and the issues involved make the Nagarwala saga irresistible. It has all the ingredients of a thriller, replete with tragedy, farce, human failings, greed, pretentiousness and misuse of authority. What we have tried to do, to the best of our abilities, is present the facts as they occurred and let the discerning reader decide whether we have succeeded in our attempt to reconstruct what happened so many decades ago.

We thank the director-general of the National Archives of India, Chandan Sinha, and his colleagues, Dr Sumita Das Majumdar and Fareed Ahmed, for their help in facilitating access to archival material; our friends Shankar Raghuraman, Archis Mohan, Jagjiwan Bakshi, Amitabh Shukla, Pradeep Sharma, Pooja Gupta, Gautam Kumar, Vidyut Patra, Anshuman Mohanty, Priyaranjan Nayak, Sukanta Sahoo, Nita Nagaraj and Jasmine Singh for their encouragement and support in this endeavour.

This book would not have seen the light of day without the support of Swati Chopra. She understood the delicate nature of the book in the context of the politics of the era when the scandal took place, and its potential future. She shared our thrust on political neutrality and our quest for a comprehensive morality.

A big thank you to Ujjaini Dasgupta, who meticulously went through the text. Her eye for detail, insightful suggestions and observant approach were invaluable.

Our deep sense of gratitude to our friend and former colleague Ananda Sen, who went through the manuscript and came up with pertinent observations regarding both the structure and the text.

Prakash Patra
New Delhi, April 2024   **Rasheed Kidwai**

SECTION I

THE PHONE CALL. THE HEIST. THE TRIAL

CHAPTER 1

THE LOOT

Ved Prakash Malhotra leaned back in his chair. Monday mornings were usually busy for banks, but the chief cashier seemed relaxed. He had no reason to not be. Malhotra had joined the State Bank of India when it was known as the Imperial Bank twenty-six years ago, and had risen through the ranks to become chief cashier at the bank's Parliament Street branch, a post specially created for him in recognition of his hard work and dedication. It was a position of trust and responsibility. That was eleven years back. Now forty-six, after a lifetime of hawk-eyed handling of cash at the SBI's local head office at a sprawling building dating back to 1873, he could afford to relax a bit.

What Malhotra didn't know was that his life was about to change—and dramatically—that 24 May morning in 1971.

It was 11.45 a.m. Malhotra was in his cabin talking to a client when one of the three telephones on his desk rang. It was the direct number (45468), not the one connected to the SBI exchange or the intercom, which meant the call was from outside. The chief cashier picked up the phone.

'Shri Haksar, secretary to the Prime Minister of India, wants to talk to you,' said the voice at the other end.

'Put him through,' Malhotra replied.

There was a pause, then another voice came on the line, purportedly that of P.N. Haksar, the secretary to the Prime Minister.

'I am secretary to the PM speaking.'

'Namaste,' Malhotra replied. 'What are your orders?'

'I have to talk to you about a very secret matter, and if there is anyone sitting in your room, he must be asked to go,' the voice at the other end said.

Malhotra placed a hand on the receiver and looked at the man sitting across the table. 'Please, wait outside,' he said. 'I have an important call to attend.'

Mathura Das, retired honorary magistrate of Delhi, was a respected client, but it was not every day that one got a call from the Prime Minister's secretary—that, too, about something 'very secret'.

Das would later recall how taken aback he was at Malhotra's 'unacceptable' behaviour. He had known Malhotra for a long time, and the chief cashier had always been courteous.

As Das got up and stepped outside the glass cabin, Malhotra spoke into the phone again, telling the person at the other end there was no one else in the room.

What followed was a series of terse, cryptic orders, not dissimilar to what readers of espionage stories would expect, but enough to arouse Malhotra's interest and kindle long dormant feelings of nationalism.

'The Prime Minister of India wants Rs 60 lakh to be sent for a work that is very highly secret in nature. She will send a person and you can hand over the money to him,' the person at the other end told Malhotra.

The chief cashier asked whether the money would be handed over against a cheque or a receipt. 'It is a very urgent and secret work. This is what the PM's orders are. Receipt or cheque will be given later,' the voice replied, almost peremptory in tone, before going on to bark out further instructions.

'Take the money in a van to the Free Church, because this money has to be sent to Bangladesh by an air force plane. This is a work of urgent nature and should not be disclosed to anyone, and you should come soon.'

In his long career at the bank, Malhotra had never been in such a situation. Handling cash demanded total attention, but this was different. 'It is a very difficult task,' he stammered.

'Then you talk to the PM of India, Smt. Indira Gandhi,' the voice replied, and a moment later, Malhotra heard a familiar voice come on the line. 'I am the PM of India Smt. Indira Gandhi speaking.'

Malhotra couldn't believe he was speaking to Indira Gandhi. At the other end, the new voice came directly to the point. 'As my secretary has just now informed you, Rs 60 lakh is urgently required in Bangladesh for an important secret work. Get it ready quickly. I am sending my courier. At the place indicated by Haksar, you hand over the money to him.'

Malhotra was now confident that the voice on the other side was that of the Prime Minister of India. He relaxed. 'How will I be able to identify the person?' he asked.

'The person will talk to you in code words and will say, "I am Bangladesh ka babu." You reply, "I am Bar-at-Law." By this you will be assured that he is my courier. Thereafter, you proceed as he says,' the person at the other end replied. 'After delivering the money, come straight to my house and you will get a receipt.'

Then the line went dead. Conversation over.

For long, Malhotra, a victim of the Partition and a migrant, had been wanting to do something for the nation. But the opportunity had never arisen and he had immersed himself in his unspectacular, though steady, bank job. Now, all of a sudden, fate had thrown him a line to redeem himself in his own eyes. It was true that what he had been told to do was fraught with uncertainty, but how many like him had had the privilege of receiving orders directly from the Prime Minister?

Malhotra would later say he was 'spellbound' after speaking to Indira Gandhi. But there was little time to waste. The chief cashier got up and stepped out of his cabin, only to see Das standing outside. It was clear the elderly client was upset at being asked to step outside Malhotra's cabin.

Malhotra, too, had sensed the older man's feelings of hurt. He apologized, touched Das's knee and said, 'I am going on an important mission of national importance.'

Das, not unaccustomed to the Punjabi way of obeisance, patted Malhotra on the shoulder and wished him success.

Malhotra then knocked on the cabin assigned to his deputy, Ram Prakash Batra, and asked him how many bundles of hundred-rupee notes he had with him. The deputy chief cashier glanced at the cash register lying on his table and replied, 'About 180 or 190 bundles.' Roughly Rs 1.8 to 1.9 lakh.

'Arrange 60 lakh ke bidda [wads]. It is for a payment,' Malhotra told Batra. 'Get the money from the strongroom currency chest and put the amount in another chest.' There was a tone of urgency in his voice.

After Malhotra left, Batra walked up to the cabin of Hakumat Rai Khanna, the cash-in-charge, who sat in the savings bank section a little away from Malhotra's room. Khanna, along with Batra, held separate keys to the currency chest in the strongroom as joint custodians.

Batra informed Khanna that the chief cashier needed Rs 60 lakh immediately. As they spoke, Malhotra entered the room. When Khanna asked Malhotra why so much money was needed, the chief cashier told him it was 'top-secret work', but promised to explain the details 'after the disbursement'.

Batra and Khanna then moved towards the strongroom, which had an elaborate security system. To enter the strongroom, three locks had to be opened. Khanna had the control key for two of the locks. He used it and the two locks opened. The cash-in-charge then inserted the second key, the one for the third lock. Khanna simultaneously inserted a key of his own and the main door of the strongroom opened.

Now two more locks needed to be opened to access the cash chest. Khanna inserted his key to open the first lock of the grille door, and the other lock opened when Batra applied his key. The two then opened the chest with two separate keys. While Batra withdrew the amount, Khanna counted the 100-rupee bundles before the wads were put in a designated trunk. Malhotra walked into the strongroom to see whether the amount was being correctly packed. Khanna again asked Malhotra the purpose behind withdrawing the huge amount, that, too, at such short notice. Malhotra repeated what he had said earlier. It was a 'heavy payment', he said, adding that he would reveal the details after the money was handed over. Malhotra then left the strongroom and returned to his cabin. Once the money was withdrawn, two coolies—Surinder Kumar and U.D. Sharma—lifted the trunk and carried it to the head cashier Rawail Singh's cabin.

Back in his cabin, Malhotra rang up the security officer S.C. Sinha, who was in the bank's adjoining old building. The call on the intercom was received by Barun K. Mitra, the assistant security officer. Malhotra asked Mitra to allot him an Ambassador as he had to go out on a 'top secret' official assignment. The chief cashier also told Mitra that he did not require a driver as he would drive the official Ambassador himself.

Mitra told Malhotra he would not be able to provide him a car without a driver. While they spoke, security officer Sinha walked in. He told Mitra that he had already spoken to Malhotra on the intercom and had told the chief cashier that a car (DLK 760) would be allotted, but that he wouldn't be allowed to drive it—

Santosh Kumar, a driver, would be at the wheel. Sinha also told Kumar not to give the car keys to Malhotra.

Back at the strongroom, Batra and Khanna again carried out the elaborate procedure to secure the vault after the money had been taken out. Batra then met head cashier Singh in his room and got the 'vault register' signed, recording the withdrawal of Rs 60 lakh in cash.

Once the necessary entries had been made, Malhotra came down from his office and walked to the bank compound gate, where the bank's cars were parked. The two coolies brought the cash box to where the Ambassador waited. Car driver Kumar and a security guard, Man Bahadur, were present at the spot. Kumar opened the trunk and the two coolies heaved the box inside. 'The dickey could not be closed' due to the size of the box, Kumar would say in his statement to the police later. Batra handed over the keys of the cash trunk to Malhotra, who got in behind the wheel and drove off.

Kumar would later complain to his boss, the security officer, that Malhotra 'took away the car by driving himself after virtually snatching the keys' from him. Malhotra did not let Man Bahadur accompany him either.

It was 12.15 p.m., barely half an hour since Malhotra had received the phone call that would change his life forever. Malhotra was to meet the courier at 12.30 p.m. 'I realized that it would be better to let R.P. Batra know that in case I was delayed at the Prime Minister's house, he should supervise my work in my absence,' he would later say in his statement to the police.

Malhotra told them that he drove back to inform Batra. 'I came back and called Batra downstairs and said, "Brother, take care of my work."'

Malhotra stopped the car across the road, barely 100 paces from the SBI's Parliament Street branch near the Free Church, a 1927 distinctive red-and-white neocolonial-style building. As he had been instructed on the phone, he got out of the car.

'[A] tall, hefty, fair-complexioned person wearing an olive-green hat approached me and said, "I am Bangladesh babu." And I replied, "I am Bar-at-Law." He said, "Let us go,"' Malhotra would say in his statement.

The two then got inside the Ambassador, but the car wouldn't start. 'I attempted. Then I asked him, "Do you know how to drive?" He said yes, and I said, "Please control the steering."'

Malhotra got off and pushed the car. Once the engine started, the two men exchanged places, with Malhotra at the wheel again. They then drove towards Parliament.

'I asked him where he had to go. He said, "Kitchener Road." I did not know Kitchener Road. Then he said that he had to go to Palam airport. I recollected that the road leading to Palam was called Kitchener Road. Then I turned towards Gole Dak Khana and then to Willingdon Hospital, and proceeded towards Palam,' Malhotra recalled in his statement.

The route the car had taken was Ashoka Road, Irwin Road, Willingdon Crescent and Sardar Patel Marg before it reached the crossing of Panchsheel Marg. This route was the fastest way to reach Palam. Malhotra said he volunteered to accompany him up to Palam airport, but the man declined, saying, 'It will not be proper.'

Sometime later, Malhotra said, the man told him he would hire a taxi. 'It's not proper if you accompany me because it is a top-secret matter. I have to catch an air force plane. So I will hire a taxi. You should straightaway go to the Prime Minister's house. She will meet you at 1 p.m.'

The chief cashier said the man asked him to stop the car near the crossing of Panchsheel Marg, still more than halfway to the airport. 'There was a taxi stand, and he asked me to stop the car there. He called for a taxi and a coolie to shift the box.'

Malhotra hesitated. 'It's national work and we can do it ourselves,' he said. By then a Fiat taxi had driven up and the three of them, including the taxi driver, a turbaned Sikh, shifted the trunk from the Ambassador to the Fiat's trunk. Malhotra then handed over the keys of the cash trunk to the man. As he got into the taxi, the man, with folded hands, said, 'My name is Aziz. Jai Bangladesh, Jai Bharat Mata.'

The man would later be traced and identified as Rustom Sohrab Nagarwala, a former army captain.

Malhotra had a close look at the taxi's number plate and noted down the number: DLT 1622. He then got into the Ambassador. Mission accomplished. He now had to meet the Prime Minister and collect the receipt from her.

Malhotra drove fast to meet the 1 p.m. deadline.

Notes

1. Three statements were made by Malhotra. The first one was to the police, on 24 May 1971. His second statement, on 25 May, was to SBI officials. It was in Urdu and more detailed. His third statement, in 1978, was to the Jaganmohan Reddy Commission, which looked into the Nagarwala affair.
2. That Malhotra had addressed Indira Gandhi as 'Mataji' during the conversation is mentioned in the statement made before the Reddy Commission and is not there in his earlier statements. Nagarwala's confession, which was recorded by a magistrate, also mentions that Malhotra had said 'Namaste, Mataji' when he had mimicked the voice of Indira Gandhi. Subsequently, Nagarwala had disowned the statement and had alleged that it was made under duress.

CHAPTER 2

THE ORDEAL

As he drove through the midday traffic towards the Prime Minister's residence at 1, Safdarjung Road, Malhotra replayed in his mind the incidents of the morning. The unexpected phone call, the thrill of speaking to Indira Gandhi, the hurried transfer of cash from the vault, the way he drove off alone in the bank's Ambassador with the huge amount in the trunk. It seemed like a dream, only that he was living it. The Prime Minister had assigned him a national task, a top-secret job, and he had done it. He felt proud and excited—this was something people read about in books, but here he was, right in the thick of it all, a real-life character in a real-life action thriller.

It was around 12.45 p.m. when he pulled into 1, Akbar Road, the official complex adjoining the Prime Minister's residence. Officials and visitors to the Prime Minister's residence would have to go through the bungalow that housed the reception desk. Malhotra parked the Ambassador and approached.

At the reception Malhotra was happy to see Suraj Balram, an inspector with Delhi Police. They knew each other for many years, since the days Malhotra had played for the New Star Hockey Club as a young man.

He walked up to Balram. 'I want to see the Prime Minister.'

'You want to see the Prime Minister? What's the matter?' a surprised Balram asked.

'I don't know. It is she who called me here,' Malhotra replied, gulping down the glass of water Balram offered him.

'But she is not at her residence. She has gone to Parliament,' Balram said, pointing out that it was the first day of the second session of the fifth Lok Sabha.

The Prime Minister, holding the home ministry portfolio, had her newly inducted ministers C. Subramaniam, Uma Shankar Dikshit, H.N. Bahuguna, Mohan Dharia, Gen. Shahnawaz Khan and a few others introduced at the Lok Sabha. Indira Gandhi had also faced a hawkish Opposition asking whether there had been heavy movement and concentration of Pakistani forces on the eastern and western sectors of the Indo-Pakistan border.

Malhotra asked him where Haksar, secretary to the Prime Minister, was. Balram looked at his old acquaintance. He seemed dead serious. Something was up. But it was none of his business. Parliament was in session, he told Malhotra, and the Prime Minister and her secretary were at Parliament House. Balram advised Malhotra, who was in a 'great hurry', to go to Gate No. 5 of Parliament House. The gate was primarily used by the Prime Minister and her officials.

While Malhotra was speaking to Balram, a car drove into the complex. Malhotra saw a man sitting on the A-2 seat at the back. Assuming it was Haksar, Malhotra eagerly approached the reception officer, asking, 'Who is he?'

'The Prime Minister's younger son,' the officer replied.

Malhotra looked at his watch. He was getting impatient when he noticed another car enter the compound. Another man was sitting in the rear seat. Malhotra ran towards the car, thinking this would be Haksar, but by the time he reached the vehicle, the man had disappeared inside the Prime Minister's residence. He asked the driver who the person was. 'He told me he was Mr Gupta,' Malhotra later said to the police. The exact identity of 'Mr Gupta' was not elaborated either by the police or the Reddy Commission, which was subsequently set up to probe the affair. The security norms in those days were not as stringent even at the Prime Minister's residence. In those days even commoners could walk up to the gate or get a glimpse of Indira Gandhi playing with her pets or seeing off guests at the portico.

Inside the compound, however, security personnel were aghast at Malhotra's strange behaviour. He shouldn't have run towards the car like that, they told him. He should have asked them first.

Getting increasingly impatient now, Malhotra sat in the reception office and waited. It was a few minutes past 1 p.m., but there was no sign of either the Prime Minister or Haksar. After a while he walked up to the reception counter again and asked if anyone knew when the Prime Minister would return. He also requested those at the counter to inform Mrs Gandhi that Malhotra was waiting at the reception. They told him it was not possible to call up the Prime Minister like that.

'When does she usually come?' Malhotra said, exasperated.

'She usually comes around 1.30 p.m.'

'What about Mr Haksar?'

Malhotra later said, 'They told me that if I was in a hurry, I could go to the Prime Minister's secretariat [in South Block].'

Malhotra drove to the secretariat, where he inquired about Haksar at the reception. He was told that Haksar had just left. Malhotra thought Haksar might have gone to the Prime Minister's residence to deliver the 'cheque' to him.

He rushed back to 1, Akbar Road, only to be told that Haksar was not there and that the Prime Minister had not returned either. 'If the work is so urgent, you could go to Parliament House,' he was told.

Malhotra drove to the Parliament House complex and approached the reception there. 'I would like to meet the Prime Minister,' he said.

He was told that Indira Gandhi had gone for lunch.

Malhotra returned to the Prime Minister's residence, but was informed that lunch had been sent to Parliament House and that she would not have her lunch at her residence.

Balram again advised Malhotra to go to Gate No. 5 of Parliament House and find out if the PM was present. Malhotra rushed back to Parliament House again and requested the sentry posted at the gate to allow him to meet the Prime Minister. The sentry informed him that Mrs Gandhi was inside a room and he couldn't be allowed in there.

Desperate by now, Malhotra mentioned the name of S.S. Chaddha, an officer of the rank of deputy superintendent of police and who was then the Prime Minister's personal security officer. He asked the sentry to inform Chaddha that he, Malhotra, wanted to meet the PSO.

The sentry declined. 'He is our sahib and he is taking his meal now.'

As Malhotra pleaded with the sentry, he saw Chaddha walking out of the building and ran towards him. Once he had caught his breath, he told Chaddha that he needed to urgently see either the Prime Minister or Haksar.

'She had called me,' he told Chaddha, who asked him to wait. The security officer then went inside, but returned a few seconds later, saying there was a meeting going on and that he would have to wait.

Malhotra insisted that Chaddha go inside and speak to the Prime Minister. 'Tell her about me and she will call me,' he said. Chaddha went back inside and returned with N.K. Seshan, the private secretary to the Prime Minister. They met Malhotra outside Gate No. 5.

'He told me about the incident,' Seshan later recalled in his written submission to the Reddy Commission.

After hearing Malhotra out, Seshan apprised the Prime Minister of the situation. He also called up Haksar, who was in South Block, asking him to 'come urgently' to the Prime Minister's office inside the Parliament building.

As Haksar reached Gate No. 5, primarily used by the Prime Minister and her staff, and briskly climbed up the five stairs, Malhotra approached him, asking if he was P.N. Haksar. Malhotra told him everything that had transpired since morning. And the words came out in a torrent. Haksar later recalled how agitated this 'well-built, burly and excited' person was. '[Malhotra] told me the story of the alleged telephone call, in which he parted with a large sum of money,' Haksar stated before the commission.

Haksar gave Malhotra a patient hearing. 'I heard the story and I told him that he should rush to the nearest police station and report the matter, as it appeared to me to be a matter of "extraordinary fraud". When I told him this, he became even more agitated and said something to the effect that he was doing his patriotic duty,' Haksar said.

Chaddha, PSO to the Prime Minister, had by then come out of Parliament House and was listening to the conversation between Haksar and Malhotra.

Haksar made it clear that no telephone call had been made to the bank by him or the Prime Minister.

'Frankly, looking at him, I got the impression that this man was excited and agitated to the point of being unbalanced.'

After advising Malhotra to go to the police, Haksar entered Parliament House and went straight to Seshan's room. He then met the Prime Minister, who had already been briefed about what had happened.

'This is an extraordinary case of fraud,' she said.

'Left me quite dumbfounded,' Haksar said.

Indira Gandhi later told the Reddy Commission that Haksar viewed the incident as 'a prank on the bank' and told her that the police were on the job.

On his part, Malhotra said, 'I was very nervous and terribly perplexed.' He wanted to meet the Prime Minister, but no one would let him. He saw her leaving the complex from a distance.

'I was stunned and taken aback. I wanted to commit suicide,' he said.

Malhotra, who was on good terms with Delhi Police officials, saw B.N. Mehra, superintendent of police (security), walking by after the Prime Minister had left. Malhotra knew Mehra well and narrated the entire incident to him. Mehra advised him to go to Vijay Chowk, where New Delhi's district superintendent of police (SP) Y. Rajpal was supervising arrangements to face a demonstration organized by the Bharatiya Jana Sangh on the issue of Bangladesh.

Seeing the condition Malhotra was in, Mehra called Om Prakash, a sub-inspector working with the security, and asked him to accompany the bank cashier to Vijay Chowk. The two left in Malhotra's car.

But once outside Parliament building at Vijay Chowk, District SP Rajpal was nowhere to be seen. However, Malhotra spotted Devinder Kumar Kashyap, assistant superintendent of police (ASP), who was also the subdivisional police officer (SDPO) in charge of the Chanakyapuri area. The young Indian Police Service (IPS) officer was standing at the outer gate of Parliament House, adjoining Vijay Chowk.

The Bharatiya Jana Sangh workers had assembled at the Boat Club and were holding a meeting demanding recognition for Bangladesh, then still a few months away from its eventual separation from Pakistan as an independent country. The protesters were to march to Parliament House, defying prohibitory orders, and court arrest. Among those who had reached Rajpath and Rafi Marg, shouting slogans, were the future Bharatiya Janata Party (BJP) leaders Atal Bihari Vajpayee and Lal Krishna Advani.

The police had managed to control the situation and taken 252 persons into custody. Hari Dev, the station house officer of the Chanakyapuri police station, said the demonstrators had 'broken the police cordons and entered the precinct of Parliament House around midday'. The officer added that after they had cleared the demonstrators, SP Rajpal had left for office.

Malhotra met A.K. Bose, the station house officer of the Tughlaq Road police station, and inquired about Kashyap. When Bose wanted to know what the matter was, Malhotra briefly told him about the mess he had landed himself in.

'I did not believe him,' Bose told the commission. Bose left the place after pointing to where Kashyap was standing with Hari Dev, the station house officer of the Chanakyapuri police station. Now that the demonstration was over, both were about to leave the spot, but Malhotra approached them. It was around 2.15 p.m.

With tears in his eyes, Malhotra again narrated what had happened. Kashyap heard him out patiently and then instructed a wireless operator to flash a message. The message, which the police named 'Operation Toofan', was: 'The vehicle number is DLT 1622, and it has a Sikh driver. Trace the vehicle, bring the driver and the taxi to the Parliament Street police station.'

Sub-inspector (security) Om Prakash, who stood a little distance away as his superiors spoke to Malhotra, later recalled that he could hear Malhotra saying, '*Main mar gaya, main loot gaya, mera saath dhoka ho gaya* [I am finished, I have been robbed, I have been cheated].'

Notes

1. Suraj Balram, the inspector attached to the Prime Minister's security (CW 63), was never questioned by Delhi Police during its investigation. He appeared before the Reddy Commission and made his statement.

CHAPTER 3

TRAILS AND TALES OF TAXI-WALLAHS

The protest was over, the slogan-shouting demonstrators had been taken into custody and calm had returned to Rajpath as ASP Kashyap, his subordinate officer Inspector Hari Dev and Malhotra reached the Parliament Street police station. The three met District SP Y. Rajpal in his room, which was part of the Parliament Street police station complex, where Malhotra once again recounted his story.

Rajpal had a look of disbelief on his face as he listened. 'It's a fantastic story,' he quipped after Malhotra had finished. The SP then asked the two officers to visit the SBI branch, barely 200 yards from the police station.

'Check the veracity of the allegations,' Rajpal told the officers as they left. Malhotra stayed back.

It was close to 3 p.m. when the inspector-general (IG) of Delhi Police L.S. Bisht, the deputy inspector-general (DIG) (New Delhi Range) P.A. Rosha and others arrived at the New Delhi district SP's office. Inspector Bose, SHO of the Tughlaq Road police station, who was summoned by his boss Kashyap through wireless message, was also there.

Rajpal, who had by then received a call from the Prime Minister's Office about the bank fraud, informed the officers that the Crime Branch would take over the case.

Kashyap told Bose that since the fraud had taken place in the New Delhi area, Rajpal wanted the district officers to try and solve the case. He said the SP wanted him (Kashyap) to take the lead, helped by Hari Dev and Bose.

Bose joined the Crime Branch team, led by SP Markandey Singh, where Godha Ram, deputy SP was present. They interrogated Malhotra. Rajpal briefed IG Bisht and DIG Rosha. 'I found the story implausible,' Rosha would later tell the commission. He said that he found Malhotra weeping and saying in between sobs, '*Main toh soldiership mein mara gaya,*' indicating that he thought he was fulfilling his patriotic duties towards his nation.

Kashyap and Hari Dev had, in the meantime, reached the bank and met R.L. Jain, the chief accountant, and S.K. Taparia, the deputy secretary of the SBI. The bank officials informed Kashyap that Malhotra had taken Rs 60 lakh in 100-rupee currency notes from the strongroom and left with the money. Jain produced the vault register that showed an entry pertaining to the removal of Rs 60 lakh from the chest. The police took the register into its possession. Kashyap told the SBI officials that their bank had been duped and someone had made away with the money.

Taparia, who subsequently became chief general manager of the SBI, informed Kashyap he had received a call from N.K. Seshan, the private secretary to the Prime Minister, asking if Rs 60 lakh had been withdrawn by Malhotra and handed over to an unknown person. Taparia's office was in the adjoining building. After Seshan's call, he had dialled the new building's telephone numbers and then walked across when he had received no response. Before visiting the branch, Taparia had informed the Prime Minister's secretariat and the SBI chairman in Bombay (now Mumbai) that he was going to the next building to take stock of the situation.

Kashyap, Hari Dev, Taparia and Rawail Singh, the head cashier of SBI, left for the Parliament Street police station, where Malhotra was being interrogated.

The breakthrough came when, at the police station, Kashyap received a message that the taxi had been traced. Next, Kashyap and Hari Dev left for Shantipath, where the taxi had been located.

The Taxi Driver's Story

Balbir Singh, the middle-aged Sikh cab driver, was standing near his taxi, DLT 1622, on Shantipath, the main road in the diplomatic enclave of Chanakyapuri. The taxi had broken down and was being repaired. It was 3.30 p.m. and the road was quite empty. Singh saw a police Jeep slow down and stop near his cab. A policeman leaned out and looked at the taxi's number plate. Then he spoke into his wireless set: 'DLT 1622 traced.' Balbir could hear the message being relayed.

Within a few minutes, five to six Jeeps arrived at the spot and the taxi was surrounded by policemen. The wireless crackled again: 'Bring the taxi along with the driver to the Parliament Street police station.'

At the spot, a policeman with a wireless set looked at the taxi. 'The car has broken down. Cannot be taken to the police station,' he said.

'Bring the taxi driver to the police station,' came the prompt reply on the wireless.

One of the policemen approached Balbir. 'Who's the driver?' he asked.

Balbir, taken aback by the sudden appearance of the police, pointed to another driver present at the spot and said, 'Maheshanand Garhwali.' The policemen asked both of them to get into a Jeep.

Back at the Chanakyapuri police station, Rajpal was deep in conversation with his fellow officers. Kashyap, he told them, may be given more time to investigate the case as his efforts had resulted in tracing the taxi. Kashyap was a young IPS officer belonging to the 1967 batch and the Chanakyapuri area was his first field posting as a subdivisional police officer. It was his first major assignment.

At the Parliament Street police station, Malhotra recognized Balbir Singh as the driver whose taxi had been hired at the Panchsheel crossing. Balbir told the police that two persons had come in a private black Ambassador and engaged his taxi. The two men had a big white trunk with them and that all three, including himself, had shifted it to his taxi's dickey.

He also recalled that he had heard Malhotra telling the other person, 'Okay, Sir, I am going straight to the Prime Minister's house.'

Balbir had then driven the other passenger towards Palam via Sardar Patel Marg and on reaching Vayudham (the Indian Air Force area) the man had asked him if he could reach the air force aerodrome within 'five to six minutes'.

Balbir said that he had replied that it might take 'about twenty minutes'. The passenger had then told him he would 'take the next flight' and asked him to turn towards Ring Road. Once they arrived in Defence Colony via the Safdarjung Hospital route, Balbir said the passenger asked him to turn left and gave directions that ultimately led to a bungalow, A-196, located opposite a school.

Fiat with a Flat Tyre

After they got out of the taxi, Balbir said, the two of them unloaded the trunk from the dickey and the man paid him Rs 7 towards taxi fare. While he was receiving the cash, Balbir said he noticed a Fiat taxi coming towards them with a deflated tyre. He indicated to the driver that one of the rear tyres was punctured.

Balbir's passenger had meanwhile lit a cigarette. Having received his taxi fare, Balbir said he drove off towards Lodhi Colony. After he had finished giving his statement, the police team, led by Kashyap, left with him for the Defence Colony bungalow, where his passenger had got off.

Balbir had told the police that the Fiat with the punctured tyre belonged to the taxi stand in Lodhi Colony. The team went to Lodhi Colony and traced the taxi, DLT 810. Dhian Singh, its driver, admitted that he had been left stranded in Defence Colony with the flat tyre because the jack had 'slipped under the vehicle' and a man wearing a felt cap had got out of a taxi about 100 metres away. He told the police that, after a few minutes, the 'tall and fair-complexioned man' with the cap had hailed another taxi. He had lifted a trunk into the next taxi with the help of the driver and left. Although he couldn't remember the taxi number, he said he had seen the car being used to transport school students to and from Jorbagh, a south Delhi locality near the intersection of Sri Aurobindo Marg and Lodhi Road.

Third Taxi Driver

The police team, according to the case diary, then spoke to some schoolchildren and learnt that the taxi would come to pick them up from the Lajpat Nagar taxi stand. Dhian Singh accompanied the team, since he had seen the driver and would be able to identify him. They went around the area and found the taxi parked at Anand Taxi stand in Lajpat Nagar. The fifty-five-year-old driver, Om Prakash, was identified. He would become a key witness in the case.

Om Prakash said he had been driving the taxi, DLT 2572, since 1955. He was 'passing through Defence Colony' and had entered A Block when he saw a man standing on the side of the road with a steel trunk, and was flagged down. 'We lifted the trunk and kept it in the dickey of my taxi,' he said.

The driver recalled his conversation with the passenger:

'It's heavy. Are these books?'
'Yes, books.'
'It's heavy. You pay extra … whatever you feel like.'
The man had agreed and asked him to drive to Delhi Gate.

Om Prakash had then driven towards Delhi Gate, via Lodhi Road. He said that while driving by the Parsi dharamshala on Bahadur Shah Zafar Marg, his passenger had asked him to stop. 'He got out and went into the dharamshala. After nearly fifteen minutes, he came out with a bag, which looked empty. *Felne wala chain laga hua tha* [a suitcase that could expand with the help of a chain],' he recalled.

Om Prakash said the man got back into the taxi and asked him to drive to Rajinder Nagar.

'New or old?' Om Prakash asked.

'*Chalo, main bata ta hoon* [Drive, I will tell you],' the passenger replied.

By the time they reached Pusa Road, about eight kilometres from the Parsi Dharamshala, Om Prakash said the passenger had got into a chatty mood. '*Kitne paise roj kamate ho* [How much do you earn in a day]?' he asked.

'*Char-panchso rupaya mahine kamata hoon* [Four to five hundred rupees a month],' Om Prakash replied.

'*Taxi wale daily 50/100 kama lete hain* [A taxi driver earns Rs 50–100 a day],' the passenger said.

'*Main time se aata hun, bandh karta hoon time se … Ho sakta hai woh din raat chalte hain … ya … galat kaam karte honge* [I come on time and wrap up on time. Maybe they (the other drivers) work day and night … or maybe they do illegal things].'

'*Kahaan rehte ho* [Where do you stay]?'

'E-8, Amar Colony.'

As the car neared Rajinder Nagar, the passenger became friendlier. 'Now I'll tell you one thing, but promise you won't tell anyone,' he said. He paused a while, then told Om Prakash about the money in the trunk. 'The trunk contains Rs 60 lakh,' he said, adding that he wanted to shift the cash from the trunk to the bag.

Om Prakash felt a stab of uneasiness. 'So much money … you are a big man,' he mumbled. 'Can't you go to a kothi [bungalow] or a hotel for that?'

'Taking this [the money] to Bangladesh. Can't take such a big trunk,' the passenger replied.

The car had by then reached New Rajinder Nagar and was near a park in a desolate area. The passenger asked Om Prakash to stop the car. As soon as the car stopped, he got out, only to get in again.

Om Prakash, already nervous, looked at the man who had opened the door and got out. He suddenly noticed that the man was carrying a revolver, which was 'in a cover' and tucked under his bush shirt.

The passenger asked Om Prakash to drive a little further, saying there was a kothi ahead. When they had driven a few metres, the man asked Om Prakash to stop near R Block. He got out, walked towards a house and shouted out to a man on the first floor. The two conversed in English before Om Prakash's passenger was allowed in. In a few minutes, he was back with one small Rexine bag and asked Om Prakash to start driving again, assuring him that he would get off once he had moved the notes to the two bags.

'Bundles of Notes'

Om Prakash said he had driven just a little distance when his passenger again asked him to stop. The taxi had reached the end of R Block, a slightly isolated place with a jungle on one side and a few bungalows on the other. The man asked Om Prakash to remain seated and not come out of the car. The passenger got out, opened the dickey and moved the cash from the trunk to the two bags.

It was a summer afternoon. Om Prakash looked up and down the road, but there was nobody around. He glanced towards the dickey and saw his passenger shoving bundles of notes into the bags. After he had finished, the man yanked the trunk out of the dickey and tossed it away near a dustbin.

Om Prakash started the engine as soon as his passenger got in again, and drove out of the area. The driver, now a nervous wreck, suggested that his passenger take another vehicle, but was told not to worry. It's 'Bangladesh fund', the man said, adding that he was going to Bangladesh. And no, he assured Om Prakash, he had not committed any 'robbery or theft'.

He asked Om Prakash to drop him off at Connaught Place. Once there, the man got off in front of a shop, Salwan Furniture, near Marina Hotel. Before leaving with the two bags, he offered five hundred-rupee notes to Om Prakash, which the driver declined. The man threw the notes in on the seat and left.

Om Prakash drove away, relieved that the man had finally left, but the afternoon's experience bothered him. When he reached Sujan Singh Park, barely five kilometres from Connaught Place, he stopped, got out of the taxi, dialled the financier of his cab and narrated the strange events of the afternoon. The man at the other end of the line asked Om Prakash to drive to the taxi stand in Lajpat Nagar, saying he, too, would be there soon.

Om Prakash did as he was told and saw a police Jeep at the Lajpat Nagar taxi stand. Kashyap was there with his fellow officers. Om Prakash re-narrated the events of the afternoon to the police team and handed over the notes the passenger had thrown into the back seat.

Kashyap asked Om Prakash to accompany them to Defence Colony, from where he had picked up the passenger. Once they got there, the police searched the area near the bungalow A-196, where the passenger had got off Balbir Singh's taxi earlier in the afternoon. The police soon found the mysterious passenger's 'olive green cap' lying in a drain. Cab driver Dhian Singh had seen the man taking off the cap and throwing it in there.

From Defence Colony, the police party left for New Rajinder Nagar in west Delhi. Their destination was the R Block house the passenger had visited to pick up the second bag. The house (R-822) belonged to Homi C. Gotla, a Parsi man.

Asked if Gotla had, earlier that afternoon, given a Rexine bag to a man who had arrived in a taxi, he revealed the identity of the visitor, Rustom Sohrab Nagarwala. 'My wife had given the case to Nagarwala,' he said, adding that the man lived in the Parsi Anjuman dharamshala in Bahadur Shah Zafar Marg.

The police team told Gotla that Nagarwala had committed 'a grievous crime'. The team then left after deploying a few plainclothes cops at the house to keep an eye on it.

Om Prakash also led the police team to the place where his passenger had thrown away the SBI trunk after transferring the cash to the two bags. By then it had grown dark and the team couldn't locate the trunk. The abandoned trunk would be found later.

Notes

1. Mrs Gotla, in her statement to the Reddy Commission, confirmed Om Prakash's version that her husband had given the bag to Nagarwala. Gotla later tried to raise funds for Nagarwala when he was in jail and maintained his friendship with him until Nagarwala's death.

CHAPTER 4

NAGARWALA'S DAY OUT

Rustom Nagarwala stood on the road outside the taxi stand in the outer circle of Connaught Place. That is where cab driver Om Prakash had dropped him. Nagarwala had left five hundred-rupee notes on the back seat after the driver had refused to take the money. So frightened was Om Prakash that he had sped off and disappeared from the scene after dropping his passenger.

Across the road was Marina Hotel. Nagarwala, carrying the two bags, scanned the streets, walked into the hotel and spoke to the concierge. He then kept the bags that he was carrying on the patio near the main gate of the hotel, nodded to the concierge and left.

He seemed in a world of his own, oblivious to everything around him. A little distance away, workers at the nearby Plaza Cinema were busy with a post-lunch agitation against the owners of Eagle Theatres, who owned Plaza Cinema, demanding a hike in bonus. Inside Plaza Cinema, it was another full house for the Rajesh Khanna-starrer *Haathi Mere Saathi*.

But neither protest nor blockbuster interested Nagarwala. He had work to do and no time to waste. A little later, he was at the office of the Marina Taxi Service. This was familiar territory for him. Nearly two decades ago, shortly after leaving the Indian Army, Nagarwala had invested Rs 10,000 in the venture, started by his friend Rajinder Singh. But that was in the early 1950s. Rajinder was no more and his son Mohinder now ran the business.

Mohinder was not in the Marina taxi office, but his younger brother, Harbhajan, was. Nagarwala made small talk with the teenager as he waited in the office for Mohinder to arrive. It was around 2.40 p.m. when Mohinder walked in.

Already impatient, Nagarwala came straight to the point. He said he was in a hurry and wanted an air-conditioned car for a trip to Nainital. He said he had a few foreign guests to entertain and wanted to take them to a hill station. Delhi's weather then was a scorching 42 degree Celsius, made more unbearable by the dry hot wind (loo) blowing across parts of north India.

For Mohinder, Nagarwala was a regular client. But this time around, Mohinder expressed his helplessness. All his vehicles, he said, were out on the street and he had no car to spare.

But Nagarwala was insistent and Mohinder conceded that he had one air-conditioned vehicle whose fitness certificate had expired. 'Don't worry,' Nagarwala told him. 'If the car is stopped, I'll pay the fine.'

Mohinder was aware of Nagarwala's influential contacts, but he declined.

'Can't you spare a small car?' Nagarwala asked again.

Mohinder shook his head. Nagarwala paused and thought for a moment, then told Mohinder to book an air-conditioned vehicle for the next day (25 May 1971). It should be sent to him at the Parsi dharamshala early in the morning, he added. Mohinder made a note in his diary and confirmed the booking.

Nagarwala seemed to have relaxed a bit. He leaned back in his chair, holding the chilled 300 ml bottle of Coca-Cola Mohinder had offered to his guest. But he was not done yet. 'Can you spare your personal car?' he asked the younger man. 'I have some urgent work for a couple of hours and have to meet a few friends.'

Mohinder could not turn down this request. Apart from being his late father's friend, Nagarwala had got him good business, promptly cleared his dues and tipped drivers generously.

'Call Paramjit,' Mohinder told one of his employees.

'Where can I buy a big-size leather suitcase?' Nagarwala asked as they waited for Paramjit, Mohinder's personal driver, who drove the family car (DLK 2125).

Nagarwala, who minutes ago had been pleading for a car, now looked more confident, his hefty, five-foot-ten-inch frame accentuating his air of authority.

'There are so many shops nearby,' Mohinder replied, specifying two shops in the vicinity.

Paramjit entered at this point. He was in his twenties. His father, too, worked for the family as a driver, and he was no stranger to Nagarwala.

'Go with him,' Mohinder said, gesturing towards Nagarwala, as he handed the car keys to Paramjit. 'Come back as soon as his work is over. Don't ask him for money. He has booked a taxi for tomorrow.' Paramjit nodded as he accompanied Nagarwala out of the office.

Mohinder's younger brother, Harbhajan, who had been hovering around in the office, followed them. The teenager was keen to show Nagarwala the shop where he could buy the suitcase. Imperial Leather Works, established in 1945, was then among the most well-known leather-bag dealers in Delhi. From the 1950s through the 1970s, it was a one-stop destination for customers.

Friends, 'New Look' Haircut and Suitcases

Nagarwala and Harbhajan picked up two suitcases from Imperial Leather Works and walked back to the Marina taxi office. The two suitcases had cost Nagarwala Rs 84. He then went back to the hotel where he had left the bags, while Harbhajan waited with the suitcases. Nagarwala returned soon with the bags and he and Paramjit lifted the bags into the dickey of the private car.

'Are there bricks inside?' Paramjit asked, surprised by the weight of the bags.

'They are books,' Nagarwala replied. He thanked Harbhajan, got into the car and asked Paramjit to take him to the Parsi dharamshala.

It took less than ten minutes to cover the three-and-a-half-kilometre distance between Marina Hotel and the dharamshala. Once at the dharamshala, Nagarwala took out all the bags from the dickey—the two suitcases and the two bags—and headed straight to his room.

Dhur Darius Bagli, wife of the Parsi priest-caretaker of the dharamshala, remembered seeing Nagarwala striding towards his room. He seemed to be in a tearing hurry. But what surprised her was that he had barely noticed her and they had passed each other at the gate without the usual exchange of greetings. She also noticed that Nagarwala had got his 'hair shortened' and 'dyed'. That was, perhaps, the first time she had seen Nagarwala like that.

Paramjit had been waiting for fifteen to twenty minutes when he saw his passenger come out of the dharamshala and walk towards the car. Nagarwala asked Paramjit to help him carry the two suitcases from his room to the car.

'Take me to Kashmere Gate,' Nagarwala told the driver. He gave directions as Paramjit drove the six-kilometre distance. The car had reached Nicholson Road when Nagarwala asked Paramjit to stop in front of a two-storey house in a lane. It was around 4 p.m. Nagarwala got out of the car, opened the dickey and took out one of the suitcases.

'I have to deliver the suitcase and will be back soon,' he told Paramjit, who saw Nagarwala climb the stairs of the house.

The house belonged to Lt Col. P.S. Keshwala. Nagarwala knocked on the door. Keshwala's wife opened the door to see a 'perspiring' and somewhat dishevelled Nagarwala standing before her. 'Come in,' she said, informing him that her husband was not at home. 'Will you have tea?'

Nagarwala declined the offer and headed straight towards the refrigerator and took out a bottle of water. In a few seconds he had emptied it.

'He [Lt Col. Keshwala] could be at the British Council library or at Mrs Badhwar's place,' Mrs Keshwala said.

'Can you spare him for two or three days?' Nagarwala asked, only half-jokingly, telling her they planned to be go out of Delhi.

'Ask him, I have no objection,' she shrugged, surprised by the unusual request.

Nagarwala then told her he wanted to keep a suitcase in their house until he returned from his outstation trip. Mrs Keshwala looked even more surprised. Nagarwala was not carrying any suitcase with him. She nodded half-heartedly as Nagarwala stepped outside.

A little while later, Paramjit, who was waiting outside, saw Nagarwala hurrying back with the suitcase, which he had kept on the staircase before stepping into the flat. He said he looked visibly 'agitated' and that Mrs Keshwala refused to keep the suitcase in her house.

'Bad day,' he sighed, as he slumped into the back seat after putting the suitcase back into the dickey. Wherever he was going, he told the driver, he was not 'finding' anybody.

As the car eased back on to the main road, Nagarwala asked Paramjit to take him back to Connaught Place. This time his destination was M/S Pearey Lal Motors at the Janpath Tolstoy crossing. The eight-kilometre distance took about twenty minutes, but they drove in silence.

Mohini Badhwar, a common friend of Nagarwala and Lt Col. Keshwala, lived above M/S Pearey Lal Motors, a commercial establishment known for repairing Fiat, Ambassador and Ford cars. Nagarwala asked Paramjit to wait until he returned, then entered the building and took the stairs two at a time.

As Mrs Keshwala had told him, Nagarwala found his friend, the lieutenant colonel, at the Badhwar residence. 'I had gone to your house and was told that you would be here,' Nagarwala said even as Keshwala took in Nagarwala's 'new look' and 'clean-shaven' appearance with a puzzled expression.

Nagarwala ignored the look on his friend's face. 'Are you interested in making some "pin" [quick] money?' he asked, and then continued without waiting for a reply. He asked Keshwala to drive him to Ranikhet, a hill station and cantonment town about 370 kilometres from Delhi, and promised to bear the entire cost of the trip. He also told Keshwala that he would pay him Rs 350 in cash.

'Is this above board?' Keshwala asked. But Nagarwala's reply, Keshwala would say later, was 'vague' and 'nebulous'. Keshwala declined the offer to join him on his trip to Ranikhet.

While conversing with Keshwala, Nagarwala had moved to a window to keep an eye on Paramjit. He gestured to the driver to wait.

Nagarwala then changed the topic and asked Keshwala to lend him his car for a few hours. The vehicle was being used by Mohini Badhwar, who was at a nearby house on Tolstoy Marg. Nagarwala called up Badhwar and requested her to spare the car for a few hours. He promised to send the car back by 6 p.m.

When Subhash, Badhwar's driver, arrived with the black Fiat (DLJ 6110), Nagarwala asked him to park the car dickey-to-dickey with Paramjit's taxi. The luggage was then shifted to Keshwala's car.

'Will you be interested in using this car?' Nagarwala asked Keshwala, pointing towards the personal vehicle of Mohinder. Keshwala shook his head.

Nagarwala then took out a Rs 10 note from his pocket and gave it to Paramjit, who had been waiting there for nearly two hours. Paramjit drove off to his workplace in Connaught Place.

Nagarwala got into the driver's seat. 'I will be back by 7 p.m.,' he said as he eased his foot off the clutch and gently pressed the accelerator.

Bags Go 'Under the Bed'

From Janpath, Nagarwala drove to Defence Colony to meet his friend Nashir B. Captain, who was the branch accountant of *The Statesman* newspaper. Captain was an old friend who had in the past stayed at the Parsi dharamshala. N.B. Captain, his wife Nergiz and Nagarwala had watched a movie together at the Sheela Theatre in Paharganj the previous evening (23 May). The couple lived in a barsati in Defence Colony.

In the 1970s, Defence Colony was a quiet, upper-middle-class neighbourhood of charming two-storey houses called 'bungalows' (they are not really bungalows) with a pretty front patch of green. The most common rentals in Defence Colony were barsatis, which had one or two small rooms with a kitchen space and bathroom built on the terrace. Originally they had been designed as some sort of shelter for domestic staff, but over the years these barsatis, with their vast terraces, became popular among young couples, people working with foreign missions and students or research scholars who could not afford high rents.

It was around 5.30 p.m. As stated by Nergiz, who worked with the British Council library, she had just returned home when she heard her husband's voice: 'I have returned home a little early.' She opened the door. To her utter surprise she found Nagarwala standing outside with two suitcases. He was panting and 'profusely sweating'. A surprised Nergiz asked him to come inside.

Nagarwala said he was 'thirsty' and asked for a glass of Coke. There wasn't any. He drank 'three bottles of cold water' as he waited for his friend to come home.

When Captain arrived after a few minutes, Nagarwala told him he had come to return Rs 1,100 that he owed him. He had earlier borrowed Rs 2,000 from Captain and had so far returned Rs 900 in instalments. He handed Captain two envelopes, one containing Rs 1,100 in cash and another that had Rs 1,500.

He told Captain he would collect the envelope containing Rs 1,500 after he returned from Nainital. According to Captain's statement to the Reddy Commission later, Nagarwala appeared calm, spoke 'normally' and informed the couple that the black car in which he had come belonged to a colonel friend of his.

He requested Captain to keep the two suitcases—one black and the other red—in his house. The suitcases belonged to a friend who stayed with him at the dharamshala, Nagarwala said, adding that this friend thought it would be unsafe to keep them at the dharamshala, since they would be travelling out of Delhi for a few days.

The Captain couple, who knew Nagarwala well, did not find anything strange in the request. The two suitcases were 'placed under the bed' in the bedroom.

Nagarwala then left the place. It was around 6.30 p.m. when he appeared outside Mrs Badhwar's house in Janpath to hand over the car keys. Mrs Badhwar saw Nagarwala carrying a 'scooter tyre in hand' and looking a 'little tired'. He had grease on his clothes. His scooter had broken down, he told her. He declined her offer of tea and left.

Enter the Cops

It must have been around this time that the police team reached the Marina taxi stand and asked Mohinder if he knew about anyone who might have hired a car for a trip outside Delhi. By then Mohinder had realized something was wrong, because earlier in the day a police team led by the Tughlaq Road police station SHO A.K. Bose had made similar inquiries in the area. The police had spoken to a driver who had informed them that someone had booked a taxi for Ranikhet. But Bose had cut short his inquiries after being asked by ASP Kashyap on the wireless to rush back to the dharamshala to join the investigation.

In the evening, when the police came for the second time, Mohinder told them that Nagarwala had booked a big car for Nainital.

Paramjit, who had arrived at the taxi stand by then, gave the police a detailed account of Nagarwala's visits in his car that afternoon. The police told Paramjit to go to the dharamshala the next day, as Nagarwala had asked him to, at the appointed hour.

Notes

1. Nagarwala in his confession said he had visited a salon for a haircut, dyed his hair and had a shave after his visit to Defence Colony. But multiple witnesses pointed out that he had done all that during the day. The dyeing was done after his visit to Defence Colony, which was noticed by Nergiz Captain when he visited the second time.
2. Nagarwala would later say that the two envelopes contained Rs 3,500 and not Rs 2,600.
3. Strangely, the police did not pursue Paramjit's lead and did not contact Mrs Badhwar and Lt Col. Keshwala.

CHAPTER 5

NAGARWALA'S ARREST

Darius Erach Bagli, the high priest of Delhi Parsi Anjuman, was also the manager of the Parsi dharamshala. He had been living there with his wife Dhur since 1951 and the couple knew Nagarwala, who was a frequent visitor to the dharamshala since the 1950s. The dharamshala had come into existence in 1925, fourteen years after the British rulers shifted India's capital from Calcutta (now Kolkata) to Delhi.

A signboard with the words 'Delhi Parsi Anjuman' greets visitors as they leave Delhi Gate and enter Bahadur Shah Zafar Marg. Behind the board, inside a compound, are the Muhgusi Parsi dharamshala, or the rest house, and the Bhiwandiwall (community) hall. The compound also has a library that houses books on Zoroastrianism, its history and culture, and the Kaikhusuru Palonji Katrak Dar-e-Meher (or the Fire Temple). Every day, when the liturgy is performed at the temple, the names and deeds of great saints and kings of Iran are remembered.

In a write-up, the late R.V. Smith, a journalist and a quintessential Delhiwala, had described an early-morning scene at the dharamshala. 'The breeze blows in from the Yamuna, the beautiful dawn prayer Hosh-Baam is recited. The opening lines, "Through Asha most high,

Asha most pure", seem to merge with the first rays of the sun, for it is the sanctity of light that the temple personifies,' he wrote in a piece that appeared in *The Hindu*.[1]

On the morning of 24 May 1971, after lighting the fire at the temple, Bagli offered a lift to Nagarwala in his car from outside the dharamshala to Connaught Place. With him was his daughter. It was around 10.30 a.m. when Nagarwala got off at the Regal Theatre, saying he had some urgent work and would have to make a 'couple of telephone calls'.

Nagarwala had been occupying Room No. 3 in the dharamshala since November 1970. He shared the twin room with another Parsi, Dinwar Kolaji, from Bombay, who was in the city on official work for the past few weeks. Any Parsi could stay at the dharamshala, depending on the availability of rooms. For single occupancy, Rs 4 a day was charged, with additional charges for meals. One could stay up to seven days at a stretch, which could be extended by another week. Beyond fourteen days, one had to pay Rs 5 a day, but the extension was at the discretion of the manager. Nagarwala had been staying at the dharamshala for nearly eight months.

On the evening of 24 May, two police Jeeps came to a halt in front of the compound and nearly a dozen policemen got out of the two vehicles. Among them were ASP D.K. Kashyap, Hari Dev, SHO of the Chanakyapuri police station, and A.K. Bose, SHO of the Tughlaq Road police station. The three barged into the premises while the other men in khaki stood guard outside.

Inside the compound, Dhur, the manager's wife, felt a tingle of alarm when she saw the officers approaching, but stood her ground,

---

1 R.V. Smith, 'The Parsi Link with Delhi', *The Hindu*, 6 January 2020, https://www.thehindu.com/society/history-and-culture/how-the-parsi-communitys-association-with-delhi-dates-back-to-akbars-time/article30492344.ece

questioning the police's authority to enter the complex that had a temple exclusively meant for Parsi Zoroastrians. The officers brushed aside her protests and asked for Bagli, the manager, who was then busy directing a play inside. The proceeds from the play were to contribute to the effort of Bangladeshis fighting for freedom.

Hearing the commotion outside, Bagli came out, along with a few others.

'Who is Bagli?' one of the officers asked.

'I am Bagli,' the manager said, identifying himself.

One of the police officers then asked him to accompany them to Room No. 3.

Bagli had no clue what was happening. The police had never entered the dharamshala premises before. He escorted them to the room, which was latched from the outside but not locked. The officers opened the door and went in. The three then started going through the belongings of the two guests, who were both away. The room had an attached bath and a partitioned cupboard for the occupants to keep their belongings in.

Bagli, who had been silent all this while, asked the officers if they had a search warrant. 'In certain cases, no search warrant is required,' he was told.

The manager realized there was nothing much he could do by staying there, and decided to inform the dharamshala management. The anjuman was, after all, managed by senior government officials belonging to the city's powerful Parsi community.

Bagli headed towards the office room, where he dialled the number of the president of the Parsi Anjuman, S.D. Nargolwala, an Indian Civil Service (ICS) officer working with the government of India. Nargolwala lived in a bungalow at 5-B Zakir Hussain Marg, a stretch that connected India Gate with south-east Delhi. The road was named after the third President of India, who had died in office in

May 1969. Zakir Hussain was also an educationist and a co-founder of the university Jamia Millia Islamia.

Revolver Wrapped in a White Shirt

While Bagli was making the telephone call to Nargolwala, the police were going through Nagarwala's belongings. By the time the high priest returned to the scene of action, Nagarwala's room appeared to have been 'ransacked', Bagli would recall later.

One of the officers held 'a revolver wrapped in a white shirt' and some cartridges. Papers lay strewn all around the room as the policemen searched the suitcases, which did not have any locks. Bagli watched as the officers finished their work. The search lasted about half an hour.

The police officers made a panchnama, listing the revolver, the documents they had found, Nagarwala's old and new passports, photographs and cyclostyled copies of his biodata. Kashyap even rolled his eyes while going through a copy of the biodata. A moment later he appeared gleeful—they had found what they were looking for, including Nagarwala's physical description.

According to the documents they had found, Rustom Sohrab Nagarwala hailed from Pune. Born on 2 March 1922 in Bombay, he studied at St. Vincent's High School in Pune between 1928 and 1936. After completing his Intermediate of Arts (IA) from the Nowrosjee Wadia College, he joined the Indian Army as an officer and was with the Army Ordnance Corps between 1943 and 1951.

The documents revealed that the former army captain could converse in English, French, Japanese, Hindi, Marathi and Gujarati. He used to run a tourist taxi service, had a professional driving licence and had also worked as a tourist guide in India. He had briefly lived in Nagoya, Japan, where he had taught English at the American Culture Center, Nagoya, and at the University in Nagoya.

Nagarwala's biodata described him as a 'friendly' companion, travel guide, shopping adviser, car driver and someone with excellent practical knowledge of India, Ceylon (as Sri Lanka was known then) and Hong Kong. It said he could work in any administrative capacity in any office, while, for the purpose of export and import, he had excellent contacts with business houses in all the 'above countries', especially in Japan. According to the biodata, he could ride horses, swim, play contract bridge and cook Indian dishes.

Inspectors Bose and Hari Dev had also found a few letters, visiting cards, driving licences, a steel badge (No. 7778) along with a licence, another steel badge (No. 856) and a few documents in Japanese. The papers in Japanese, later translated, pertained to Nagarwala's application for a licence to the Kobayashi Licensing Authority, Japan, regarding 'cam, cam gear, cog wheel, etc.'. Another document the officers found was from the licensing authority rejecting his application on 12 April 1966. A few photographs of Nagarwala and a copy of the Indian Army's Officers' Record of Service book – 439 were also among the documents seized.

While the search was on, a telephone call was received at the dharamshala. A policeman came running to inform the officers that DIG P.A. Rosha was on the line. However, Rosha seemed to be unaware that the team had reached the Parsi dharamshala in pursuit of the man who had allegedly fled with Rs 60 lakh. His call was in response to S.D. Nargorwala's call to him. Nargorwala had complained to the DIG about the raid at the dharamshala without a 'search warrant' and accused the police of acting in a 'high-handed manner'.

But Rosha was firm. He informed the senior bureaucrat that he had himself taken 'the responsibility for this action' and ordered a search of the premises as it was 'justified and in accordance with the law'. Rosha told Nargolwala that Bose had briefed him about the developments that had led the police to the dharamshala.

Around 7.30 p.m., another telephone call was received at the dharamshala's office. This time, Inspector Bose picked up the phone. A woman was at the other end of the line. She inquired about Nagarwala. Bose informed her that Nagarwala was not available at the moment and that he could note down a message for him. The lady replied that Nagarwala had asked her to ring him up at that time, which was why she was calling.

Bose tried to get her name and address, but was unsuccessful. She refused to part with any information and disconnected the call. But overall, the police search at the dharamshala had yielded a lot of information. They now knew all the details about Nagarwala, and, if everything went to plan, he would be in handcuffs soon. The New Delhi district police, led by ASP Kashyap, had made a breakthrough in a sensational case in record time.

The ASP and his two inspectors had been on the job since morning and needed a quick wash and change of clothes. Hari Dev and Bose, who had years of experience behind them, asked sub-inspector Surender Singh, Hawa Singh, who was Bose's assistant wireless operator, constable Nand Lal and the two taxi drivers Balbir Singh and Om Prakash to stay back at the dharamshala. They had to keep an eye on the place, the officers said, as the alleged culprit might come back at night. The five men were given Nagarwala's photographs, seized from his room, so that they could identify him as soon as he arrived. A police Jeep was parked at a distance from the dharamshala, in case there was any trouble.

Bagli and his wife were given Rosha's telephone number and asked to contact the DIG as soon as Nagarwala returned to the dharamshala, or provide any information that could help the police track him.

Dinwar Kolaji, Nagarwala's roommate, returned from his office and found the door of the room open. He pushed open the door, entered and froze. All his belongings, including his clothes, lay 'scattered' all around. Kolaji rushed to Bagli's room and was told the police were looking for Nagarwala, so they had searched his room.

'Nagarwala Is at the Dharamshala'

Around 8 p.m., Balbir Singh noticed a scooter-taxi stop outside the dharamshala. A man, carrying a scooter tyre and tube and a Rexine bag, walked into the compound.

Balbir, however, failed to recognize Nagarwala, who had had his hair trimmed and dyed. The policemen, who had been shown photographs of Nagarwala a few hours earlier, also didn't recognize him.

Mrs Bagli was sitting with two friends when she saw Nagarwala enter the premises. Already upset, she bolted her room from the inside. Her husband, too, was in the room, tense and lost deep in thought.

Mrs Bagli dialled the number the policemen had given her. 'Nagarwala is at the dharamshala,' she spoke into the phone even as her two friends rushed out to inform the policemen at the gate that the person they were looking for had arrived.

Unaware of the developments, Nagarwala walked into his room to find it turned upside down. Like his roommate, Nagarwala rushed to Bagli's room and banged on the door. Bagli did not want to come out and talk to him. Mrs Bagli opened the door and informed Nagarwala that Bagli was not at the dharamshala.

Nagarwala was furious. 'Who ransacked my room?' he demanded. Mrs Bagli, who, too, was seething inside, bluntly told Nagarwala that the police had searched his room. She added that they suspected he had stolen Rs 60 lakh from a bank.

'It's all rubbish!' Nagarwala shouted. 'What right do the police have to search my room?'

The angry exchange between the two caught the attention of Hawa Singh and Nand Lal, the two policemen who were outside the compound. They ran to the manager's room and caught hold of Nagarwala.

'I will get you suspended!' Nagarwala screamed at Hawa Singh. The assistant wireless operator pulled out his service revolver, pointed it at Nagarwala and asked him to follow his instructions. Nagarwala struggled to free himself but couldn't. The policemen dragged him outside, where others, including the two drivers, joined them. Nagarwala was made to sit on a chair in the compound while the policemen waited for their seniors to arrive. Balbir Singh and Om Prakash took a close look at Nagarwala and confirmed that he was the one they had driven around the city earlier in the day.

At the Tughlaq Road police station, a message crackled on the wireless set: 'Nagarwala came to dharamshala and has been arrested.' Kashyap, Hari Dev and Bose, who had by then had a quick wash at the police station, rushed to the dharamshala, covering a distance of seven kilometres in fifteen minutes.

Kashyap asked Sub-Inspector Surender Kumar Singh to check the tyre the police had seized from Nagarwala. A few hundred-rupee notes fell out when the policeman deflated the tube. 'I don't know how many were in there. But there were two bundles. Hari Dev took the notes,' Hawa Singh said, adding that when he lifted the scooter tyre (manufactured by Firestone) to hand it over to Hari Dev, the notes had bulged out. The tyre was deflated and two bundles were found. Hari Dev took charge of the tyre, the money and the suitcases.

The officers then took Nagarwala and the two taxi drivers to the Parliament Street police station, leaving Hawa Singh and Surender Kumar Singh to guard Nagarwala's room and keep an eye on the dharamshala.

Shortly after the officers had left, the dharamshala received another telephone call. Bagli asked Hawa Singh to answer it. A senior Delhi Police officer of the rank of superintendent of police (SP) was supposedly on the line. The caller said that Nagarwala was 'innocent'.

'I told him that Nagarwala had already been taken to the Parliament Street police station by D.K. Kashyap sahib,' Hawa Singh told the Reddy Commission later.

Notes

1. Conflicting versions were given by Hawa Singh, Surender Kumar Singh and Hari Dev before the Reddy Commission regarding the seizure of the tyre and the tube containing Rs 30,000 in cash, and also about the timing of the seizure of the licensed revolver from Nagarwala's room.

CHAPTER 6

THE INTERROGATION

Ved Prakash Malhotra cursed his fate as he sat outside the Parliament Street police station, a walking distance from the SBI head office, where he held a position of authority and commanded respect. But after what had happened that morning, especially his brief but devastating interaction with P.N. Haksar, secretary to the Prime Minister, all that seemed in the distant past, perhaps irreversibly over.

As Malhotra sat in silence, his mind heavy, there was a sudden flurry of activity. It was Nagarwala, escorted by policemen, being walked towards him.

Malhotra stood up, shaking with anger, as he remembered the morning's telephone call that had changed his life. 'You must arrest the lady, his accomplice, who had spoken to me,' he shouted. Tears welled up in his eyes as he spoke. He gave vent to his emotions. 'I am innocent ... He has got me involved,' he said, gesturing towards Nagarwala.

In police functioning, bringing alleged criminals face to face with their victims is a multipurpose tool. For one, it instantly establishes eyewitness identification, a standard legal requirement.

One of the officers who had heard Malhotra's outburst leaned towards him. 'No lady was involved,' he told the cashier. 'He is the one.' It was the burly man standing before them, the officer explained, who had spoken to Malhotra in the voices of both Haksar and Indira Gandhi.

Malhotra was stunned. By then Nagarwala had walked up to Malhotra and apologized for his actions. Then, looking at the policemen, he said, 'He [Malhotra] is innocent.'

Before Malhotra could react, the policemen whisked Nagarwala away to the Ashoka Road side of the police station, where suspects were confined for interrogation. Now one more task remained, and it was a difficult one. The entire stolen cash had to be recovered.

Nagarwala was not an easy nut to crack. Veteran interrogators such as Hari Dev, popularly known as Panditji in Delhi Police circles, and Bose had quite a job to do. One bullied and threatened, the other acted friendly and sympathetic as the game of good-cop-bad-cop started, with Bose playing the good cop in the first round of interrogation.

But no amount of questioning and cajoling helped. Nagarwala kept repeating his statement. He refused to budge from what he had been saying right from the beginning—that more people were involved in the loot and the Rs 30,000 in cash that had been recovered from the scooter tyre was his 'share of the booty'. The 'rest of the money', he insisted, had been taken away by a 'party' whose identity he was not aware of.

SP (CID) Markandey Singh, New Delhi District SP Y. Rajpal and a battery of ace investigators joined the interrogation, but nothing significant emerged. The accused gave nothing away.

As the clock ticked late into the evening, the cops came up with an ingenious idea. DIG Rosha, who was in civilian clothes and had not yet met Nagarwala, should pose as a senior SBI officer and bargain with him.

Rajpal and Rosha walked towards Nagarwala, who was 'standing on the pavement' on the Ashoka Road side of the police station compound. It took five minutes for them to convince Nagarwala that Rosha, 'the bank official', would ensure a substantial reward for him if he provided credible information leading to the recovery of the 'balance amount'.

The strategy worked. Nagarwala agreed to lead the cops to the place where the money was hidden. But he laid down two conditions. The police should not ill-treat him because he had, in the past, suffered a 'paralytic stroke' and already had a 'heart ailment'; and he wanted 'plainclothes people' to accompany him, not those in uniform.

Bose, who was playing the good cop, had gained Nagarwala's trust. It was apparent that the accused was more relaxed when he talked to the inspector. So it was decided that Bose would accompany Nagarwala and extract from him as much information as possible. After all, Nagarwala had been parting with small bits of information while speaking to Bose. He had told him that after he had had a haircut at Connaught Place, he had gone to have a meal at Wenger's.

Nagarwala, however, came up with another condition. He told Kashyap, Hari Dev and Bose that none of his 'Parsi' friends—Gotla, Captain, Bagli and Keshwala—were involved and should not be harassed. As for himself, he said, he was prepared to 'confess his guilt' and added that 'Malhotra is innocent', repeating what he had said earlier but without any prodding.

To Bose he confided that the lady who had called up the dharamshala number while the police were waiting there was his 'girlfriend', but said she had nothing to do with the case. He said he had wanted to take her to Ranikhet on a holiday and pleaded with Bose 'not to pursue' the matter further. The inspector nodded and continued with his efforts to extract more information.

Now that Nagarwala was ready to cooperate, the police prepared a disclosure memo and seized the bank's car, DLK 760, which Malhotra had used to transport the cash. The car was already inside the police station compound, parked since the afternoon when Malhotra had come to lodge his complaint.

Bose, Hari Dev, Kashyap, Markandey Singh and the two taxi drivers, Balbir Singh and Om Prakash, accompanied Nagarwala to A-277 Defence Colony, the residence of the Captains. As agreed, four or five police officers[2] went with Nagarwala to the barsati. The others waited outside at a distance. Nagarwala was 'panting' and rested twice as they climbed the stairs.

N.B. Captain was sleeping on the terrace when the doorbell rang. There were several knocks on the door. It must have been around 10 p.m. or a little later. Captain opened the door and found Nagarwala with four or five people standing behind him. Nagarwala introduced the policemen as his friends. The suitcases belonged to them, he said, adding that he had come to collect the suitcases.

'When did you dye your hair?' asked Nergiz, who had followed her husband to the door. Nagarwala gave a nervous laugh.

After Captain unlocked the bedroom door, two of the policemen who had come with Nagarwala entered, dragged the two Rexine suitcases—one black, the other red— out from under the bed and left the room. Before going down the stairs, Nagarwala told the Captains that he would meet them 'after his return from Nainital'. Stopping on their way down the stairs from the second floor, Markandey Singh 'opened' the suitcases and saw the notes.

There were no proper streetlights outside, but as they were leaving, the police saw Captain waving at Nagarwala from the second floor before the group disappeared into the dark.

---

3   According to police statements, the number of officers going to the Defence Colony barsati floor varied, and hence became a subject of contention.

The Interrogation

After the cops reached the Parliament Street police station, the bags were opened and Malhotra was called to identify the cash. He took a quick look at the wads of currency notes and 'identified' them as the money he had handed over to Nagarwala. The black suitcase contained Rs 28 lakh, all in hundred-rupee notes.

When the notes in the red suitcase were being counted manually, Om Prakash, the taxi driver, the recipient of Nagarwala's generosity earlier in the day, 'threw' five hundred-rupee notes into the suitcase, which the police seized.

The red suitcase yielded Rs 31,94,300. In all, the police had recovered Rs 59,94,300. The suitcases were then sealed and a recovery memo prepared and signed by the witnesses.

There was still a shortfall of Rs 5,700. Nagarwala revealed that he had 'returned' Rs 2,600 (twenty-six hundred-rupee notes) to his friend Captain of A-277 Defence Colony.

Nagarwala then saw DIG Rosha inside the police station instructing his officers and realized he had fallen for their trap. His face fell. 'Sir, you are a police officer, not a bank official,' he said, according to Rosha's statement.

The News Spreads

In newspaper offices, 24 May, with the mercury touching 43 degree Celsius, had so far been an uneventful day. Then, sometime in the afternoon, the lone telephone rang at the crime reporters' desk at *The Statesman* office in New Delhi. According to *India Today*, a reporter picked up the phone.

'*Daka par gaya 60 lakh ka sarkari bank Parliament Street mein* [There has been a robbery at a government bank on Parliament Street],' the voice at the other end said. The caller spoke in a hushed voice, but the reporter recognized it as that of his dependable police contact.

In a moment the atmosphere changed in the newsroom. Soon after that, city reporters of all major dailies were on their toes. It was big news—someone had decamped with Rs 60 lakh following a telephone call to the bank. The call had come apparently from the Prime Minister, asking a bank official to hand over the money to her 'courier'. Soon, an army of reporters were on the ground, doing the rounds of various police stations and the SBI branch on Parliament Street.

It wasn't only the press. Among the visitors were senior Delhi administration officials, the joint secretary in the Prime Minister's Office B.N. Tandon and his younger brother G.N. Tandon, an employee of Bharat Heavy Electricals Limited. The Tandon brothers were no strangers to District SP Rajpal, who lightheartedly told the younger Tandon to see the cash on display at the police station as he might 'never get a chance' in his lifetime 'to see so much money'. G.N. Tandon went in to see the currency notes.

Assistant Inspector-General of Police Gautam Kaul, a young IPS officer and a first cousin of Indira Gandhi, had been at the police station ever since the news had broken. Kaul, a 1965-batch IPS officer, was in charge of the police's press-relations wing. Kaul rang up several newspaper offices, informing them that Delhi's IGP, L.S. Bisht, would address a late-night press conference.

At the press conference, the seals on the suitcases were broken to display the seized cash for the benefit of press photographers. Rosha, being the head of the New Delhi range, did most of the talking at the press meet. Nagarwala was paraded before the media. Once the press conference was over, Kashyap resumed his interrogation.

Nagarwala's tone had changed after the recovery of the cash and he had become 'more communicative'. He told Kashyap that he had 'changed the voice himself' and spoken to Malhotra, mimicking the voices of both Indira Gandhi and P.N. Haksar. He also said he had called the bank from a telephone booth on its premises.

Like the others, Kashyap at first found it hard to believe that a man could mimic a woman's voice. Prodded by the investigators, Nagarwala then mimicked the Prime Minister's voice for the police to hear. He did that 'two to three times' to convince those present that it was indeed him.

'Why not arrange a telephonic conversation between Malhotra and Nagarwala, and tape-record it?' a police personnel suggested. Everyone agreed. It was already late and a recorder had to be arranged. The New Delhi district police did not have one. So an officer was sent to the CID wing of the special branch to fetch a tape recorder.

Bose was, however, 'completely satisfied' that Nagarwala could mimic the voice of the Prime Minister. On the police's request, Nagarwala showed two magic tricks with a handkerchief and a glass of water. Nagarwala had told his interrogators that he used to perform such tricks for the jawans when he was in the army.

After the recorder arrived, the police wanted to record the conversation 'without [Nagarwala's] knowledge', but Nagarwala said he was 'too tired' and promised to repeat the conversation 'the next morning'.

When Nagarwala re-enacted the telephone conversation he had had with Malhotra the previous day, he spoke from the police station and Malhotra was made to receive the call at SP Rajpal's office, which was in the same compound, barely 100 metres away. The conversation, repeated two or three times, was 'taped' without Nagarwala's knowledge. Finally, the senior officers were 'satisfied' that Malhotra could mimic Indira Gandhi's voice.

While the recording was done 'for the satisfaction of senior officers', Kashyap wanted to record the conversation for his 'personal use'. The tape recorder was in the personal custody of the ASP.

Kashyap promptly noted in the case diary: The accused demonstrated the voices of Mr Haksar and the Prime Minister, which was 'certified by Malhotra to be correct'. A case diary is a record of daily investigations in a case. Under Section 172 of the Criminal Procedure Code (CrPC), a police officer probing a case is required to maintain a daily record of the investigation being done. A court can ask for the case diary as part of the trial. However, the case diary may not as such be used as evidence.

By now, Nagarwala had become even more communicative. He said it was not a planned act and the idea to cheat the bank had come to him when he had gone to the bank to get change for a hundred-rupee note. He said he had no accomplices, elaborated on his biodata, which was already with the police, and spoke in detail about his background in the armed forces, his accidents and his visits to Japan in search of work.

'Wanted to Do Something Sensational'

Asked what his motive was, Nagarwala gave a lengthy explanation. He said he had been greatly affected by the 'loot and murder' in 1947, during the Partition—he was posted in Ambala then. And he also found it impossible to 'tolerate' what was going on in Bangladesh then. His motive, he revealed, was to loot the bank and do something 'sensational' to highlight the cause of Bangladeshi freedom fighters.

Nagarwala said he wanted the government to recognize an independent Bangladesh, but that he repented what he had done (looting the SBI). He said he was 'much pained by ruining [the] life of an innocent person [Malhotra]'. He admitted his guilt, said he was 'afraid of publicity' in newspapers and repeated that he would confess to his crime before the court. In fact, soon after the cash was recovered, Nagarwala made the offer to confess in court.

The investigators could not have asked for more. The officers had been confabulating among themselves about this. As per their plan, Malhotra was to be the 'star witness' because it was his tip-off about the taxi number that had led to the breakthrough. Not much else was required to be done in the case. Among the things left to be done, the police needed to send somebody to Ranikhet to check the veracity of Nagarwala's assertion that he had intended to go there to return money to a friend, a retired army official. Within Delhi, Bose was to make a visit to Captain to recover the envelopes containing Rs 2,600, which was part of the bank's money. The investigators insisted on going through the due process.

A personal search of Nagarwala, according to the seizure report prepared by the police, yielded four keys, one handkerchief containing Rs 32 in cash, a wristwatch, a golden-cut Omega and $3 of one-dollar denomination each.

The seizure memos also mentioned one tyre (Firestone) along with the tube (National), and the bank's steel trunk 'whose size was about 1-1/2 feet in height, 2 feet in breadth, about 2-3/4 feet in length'. The trunk had two kundas (handles) at the front and two handling kundas on the sides. It had a 'jasti colour'—made of or treated with galvanized zinc.

The olive-green felt cap, found opposite the bungalow near the Government Higher Secondary School, Defence Colony, was mentioned in a separate memo, apart from the cash and the items seized from the dharamshala. Although the revolver had been seized from Nagarwala's room on the evening of 24 May, the case diary mentioned that a police team, led by Kashyap, had made another trip to the dharamshala after the accused had disclosed that he possessed 'a revolver .38 bore', which was in a suitcase 'underneath his clothes'. The suitcase was opened with one of the keys found on Nagarwala. A revolver with twelve cartridges had indeed been found, which led to another case being registered under the Arms Act 1959.

Nagarwala would later tell Jagdish Prasad, a CID officer with Delhi Police, that it was a 'private revolver of .38 bore'. When he was in the army, there was no need for a licence for a private revolver. But on his release from the army, he said, he had rushed to Japan for treatment and forgotten about the weapon.

Nagarwala said he was checking his belongings after his return from Japan when he found the revolver, which he had brought with him to Delhi from Poona (now Pune). He said he had thought of depositing it with the government, but, in view of the legal implications, had decided to keep quiet.

Senior officials again confabulated among themselves and concluded that there was no need to ask for Nagarwala's police remand, since he was going to admit his guilt in court and the stolen property had also been recovered. Nagarwala, they decided, should be charge-sheeted at the earliest. There should be no delay—Nagarwala should be presented before the magistrate the very next day, they all agreed. Although Rajpal would later say that Kashyap felt so, Bose attributed the decision to Rajpal later.

Hope of Reward and Disappointment

Pleased with Delhi Police for their quick and efficient recovery of the stolen money, SBI officials informally assured senior police officials of a cash reward of Rs 50,000 for the team that had cracked the case. Kashyap could barely conceal his happiness. He had solved a sensational case—that, too, within a few hours. He had also promised his personal orderly that he would gift him something for his day's hard work. The orderly would later say that Kashyap had told him that if he 'gets something in this case', he would also give him 'something'.

Kashyap hoped to get the lion's share of the reward. So did the two inspectors, Bose and Hari Dev. But the money never came.

Inspector Bose, who subsequently left Delhi Police, would tell his friend Jagdish Chandra Dhir, Kashyap's brother-in-law, that they were not given proper rewards because of certain 'political considerations'. While deposing before the Reddy Commission, Bose would say that he left the force because he 'felt no future prospects for me' and that he was disappointed. 'My work was not appreciated in any manner … [in terms of] promotional avenues and cash rewards,' he said. Bose resigned from the service and joined as a security officer with the DCM Group in Kota.

In his statement, DIG Rosha admitted before the commission that it had been 'informally discussed that a substantial reward would be given to the police officials'. The amount was Rs 50,000, he recalled.

At a meeting in Parliament House, where IGP L.S. Bisht and District SP Rajpal were also present soon after the case was solved, Rosha had suggested that 'since the name of the Prime Minister' was involved, 'no reward should be accepted or announced until the case is adjudicated'. Bisht had agreed with him and the decision was subsequently conveyed to the bank officials. The decision demoralized the officials who were part of the investigation. As Jagdish Chand Dhir would say, he noticed a change in the mood of both Kashyap and Bose.

Justice Reddy, who was severely critical of the investigation in the case, mentioned the 'expectations' of Delhi Police even in 1978 about the possibility of getting the reward amount.

Salt-Free Food

At the Parliament Street police station, Nagarwala was given food 'without salt', as he had requested. He carried his own medicines (Equibrom tablets), which he had been taking since his paralytic stroke and for the heart ailment he suffered from. At night, the high-profile accused was lodged in a cell at the police station. The two taxi drivers—Balbir Singh and Om Prakash—spent the night in an adjoining cell, 'keeping an eye' on Nagarwala, lest he did something drastic.

In Bombay, Nagarwala's seventy-five-year-old mother, Goolbai, was shocked. She broke down when she heard the news of her son's arrest on All India Radio that evening. Fearing that the police might knock on her door any moment, she 'destroyed the occasional letters' her son used to write to her.

'Russy was dogged by misfortune,' she would later write to Indira Gandhi, seeking her intervention in the matter.

Notes

1. The timing of the recording—whether on the night of 24 May or during the day on 26 May—is disputed.
2. The second visit of the police to the dharamshala has been disputed. It was claimed by the police that the revolver was seized during the second visit.

CHAPTER 7

JUDGMENT DELIVERED

Nagarwala waited for daybreak with an anxious heart. The dal-roti served to him was hardly appetizing. Rather it led to a gastritis attack. After the morning's chai and biscuit, he had to sit for a long time at the Parliament Street police station. Then in the afternoon, on 25 May, he was produced in the court of S.P. Karkare, the judicial magistrate in charge of the Parliament Street police station, for a one-day judicial custody. The police case diary mentioned: 'Since no other compliance of the investigation remains to be done and the accused is insistent on confessing [to] the crime, therefore, it is necessary to get his statement recorded under Section 164 [of the] CrPC. Thus a request has been made to grant one day's judicial remand of the accused.'

Karkare went through the papers and remanded Nagarwala to judicial custody and ordered that he be produced on 26 May. 'If the police wants to get the confession of the accused under Section 164 of the CrPC, a statement should be made to my link magistrate, Shri G.S. Aggarwal,' the magistrate's verdict read.

The function of a link magistrate is to record confessions, dying declarations, and the holding of identification parades of accused persons and case property, etc. The link magistrate has jurisdiction over the same area as the magistrate directing the order.

The SBI, too, moved an application seeking custody of the cash retrieved from Nagarwala. Karkare approved it, asking the police to hand over the money on 'superdari' (custody) and directed the bank to execute a bond assuring the court that it would produce the seized property as and when required by it.

Nagarwala was then sent to Tihar Jail. Also known as Tihar Ashram, the prison house is the largest complex of prisons in South Asia. It derives its name from the village, now located in west Delhi near Janakpuri and Hari Nagar. The Tihar prison house is supposedly a correctional institution expected to convert its inmates into law-abiding members of society and empowering them with livelihood skills, education and respect for the law. It's stated objective is also to better the inmates' self-esteem and strengthen their desire to improve. Tihar, unfortunately, like other prison houses, is notorious for custodial deaths. The 2021 National Crime Research Bureau report on prison statistics notes that the number of deaths in jails in 2020 were 1,887, out of which 1,642 were classified as 'natural deaths' and 189 due to 'unnatural causes'.

In the jail, on the first evening itself on 25 May 1971, curious prisoners, by now aware of the sensational SBI case, thronged around Nagarwala to take a look at the man who had mimicked the voice of Indira Gandhi. Two of them—Mohinder Kumar Shastri, a science graduate from Punjab University and MA in sociology from the Aligarh Muslim University, and Gulzari Lal Tandon, a cloth merchant from Delhi's Chandni Chowk area—would go on to become close friends with him.

At night, Nagarwala was given a cot between two others occupied by Shastri and Tandon. The jail authorities had asked both of them to 'keep an eye on Nagarwala' at night so he didn't do anything 'drastic'. To Tandon, Nagarwala appeared to be a 'carefree man, not perturbed'. He behaved 'as if nothing had happened'.

The three tried to chitchat before going to bed. Shastri, who was well versed in law, cautioned Nagarwala that 'in case he made the statement [confession], he can be convicted'. But Nagarwala did not pay attention to his advice. He was 'confident' that after he had made the statement, he would be released. A group of other inmates in the room heard their conversation with rapt attention. All of them held Shastri in high regard. After all, he was well educated and understood the intricacies of law. His advice was taken seriously. But Nagarwala remained confident he would be released.

The next day, on 26 May 1971, Nagarwala was taken to the court. Shastri, who, too, had to appear in the court, accompanied him in the jail vehicle. They were among twenty-eight others who were to be produced in their respective courts that day. Shastri persisted with his advice to not make the statement of confession, but Nagarwala, who had made up his mind, told him that he 'takes life as it comes'.

Nagarwala appeared in the court of G.S. Agarwal, JMIC, in New Delhi around 3.30 p.m.

'He [Nagarwala] insisted that I record his confessional statement,' Agarwal said. He warned him that 'he is not bound to make a confessional statement and, in any case, if he made any statement, it might be used as evidence against him'. Agarwal explained to him at length that his statement would be recorded after making sure it was voluntary. Nagarwala did not budge from his position and reiterated that his statement be recorded.

'I again remanded him to judicial custody for one day to give him time to think about it. I ordered that he be produced on 27 May,' the magistrate told the Reddy Commission later.

Agarwal acceded to the request of Nagarwala that, he, being a former army officer and also physically disabled, be given a 'B' class jail, with better facilities.

The next day, on 27 May, Nagarwala was produced in Agarwal's court again. 'I made him sit in my courtroom for about two hours and did not allow any policeman to enter the court room in this period,' Agarwal said. He again asked whether Nagarwala's statement was 'voluntary—without any inducement, threat or promise from any quarter'. Nagarwala persisted with his request. It was done 'in camera', as per the wish of the accused. Agarwal wrote the statement as Nagarwala spoke.

He gave the Parsi dharamshala at Delhi Gate, New Delhi, as his address, and told Agarwal:

> My case is that of a flight of fancy, which I put into execution in the heat of the moment. My motive was to do something fantastic for Bangladesh. At the same time, I would get a bit of limelight and thereby come to the Prime Minister's notice.
>
> The whole idea was entirely my own. No other person or persons is involved. By my stupid and foolish actions, I have jeopardized the career of an innocent man, Shri V.P. Malhotra, chief cashier of the State Bank of India, for which I am truly sorry. I have also endangered my good name and reputation as I am facing charges of cheating and fraud.
>
> It was never my intention to cheat or defraud. I have voluntarily returned the money to the bank through the police. It was I and I alone who led the police initially to me. It was I and I alone who returned the money to the police without any threat or coercion on their part. I have never made the slightest attempt to escape or run away with the money. It was purely a big hoax.
>
> I have given my fullest and wholehearted cooperation to both the bank and the police, and now to the judiciary. I do not have any intention of cashing in on any of the publicity offered by the press or new magazines.
>
> To the State, I have never been convicted for any criminal offence. My record both in the army and in the civil world is perfectly clean. I pray to the court that in view of my clean record and career, and my future prospects, it shows me mercy and deals

with me leniently. This is my first offence as such. I have made a clean-cut confession of my guilt and plead guilty.

The confession also gave Nagarwala's version of what had transpired on 24 May 1971:

On 24 May 1971 nothing had been prearranged or preplanned. I happened to be in the vicinity of State Bank of India, Parliament Street, New Delhi, around 12 o'clock in the afternoon. I went into the bank to get change for a hundred-rupee note. As it was hot outside, I sat down on one of the couches near the trophy showcase to rest for a few minutes. I noticed two public call booths.

Suddenly, on the spur of the moment, my thoughts started churning and my blood ran hot with the excitement of adventure. I looked up the telephone directory and under the SBI listing I saw the name of one Mr V.P. Malhotra, chief cashier, telephone 45468. I took a stroll down the bank counters until I reached Mr Malhotra's office. He was sitting with a few visitors, and I observed him from outside through the glass partition of his office. I returned to the telephone booth and dialled his number and asked for Mr V.P. Malhotra.

When Mr Malhotra identified himself as the person speaking, I told him that the PM's secretary, Mr P.N. Haksar, would like to speak to him. Then I pretended to be Mr Haksar and the PM alternately during the course of my telephonic conversation with Mr Malhotra. I hereby give the sequence of the telephonic conversation.

Me (as Mr Haksar): Mr Malhotra, I am speaking on behalf of the Prime Minister. A matter of great national importance has come up. The PM and I am depending on you to use your discretion and initiative in this matter. A sum of Rs 60 lakh has to be made ready for the relief of Bangladesh almost immediately. Can you do it?

Mr Malhotra: Please wait a minute. I shall check and let you know. [Then there was pause of two minutes.] Yes, sir, I can have the money ready within twenty minutes.

Me (as Mr Haksar): Good, now listen carefully to my instructions. After I have finished speaking, the PM will also speak to you personally. A courier will await you outside the gate of Freemason Church opposite the SBI building. You will start with the money in your car. The courier will then identify himself to you by code words, which the PM alone knows. You will take the courier with you in the car, along with the money, and accompany him to Palam airport if necessary.

Mr Malhotra: I am sorry, but I cannot take the money out of the bank without a receipt. However, I am prepared to bring the money to the PM's residence and obtain a memo receipt from her. That, too, is highly irregular, but I am prepared to do it.

Me (as Mr Haksar): That would mean you will be noticed by everybody around, and as the matter is top secret, the PM cannot be involved officially or unofficially. Besides, the time is too short and the courier cannot be delayed. However, I am now putting you through to the Prime Minister herself. Please speak to her. [Pause of five seconds.]

Me, in the voice of the PM: Mr Malhotra, this is PM Indira Gandhi speaking.

Mr Malhotra: Namaste, Mataji. I am an old soldier and I am prepared to do as you order.

Me as the PM: Very good, Mr Malhotra. When you meet the courier, he will ask you, '*Aap kis desh ka, babuji?*' And you will reply, '*Bharat ka.*' The courier in return will say '*Main Bangladesh ka, babuji.*' Once this identification is complete, you will follow the instructions of the courier. Under no circumstances should he be delayed. After you have handed over the money to the courier, please report to me at my residence. Thank you.

After having the conversation, I came out of the booth. About half an hour later, I was standing outside the SBI building near the entry gate. I noticed a car driving out of the SBI building, cross the road and park at the gate of the church.

Soon after, I approached Mr Malhotra outside the church and exchanged the code words with him. Mr Malhotra and I drove towards Palam airport along Parliament Street, Ashok Road, Willingdon Crescent and on to Sardar Patel Marg. When we reached the Panchsheel Marg junction, I asked Mr Malhotra to stop near a taxi stand located there. I asked him to transfer the money into a waiting taxi. After that, I told Mr Malhotra to proceed immediately to the PM's residence in his car and that I would go to Palam in the taxi with the money. This was done.

I stopped the taxi next to a Defence Colony stand in A Block, which runs parallel to the railway line. I offloaded the money, which was in a big, heavy trunk, with the help of the taxi driver. I then let the taxi go and waited for a few minutes on the side of the road so that I may be observed by the passersby. Soon, I stopped an empty taxi coming along the road and loaded the trunk into the boot with the help of the taxi driver. I asked the driver to take me to Delhi Gate. I made him stay just outside the entrance of my residence (Parsi dharamshala).

I am absolutely sure the driver noticed my movements there on. I brought along an empty suitcase, plus a collapsible leather bag and gave it to the driver. I also told him I had brought this from the room where I live. I asked him to drive to Kashmiri Gate and then on to Rajinder Nagar. I told him I had a large amount of cash in the trunk and would like him to stop at a quiet place where I wanted to transfer the money into my suitcase and bag. He did as I asked.

The taxi driver kept watching the road and saw that I was transferring big bundles of currency notes into my suitcase and bag. I wanted him to see all this and feel uneasy, which he did. I abandoned the empty trunk and asked him to take me to Connaught Place. Along the way, the driver was getting nervous and started asking questions about the money. I offered him Rs 500 in cash and told him not to mention it to anybody, only so that in case the police came to him he could tell.

I was sure at the time that this taxi driver would safely lead the police to the Parsi dharamshala. And this is exactly what happened.

On reaching Connaught Place I dismissed the taxi and took the particulars of the driver's name, his residential address and his taxi number. I bought two new suitcases, and in another taxi took them to the dharamshala, together with my own suitcase and bag. Once there, I again transferred the money into the two new suitcases and took them to Defence Colony. I went to a friend of mine and asked him to keep the new suitcases, which were locked, and told him I would collect them later.

I then proceeded to Connaught Place and went for a shave and a haircut. On my return to the dharamshala around 8.45 p.m., I noticed that my room had been searched and immediately guessed that the police had at last followed the trail. There were no policemen to be seen, so I pretended to be very angry in front of a couple of fellow residents at the dharamshala. I also banged on the manager's door and shouted at him, wanting to know what had happened in my room in my absence. I then awaited the arrival of police officers. After some time, two armed police constables came and made me sit down on a chair. After fifteen minutes the whole police party reached and took me into custody.

The magistrate's handwritten document runs into eight pages. It took about an hour to complete the recording of the statement. Nagarwala went through the papers and signed on all the pages. Agarwal then handed over the statement of proceedings to his staff, sealed in a cover, to send to the trial court.

Agarwal referred the case to Additional Chief Judicial Magistrate N.L. Kakkar, stating that as he had recorded the confession, he '[had become] a witness in the case' and it should be 'transferred to some other court'.

At this stage, Delhi Police mentioned that as per the challan, the offence had been committed in the Chanakyapuri area and the judicial magistrate looking after Chanakyapuri should hear the case. ACJM Kakkar ordered that the case be tried by the judicial magistrate first class in charge of the Chanakyapuri area, K.P. Khanna.

It was a last-minute decision by the police to change the place of occurrence of the offence, from the Parliament Street area to the Chanakyapuri police area. The argument was that the cash exchange (Rs 60 lakh) between Nagarwala and Malhotra had taken place in the Chanakyapuri area.

But the real consideration was for obvious reasons. The young IPS officer D.K. Kashyap, ASP of the Chanakyapuri area, had taken the initiative and it was his team that had cracked the case and deserved the credit.[3]

The case came up before Khanna, a magistrate who was on deputation from Uttar Pradesh. Nagarwala was produced by judicial guards and no police officer was present. Copies of all the documents, running into twenty-four pages, were given to Nagarwala. He requested that he be 'charged'. Khanna asked the guards to produce him after the lunch break.

Khanna would later tell the commission that he had no idea that Nagarwala would plead guilty before the lunch break.

---

3 P. Jaganmohan Reddy, 'P. Jaganmohan Reddy Commission of inquiry, Regarding Nagarwala Case: Report October 1978', Government of India, 1978, p. 104.

At 2.30 p.m., the court framed the charges and explained them to Nagarwala, who said 'he knew English and could understand the charge'. He pleaded guilty and the judge asked the guards to produce him at 4 p.m., when the order would be pronounced.

The magistrate held Nagarwala 'guilty' under Sections 419 and 420 of the IPC and sentenced him to two years' rigorous imprisonment and a fine of Rs 2,000 under Section 420 of the IPC.

'I do not remember having noticed any anger, surprise or pleasure' on the face of Nagarwala when the judgment was pronounced, Khanna remarked before the Reddy Commission.

Nagarwala was taken back to Tihar Jail. A sub-inspector, Roop Chand, who accompanied him to the jail, deposited Rs 100 towards the prisoner's expenses.

The transfer of cases and the quick trial evoked sharp criticism in the media the next day and even prompted Opposition leader Morarji Desai to pen an article in *The Motherland* newspaper on 3 June 1971. *The Motherland*, in its 27 May edition, had alleged that ASP D.K. Kashyap had produced the accused before Agarwal for getting his confession recorded under duress.

Notes

1. Nagarwala later said the confession was 'tutored'. The statement did not mention the recovery of Rs 30,000 from the tyre. It does not refer to his meeting with Lt Col. P.S. Keshwala, Mohini Badhwar, Mr Gotla or even the Captain couple.
2. The statement also does not mention the air force plane, Nagarwala's hiring of the air-conditioned car to go to Ranikhet or the purpose of his visit. It does not mention to whom the Rs 30,000 belonged or whether it was part of the Rs 60 lakh stolen from the SBI. He doesn't talk about the intention behind dyeing his hair or the bargain made by the police and their acceptance of his terms for the recovery of the amount.

CHAPTER 8

TWISTS AND TURNS

By the time Sub-Inspector Roop Chand of the Chanakyapuri police station handed Nagarwala over to Tihar officials on 27 May, depositing Rs 100 with the jail authorities on his behalf for prisoner expenses, Rustom Sohrab Nagarwala's life had turned upside down. And not merely because of his changed status from an accused to a convict.

Nagarwala was now a C-class prisoner, which meant he had to do physical labour as part of his punishment. Until the mid-1980s, Tihar, like many prison houses in Punjab and Haryana, had inmates who were divided into two categories: B, or 'better-class' prisoners, and C, or 'common' prisoners. For instance, political undertrials and those with higher educational qualifications could be lodged in a 'better' class, but convicts such as Nagarwala had to be kept in class C. In 1985, Tihar Jail authorities scrapped this provision for different classes and introduced a uniform 'ordinary class' category for all inmates.

Inside the jail, Nagarwala had become an object of interest, with inmates increasingly curious to meet him and know more about his version of the story. It had, after all, been proved that he had imitated the voice of Prime Minister Indira Gandhi and almost succeeded in pulling off a Rs 60-lakh heist.

At times the curiosity and questions bordered on taunts. 'How come your hair is black?' Harnarayan Agarwal, a fellow prisoner, asked Nagarwala once.

'It will always remain black,' was Nagarwala's prompt reply.

But Agarwal came to believe that Nagarwala could mimic the voice of Indira Gandhi. He recalled how Nagarwala had once narrated an entire conversation he purportedly had had with the Prime Minister in Hindi. 'He could copy her voice,' Harnarayan said.

But Nagarwala was completely dejected after his conviction. He was hoping he would go scot-free and that the police would help him get released. He resented being in the C-class category of prisoners. He had to do manual work and could not claim the B-class facilities that he had secured from the court only three days back.

The jail authorities had assigned Nagarwala to the carpentry section, where he had to build cane chairs. The only solace he now had was the company of Shastri, who, too, had been assigned to the carpentry section. 'I found him perturbed due to his conviction. He repented a lot,' Shastri said. He later recalled before the commission that Nagarwala had asked him for legal advice.

Shastri did not take long to come up with some simple advice. He told Nagarwala he could always 'claim a retrial' and appeal against the conviction in a higher court. Nagarwala considered the suggestion, but his mood didn't lift. Money was a problem, and that seemed to bother him. How would he manage the resources to fight the case?

Shastri had a solution for that too. He told Nagarwala about Rajendra Kumar Maheshwari, a young Delhi-based lawyer who had taken up for free the case of a murder convict serving a life sentence. Shastri said Maheshwari might fight his case for fame.

Shastri volunteered to approach Maheshwari, who used to visit the jail often to meet his other clients, and tried his best to cheer up Nagarwala. His trial was illegal, Shastri said, and explained to Nagarwala that the law required his 'confession' to be corroborated by two 'independent witnesses'.

'Was that done?' he asked.

Shastri insisted that proper procedure had not been followed by the court and the case would fall flat if Nagarwala approached the higher judiciary. Nagarwala must appeal to set aside the conviction and seek a retrial, he counselled.

Nagarwala, who had pinned all his hopes on his confession, thinking he would be set free once he had made a clean breast of everything, did not heed Shastri's advice.

Fellow prisoner Gulzari Lal Tandon also tried to cheer Nagarwala up. The cloth merchant from Delhi, who also worked as a munshi, or an informal supervisor on the jail premises to keep an eye on prisoners, told Nagarwala that Maheshwari would take up his case 'for name and fame'. The lawyer, he added, had promised Gulzari Lal that he wouldn't charge any fees.

Whether such assurances lifted Nagarwala's mood is not known, but the former army officer seemed to have partly reconciled himself to his altered status after the initial shock of conviction. Although he mostly kept to himself, he appeared to be more in control while interacting with the other inmates, who invariably sought him out to hear about the case that had made such a splash in the news.

Different Versions

Nagarwala, however, had different versions of events for different people. To one inmate, Gurdeep Singh, for instance, Nagarwala narrated the events as they had appeared in the papers. Gurdeep had been following the developments through newspapers. Nagarwala did not even hesitate to mimic the voice of Indira Gandhi. Gurdeep would recall later that the voice 'imitated by him' was 'not, in fact, a female voice'.

To Shastri, Nagarwala had another story to tell. He said he had been working with Prime Minister Indira Gandhi on 'secret jobs' and would deliver money to people as directed. He said he had done so several times, but that this time he could not find the person who was to receive the money at the appointed place. As he had no instructions on how to deal with such a situation, he thought of keeping the money for his 'personal use'.

Shastri would tell the Reddy Commission that Nagarwala was clear that it was 'unaccounted money' and was certain that no one would report him or take any action against him, and that he had 'no fear of any danger' to him. Nagarwala, Shastri said, felt it was 'due to the fault of Malhotra' that the case had been reported against him. He quoted Nagarwala as saying that Indira Gandhi had 'telephoned' Malhotra and that, ultimately, the money was to reach her son, Sanjay Gandhi. That part of the job, Nagarwala told him, had to be done by someone else, but that person did not turn up.

Nagarwala also told Shastri that when he was in police custody, some persons sent by Indira Gandhi had met and assured him that if he made a confessional statement, they would see to it that nothing would happen to him. And, of course, that he should not 'name or entangle' Indira Gandhi in the case. Shastri claimed that Nagarwala made the confession not only on the advice of the police, but also on that of 'special men' of the Prime Minister. He, however, eventually realized that he had been deceived with false assurances of immunity.

To Rajendra Singh, another inmate at Tihar lodged in a family-murder case, Nagarwala had a different version yet. The gist was more or less on the lines of his statement of confession, but Nagarwala told Rajendra that he was 'tempted seeing bundles of currency notes' at the bank, sat down on a bench, lit a cigarette and hatched the plan. 'By the time the cigarette smoke was over', he said, he had thought of 'the complete plan'.

'[Nagarwala] left me in no doubt by his narration [of events] that there was no second man in the act,' Rajendra would tell the commission. He also mentioned Nagarwala's brown hair. 'He got himself shaved and had his hair dyed to disguise himself [after cheating the bank].'

Nagarwala was older than Rajendra and appears to have made an immediate impression on the younger man. 'I never disbelieved him,' the latter said, adding that Nagarwala appeared to have held a 'grudge' against Indira Gandhi. He said Nagarwala had collected 'intelligence' inputs about the Vietnam War and met her, but failed to bring her around to see his 'viewpoint'. At that time he had met Haksar too, and so was familiar with his voice.

In the first week of June 1971, Nagarwala had an unexpected visitor and was summoned to the office of the jail superintendent. The visitor was Jagdish Prasad, a deputy SP with Delhi Police's intelligence-gathering unit, the Special Branch, who had been tracking the case from the very first day.

The main purpose of the officer's visit was two things. One, to find out if the Rs 30,000 that was found in the tyre was part of the bank money; and two, to probe Nagarwala's links with foreigners, particularly his meeting with an official of the US embassy.

Nagarwala narrated the events more or less on the lines of what he had told the police but with a little variation, which could have had a bearing on the case. He claimed that he had intentionally left several clues for the police to track him down. He said the Rs 30,000 was part of the bank's money and that he had given Rs 3,500—and not Rs 2,600—to his friend Captain at his Defence Colony residence. He insisted that Rs 6,000, which he had spent on 24 May, was his own money, but did not disclose the source of it.

'The entire amount spent by me that day was Rs 6,000, which I was carrying with me. I did not spend a single penny from the bank amount,' he insisted.

To substantiate his assertion, he pointed out that Sub-Inspector Roop Chand had deposited Rs 100 on his behalf towards prisoner expenses, implying he did not have any money on him.

Nagarwala tried his best to stay aloof in prison, but curious inmates would not leave him in peace. At their request, he would mimic the sounds of cats and dogs during the carpentry workshop. 'I could make out he was good at mimicry,' Rajendra told the commission.

The two had travelled together a couple of times between Tihar Jail and the Tis Hazari court to attend case hearings. Rajendra had seen Nagarwala interacting with his 'Indian and foreign' friends from the jail van while waiting for their turn to be called to their respective courtrooms. He was not a 'well-off person', Rajendra would say.

Another person who was impressed with Nagarwala's mimicry skills was N.S. Thakur, deputy superintendent of Tihar Jail, who was in charge of the carpentry workshop. Thakur, too, was curious about Nagarwala's ability to mimic voices. Nagarwala, Thakur said, had once asked him if he could identify the Prime Minister's voice when they spoke on the jail intercom.

Thakur was impressed. 'To me [it was a] truthful reproduction of Mrs Indira Gandhi's voice,' he said. After that, Thakur recalled, Nagarwala imitated the voice of P.N. Haksar. Thakur quoted Nagarwala as saying that he had done all that 'for fun'. In the workshop, 'he was seen more with foreigners'.

A True Friend

One of those who called on Nagarwala as he waited in the jail van outside the Tis Hazari court was Nusli Pudumjee, a childhood friend from Pune. He, too, was in the Indian Army and was now well settled. Pudumjee knew almost all the details about his friend's life, his exploits and his temperament. He probably knew Nagarwala better than anyone else.

Pudumjee had gone to Europe with his family. His brother-in-law was India's assistant high commissioner to Scotland. A friend from Pune had given him the news of Nagarwala's arrest through a letter. The friend had also enclosed a few newspaper clippings related to the crime and the arrest.

Back in India after a few days, Pudumjee contacted a friend in Delhi, industrialist Bansi Dhar Gupta, to arrange a meeting with Nagarwala. Gupta, who knew Nagarwala through Pudumjee but had had a bitter experience with him in the past, cautioned Pudumjee and asked him to stay out of it as the matter had taken a 'political turn' and anybody who visited Hajee (as Nagarwala was called among his friends) would 'unnecessarily come under surveillance'.

But Pudumjee did not want to let his friend down. He had known Nagarwala since 1939 and was determined to meet him. 'It was my duty' to find out if there was anything that 'I can do for him', he told the Reddy Commission.

Pudumjee got in touch with the lawyer Maheshwari to find out when Nagarwala would be produced in court. He headed straight from Delhi's Palam airport to the court complex. Maheshwari then took him to the jail van in which Nagarwala was waiting. 'I joked with him that if he did get his hands on Rs 60 lakh, I would have expected him to be in Hong Kong, where we could have met and had a good time,' Pudumjee remarked, recalling their conversation.

When the conversation turned serious, Pudumjee told his friend that he had not expected him to act in such a 'stupid manner'. Nagarwala had laughed and replied that he should not take him 'for a fool' and that it was a 'long story', which he would one day tell him.

Pudumjee had read in the newspapers that Nagarwala had done what he did to help the people of Bangladesh. 'Since when did you become a philanthropist?' he had asked his friend. 'And he laughed and promptly replied that this, too, he would "let me know at a later date".'

Before he left, Pudumjee gave Nagarwala some money for cigarettes and 'other comforts'. Pudumjee later told his friend Gupta that Nagarwala had not told him anything about the case, perhaps because the police were there.

Back in Tihar, Nagarwala and Tandon had to share a cell for about a fortnight because of a space crunch. On the day of his conviction, the BJS had held a protest demonstration against the government, leading to the arrest of many party leaders and workers for defying prohibitory orders. The agitation was aimed at exerting pressure on the Indira Gandhi government to recognize Bangladesh as a separate country. Most of these workers wanted to speak to Nagarwala, but he avoided them.

But the constant attention irritated Nagarwala, and one day he even complained in court that he had become some sort of an 'exhibit' in jail, and that the demonstrators 'neither leave me in peace, nor allow me to sleep during the night'.

A few BJS leaders, among them L.K. Advani and Kanwar Lal Gupta, however, did manage to speak to Nagarwala. Advani would later recall that when he had asked him about the case, Nagarwala had more or less confirmed what he had said in his confession and that he was 'worried' about engaging a good lawyer for his appeal.

Kanwar Lal Gupta met Nagarwala separately and asked him to mimic the voice of Indira Gandhi. But he was not convinced by his mimicry.

Nagarwala had a few friends in Delhi. Homi C. Gotla, a fellow Parsi who worked with Indian Explosives and from whom he had borrowed the Rexine bag to move the money from the trunk in the New Rajinder Nagar area, was one of them. The two had shared a room at the Parsi dharamshala for four months in 1970, when Gotla had moved to Delhi. He later moved to the rented accommodation in New Rajinder Nagar, where Nagarwala would drop in occasionally and dine with Gotla and his wife.

Nagarwala had been in jail for some time when Gotla received a call one day. 'Sometime after he was convicted and imprisoned, I got a call from a police officer [who said] Nagarwala wanted to see me,' Gotla said.

He and his wife visited Nagarwala in jail. 'We spoke from across bars. He was in a pensive mood, but trying to put up a cheerful appearance. We had taken food, cigarettes, sweets, biscuits and a flask of soft drink. As per jail rules, we were not allowed to give food to a prisoner. The meeting lasted for fifteen minutes in the presence of jail personnel,' Gotla recalled.

As they were about to leave, Nagarwala told them, 'I have not done anything that should make you or any of my friends feel ashamed of me.'

Nagarwala had reason to feel hurt. None of his friends had visited him in jail. Captain, in whose Defence Colony home Nagarwala had kept the two cash-filled suitcases, had even rebuffed Nagarwala after he had tried to get in touch through Maheshwari.

Nagarwala had later sent a letter through Maheshwari, in which he said he would repay the money he owed Captain once he was a free man. '[In the letter] he also asked me to inform Bagli [the manager of the Parsi dharamshala] to settle his dues to the dhobi [washerman],' Captain later said.

Petition and Retrial

Nagarwala's arrest and hurried conviction were creating ripples in political circles. On 7 June, Urmilesh Jha, private secretary to the socialist leader Raj Narain, who had been defeated by Indira Gandhi in the 1971 Lok Sabha elections in Raebareli, filed a writ petition through his advocate, the eminent lawyer P.N. Lekhi, challenging the 'validity' and 'constitutionality' of the trial and naming as respondents Union Finance Minister Y.B. Chavan, the SBI and Delhi Police officials, among others. The Delhi High Court admitted the petition and issued notices to the respondents.

The combined Opposition sought to file a revision petition challenging the conviction. 'For this purpose a meeting was also held, which was attended by A.B. Vajpayee, Morarji Desai [both non-Congress future Prime Ministers] and Raj Narain. It was unanimously felt that Mrs Gandhi was involved in the case, and the way the case was conducted gave rise to nagging doubts. Though each of the Opposition leaders who attended the meeting felt a retrial was necessary to bring out the truth, no one was prepared to sign the revision petition. Ultimately, it was Urmilesh Jha, private secretary to Raj Narain, who gathered the courage to challenge the conviction of Nagarwala,' Lekhi would later say to *The Illustrated Weekly of India*. The lawyer had attended the meeting and later filed the revision petition.

Nagarwala had taken exception to Jha intervening in his case. During his meeting with the intelligence officer Prasad of the Delhi Police Special Branch, he said he had written a postcard (an unsealed letter) to an advocate, S.K. Lal, seeking a consultation. Lal's name had been suggested by some of the inmates in the jail. 'I was surprised to read in the papers that one Eleshwar [Urmilesh] Jha, who is not known to me at all, has filed a writ against my conviction. I feel that these people are creating difficulties for me,' Nagarwala wrote in his letter to Lal.

Maheshwari, meanwhile, had a tough time extracting information from Nagarwala. He made a trip to Pune and Bombay to meet Nagarwala's family and friends. He met his mother, the seventy-five-year-old Goolbai, who lived with her nephew, also named Rustom, the son of her late brother, Sir Ardeshir Dalal. Her daughter, Armaity Sohrab Shroff, two-and-a-half years younger than Nagarwala, was present when the lawyer met them at Malabar Hills in Bombay.

Maheshwari wanted information to fight the case. 'I know nothing,' Goolbai said, pleading with him 'to do something'. The lawyer told them Nagarwala was completely non-communicative and at times even lost his temper.

Goolbai told Maheshwari that he was the one who should know all about the case, being in touch with Nagarwala. 'But when he does not know anything, who else can know better?' She paid the lawyer Rs 1,000 in cash and gave him some gifts. Maheshwari made one more visit to Bombay, but Goolbai had nothing new to tell him. This time, she gave him Rs 800, and sent a greeting card and flowers for her son through him.

On 21 June, Maheshwari filed an appeal before Delhi Sessions Judge R.N. Aggarwal, pleading that Nagarwala's conviction be set aside. His contention was that Nagarwala was enduring 'strong interrogations', being 'tortured' and that his confession of guilt was made under duress from the police. He alleged that in a violation of rules, on 27 May, Nagarwala, who was in judicial custody, was taken from Tihar Jail to the Chanakyapuri police station, where he was 'allowed to have [a] bath and shaving, etc.', and had a 'good breakfast'.

Maheshwari claimed that Nagarwala was 'induced' by police officials, including Kashyap, to make the confession as 'dictated by them'. The police, the lawyer said, had promised Nagarwala that he would be set free after he confessed and that he would also get an 'unqualified reward'. Being a former military officer, the lawyer contended, Nagarwala 'took the inducement and the promise' at face value and acted on the police's 'advice and direction'.

Judge Aggarwal set aside the conviction and directed the case to be transferred to the court of Additional Chief Judicial Magistrate N.L. Kakkar. While setting aside the conviction, the sessions judge remarked that the proceedings on 27 May were conducted in 'undue haste', resulting in a 'miscarriage of justice'.

Nagarwala, the judge ruled, had not been given a 'reasonable opportunity after the documents were supplied to him to reflect and have consultation'. The accused, the judge said, was produced before the magistrate before lunch and was supplied documents that ran into twenty-four pages. It is 'difficult to believe', Aggarwal said, that the magistrate was able to supply a copy of the confessional statement to the accused within such a 'short [time] frame'. 'All proceedings were finished in less than two hours of the recording of the confessional statement,' the judge said, concluding that there had been 'no proper compliance of the provisions of the Criminal Procedure Code [Section 251-A of the CrPC]'.

On the same day, Nagarwala applied for bail on the ground that the judicial magistrate, who had earlier heard the case, had allowed him B-class facilities in jail. He was granted bail against a surety of Rs 25,000. It is intriguing, however, that Nagarwala did not take up the offer of bail. Instead, he opted for a cell in the barracks. According to his fellow inmate Shastri, Nagarwala did not try to get out of jail, as he feared he would be 'killed by the agents' of Indira Gandhi.

Gurdeep Singh, who had around this time been shifted from C to B class after he cleared his graduation, found Nagarwala 'very worried after his application for retrial was granted'. He did not talk much with the other prisoners, Gurdeep said, and recalled that Nagarwala, who had become even more reserved, kept to himself, although otherwise he 'was a normal man'.

Shastri and Gurdeep both recalled that Nagarwala had become friendly with a fellow inmate, Colonel Amrik Singh, who was in jail in a contempt-of-court case. Amrik Singh spent most of his jail term in the prison hospital in the complex, and he and Nagarwala were 'fond of talking to each other at the hospital'. Amrik Singh was also close to Dr Baldev Das Makhija, one of the jail doctors.

A week after his conviction was set aside, Nagarwala replied to his friend, E.R. Viccajee, seeking financial help. Viccajee, the director of Warden & Co., Bombay, and an old school friend, had earlier written to Nagarwala through the jail superintendent, offering to 'raise money either by himself or through their mutual friends' to pay for his 'fine' to shorten his jail term.

In his reply, Nagarwala admitted that he had been unable to 'repay you [Viccajee] for your past kindness' and appreciated his friend's gesture. '[I]n our present-day world, where dog eats dog, your gesture is truly a noble one,' he wrote.

Nagarwala said he intended to go all the way—sessions court, high court and the Supreme Court, if needed. But for that he urgently required funds, and urged Viccajee to immediately send Rs 4,000 for court expenses and lawyer fees. He wanted Viccajee to send the amount to H.R. Gotla at his New Rajinder Nagar address.

Viccajee did not respond. Nagarwala then sent another letter on 20 July, thanking him 'for offering to help and pass the hat around for Hajee'. He again mentioned that he had failed to honour his past debts and requested Viccajee again for the money for legal and personal expenses. 'My case will most definitely go to the Supreme Court,' he wrote. This time he requested his friend to send the money to his lawyer Maheshwari's Delhi address. When there was again no response from Viccajee, Nagarwala wrote to him a third time.

Nagarwala also wrote to Khusro Faramurz Rustamji, better known as K.F. Rustamji, a former Border Security Force (BSF) director-general, requesting the police officer to meet him in Tihar. Nagarwala had first met Rustamji in Jabalpur at the Parsi Club and, in 1950–51, stayed with him for a couple of days in Aurangabad after an accident. Rustamji did not reply to the letter.

On 27 July, Nagarwala appeared in the trial court of additional chief judicial magistrate Kakkar. On 9 August, all copies of the previous orders and other documents were given to Nagarwala, and the case was posted for evidence on 1 September.

More than two and a half months had passed since Nagarwala's arrest and conviction, but Nagarwala preferred to remain in Tihar, in what he felt was the relative safety of prison rather than walking free on bail. But the experience of the past few months and the media coverage of his case seemed to have aggravated his stress levels and made him bitter.

'But for you, I would have been a free man,' he once told Virender Kapoor, who worked for *Motherland* and had extensively covered the Nagarwala episode for the newspaper.

Bhawan Singh, the newspaper's photographer who was with Kapoor, wasn't spared either. 'You have taken enough pictures of my rather ugly face. Why don't you bother yourself with pretty faces now?' Nagarwala told Singh 'in his clipped English accent'.

Notes

1. The foreigner angle came up more than once as the controversy unravelled, but the Reddy Commission ignored certain telltale signs about Nagarwala's foreign links.
2. The Tihar Jail records, produced before the Reddy Commission by V.K. Sharma (CW 239), show that R.K. Maheshwari, the lawyer, had met the prisoner only four times and that all the meetings had taken place in June (21, 24, 26 and 29). The only other visitor he had was 'Omi Gotta' (R-822), from New Rajinder Nagar.

CHAPTER 9

LETTERS TO INDIRA

As directed by the sessions court judge R.N. Aggarwal, the fresh trial in the Nagarwala case had started in the court of Additional Chief Judicial Magistrate N.L. Kakkar. But before the case could be heard on 1 September, Nagarwala petitioned the high court and got the proceedings in the lower court stayed on the ground that a missing document needed to be reconstructed and given to him.

That was in July 1971. Then, on 17 September, Nagarwala wrote to Indira Gandhi. The tone of the letter, sent from jail, gave the impression that he was familiar not only with the Prime Minister but also with her office.

Mrs Gandhi was away in what was then the USSR, her first visit to the Soviet Union since the two countries formalized the Indo-Soviet Treaty of Peace, Friendship and Cooperation in August that year. Closer home, India was on its way to officially getting involved in the Bangladesh liberation struggle.

The 1971 Indo-Soviet Treaty was probably the most seminal foreign policy arrangement New Delhi had entered into in the twentieth century. It had a profound effect on the politics and geography of South Asia, cementing what many thought was India's pre-eminence in the region.

It was against this backdrop of regional geopolitics that Nagarwala wrote to the Prime Minister in what was certainly a calculated move. He also wrote a covering note addressed to Indira Gandhi's social secretary, Usha Bhagat, where he requested her to pass the letter on to the Prime Minister.

Bhagat had served Indira Gandhi as her secretary since 1953, when the former was a young kindergarten teacher. In her book *Indiraji through My Eyes*, Bhagat wrote how her association with Indira Gandhi would continue for thirty-one years until the latter's assassination in October 1984. In the period between 1953 and 1984, Bhagat assisted her in both official and personal matters. A book reviewer in *Hindustan Times* described how one of Bhagat's responsibilities was to keep Indira Gandhi informed.

In his covering note, Nagarwala mentioned that in the past, Bhagat had 'always been most prompt and helpful' in forwarding his letters to the Prime Minister. Once again, he wrote, he wanted to trouble her to put this letter in front of the Prime Minister 'alone' as soon as she returned from her trip to the USSR. He concluded the letter by saying, 'You must be aware of my case from the newspapers. I only hope that you do not think too badly of me.'

The suggestion was hard to miss. Any third person reading the letter would get the impression that Nagarwala was quite familiar with Bhagat, who had her office in the Prime Minister's residence. His letter to Mrs Gandhi also hinted at an apparent familiarity with the Prime Minister. 'As my case is still subjudice, I will not talk about it in this letter,' Nagarwala wrote. 'Someday, God willing, I hope to call on you and relate the true sequence of events exactly as they transpired. They will be quite an eye-opener for both the nation and you. I am sure.'

Nagarwala also complained against the jail authorities in his letter. 'Ever since my sojourn in jail, I'm constantly threatened by certain elements who are fully convinced that I am some kind of a secret agent of the Prime Minister,' he wrote. 'At the smallest opportunity they hurl the filthiest abuses at both you and me, and follow it up with bad gestures.'

He said he had brought this dangerous situation to the attention of the jail superintendent, Arjan Das Sapra, but the official had merely taken some half-hearted measures, with the result that a B-class inmate had assaulted him physically on a minor pretext.

Some strong words then followed in the letter. 'The next time it is going to lead to bloodshed. I have no qualms about being killed in the defence of the honour of women hood [sic] but it seems such an utter waste to die at the hand of such ruffians and cut-throats when it can be avoided.'

At times, the tone of the letter bordered on the personal. 'Dear lady,' Nagarwala wrote, addressing the Prime Minister, 'where on earth do you get such fifth-rate persons to man your police force and the CBI? I really don't know! Please, please send a man of integrity and of average intelligence whom I can talk to freely and in confidence.' He was probably alluding to his interrogation in jail by a CID officer of Delhi Police.

Nagarwala mentioned as his address the house of his lawyer, using the label 'C/O R.K. Maheshwari, Advocate, Chandni Chowk, Delhi - 6' on the letter. He would write another letter too, in the wake of India's intervention in the Bangladesh war.

Malhotra's Arrest

While Nagarwala's arrest and lightning-fast trial dominated headlines, another man's life, too, had dramatically changed. On 29 May, five days after Nagarwala's arrest, Delhi Police took Ved Prakash Malhotra, chief cashier of the SBI's Parliament Street branch, into custody. The instruction to arrest Malhotra apparently came after a meeting chaired by Minister of State for Home Affairs K.C. Pant and attended by senior police officers, including IGP L.S. Bisht, DIG P.A. Rosha and New Delhi District SP Y. Rajpal.

The police was initially reluctant to arrest Malhotra because he was the key witness in the case. There was no doubt that it was Malhotra's incredible naïveté that had landed him in this mess, but he was the one who had provided the taxi number that had led to Nagarwala's arrest and the recovery of the cash. While Malhotra, all the senior officers agreed, was not an accomplice but a victim, the decision to arrest him was probably driven by the criticism in the media and by the Opposition that Malhotra knew those who mattered, including the Prime Minister.

Inspector Hari Dev of the Chanakyapuri police station arrested Malhotra under the IPC's Section 409 (abetment). The chief cashier was first remanded in police custody and later sent to judicial custody on 2 June.

After a week in jail, Malhotra was granted bail on 9 June by the sessions court. There is no record of any meeting between Nagarwala and Malhotra in Tihar Jail.

High Court Nod

The Delhi High Court on 23 September directed the trial court to proceed with Nagarwala's case after the missing document the accused had sought was prepared and given to his counsel. Nagarwala, however, petitioned the sessions judge to transfer the case from Kakkar's court. The magistrate, he claimed, 'had tried to rush through the proceedings and … was acting under the influence of the prosecuting sub-inspector'. The sessions judge rejected his plea.

Along with the fresh trial, Nagarwala's trial under the Arms Act for possessing an unlicensed revolver and ammunition, seized from the dharamshala, had also started. The court fixed 11 October as the date for evidence for the prosecution.

But before the Arms Act case could be heard, Nagarwala, on 5 October, filed a petition seeking to implead Malhotra as a co-accused in the main case and a joint trial in which both Nagarwala and Malhotra are tried, adding another twist to the case. Nagarwala, in his petition, said the prosecution had gone 'too far' in making a reference to the statement recorded by the magistrate under Section 164 of the CrPC, and the magistrate concerned needed to be cross-examined to determine the veracity of the confessional statement.

The magistrate dismissed the petition, saying there was no 'force in it', and indicated that Nagarwala was trying to delay the proceedings. The order pointed out that in Nagarwala's confession recorded by the magistrate, he had suggested that Malhotra had nothing to do with the crime. The matter 'cannot be considered at this stage', the magistrate said in his order, as 'no new material' had come on record after 9 August to show that the witness (Malhotra) had committed a crime.

But Nagarwala was not willing to give up. He approached the court of sessions judge Aggarwal. On 14 October, Judge Aggarwal, too, rejected the petition, saying, 'Malhotra was a victim of fraud and not … a party to the fraud.'

'[T]here is no material on the record that there was any conspiracy between Nagarwala and Malhotra to deprive the bank of its money,' the judge said, making it clear that there was 'no justification for a joint trial'.

Nagarwala challenged this judgment in Delhi High Court, which, too, dismissed his appeal on 29 November. 'Malhotra is a star witness of the prosecution in the case against Nagarwala. It is his solitary statement of having received a telephone call that is the basis of his removing Rs 60 lakh from the bank and then handing it over to the petitioner [Nagarwala],' said Justice Vyas Dev Mishra.

'His [Malhotra's] statement prima facie shows that he has been cheated … Why and under what circumstances the police decided to arrest him and investigate a case against him for an offence under Section 409, Indian Penal Code, is best known to the police,' he added.

What followed were stern words directed at the prosecution. '[E]ither the prosecution is doubtful about the truth of the statement of the witness or has started this fake investigation so that the sword of Damocles may be kept hanging on the head of the witness to make sure that he supports [the] prosecution's version at the trial. Again, this aspect is not germane to the decision of the present revision and it will be for the trial court to decide what weight should be given to the statement of this witness [Malhotra],' the operative part of the high court's judgment said.

'I am, however, constrained to remark that had the police shown some diligence in completing [the] investigation of the case registered against Malhotra, as was done in the case of the petitioner, they would have provided no reasonable grounds of doubt in the mind of the petitioner about their bona fides. I can only hope they will be able to complete the investigations at a very early date,' Justice Mishra added.

By November, winter had set in, and it had become quite cold in Delhi. Nagarwala's dependable friend, Pudumjee, had received requests through 'one or two postcards' from the jail asking him for warm clothes. Pudumjee picked up some warm clothes lying in his house and sent them through Mahabir Pandey, a driver who worked for Delhi Race Club. But Nagarwala sent the clothes back with the driver, saying he couldn't wear such clothes in jail. He asked for other types of clothes, specifying what exactly he wanted. This time his friend bought them in Delhi and sent them again through Pandey.

The trial had, meanwhile, resumed, although at a snail's pace. Following the high court's dismissal of Nagarwala's revision plea on 29 November, only two witnesses—the two taxi drivers—had been examined by the trial court. Then 3 December arrived with momentous news—the military confrontation between India and Pakistan had started.

By 16 December the liberation war was over with the surrender of Pakistani forces, ending the months-long Bangladesh genocide and clearing the way for the eventual recognition of Bangladesh as a separate nation.

Backdrop of the War

In 1970, the Awami League under Sheikh Mujibur Rahman had won 169 of the 313 parliamentary seats in Pakistan, but was denied the office of Prime Minister. Not only that, Pakistan's military dictator General Yahya Khan had Rahman arrested, and imposed martial law on East Pakistan, as Bangladesh was then known. Independent researchers believe that between 300,000 and 500,000 people died in this period. The Bangladesh government puts the figure at 3 million. According to one estimate, over 300,000 Bengali-speaking women were raped.

As the Mukti Bahini retaliated through guerrilla warfare, blowing up railway lines and bridges, the Pakistan Army launched a barbarous offensive. Indira Gandhi bided her time. Then, on 3 December 1971, a pre-emptive strike on eight airfields from Srinagar to Barmer ensured that India did not have to initiate the war.

Indira Gandhi was in Calcutta that day and rushed to Delhi to address the nation. 'War has been forced on us,' the Prime Minister said in her measured radio speech. Three days later, she recognized Bangladesh as an independent nation.

The Indian Army, Air Force and Navy fought spectacularly—a Pakistani submarine, *Ghazi*, sank off Visakhapatnam harbour and a surprise attack was launched on the port city of Karachi. As India cruised towards victory, the United States tried to intervene, moving its Seventh Fleet towards the Bay of Bengal. China maintained its neutrality, but the USSR moved a fleet from Vladivostok to counter the Americans. All through, Indira Gandhi remained calm and a picture of confidence.

On 16 December—thirteen days after the war had broken out—the Pakistan Army commander, Lieutenant General Amir Abdullah Khan Niazi, surrendered Dacca (as Dhaka was then known), handing over his service revolver to Indian Lieutenant General J.S. Aurora.

Another Letter

Amid these momentous developments, on 7 December 1971, Nagarwala wrote another letter to Indira Gandhi. This time, though, he preferred not to send the letter through Bhagat. 'I am overjoyed at the news of your long-last recognition of Bangladesh. My one-man personal vendetta against you now is completely over. I apologize for having caused you moments of anxiety by my actions,' he wrote.

Nagarwala said that while he did not wish to justify his behaviour for the time being, as his case depended entirely on the judiciary, he wanted to be released on a personal bond and to have all judicial proceedings postponed until the Emergency (declared during the war) had been lifted.

Nagarwala said he should be given the opportunity to work for the country in its hour of need. He said he wanted to visit Bangladesh and its refugee camps, meet the armed forces that were facing the enemy on all fronts and then set out on a lecture tour throughout India to raise funds for legitimate government agencies and rally his countrymen to combat the common danger.

All this was solely his idea, he said, and added that he would carry out all the propaganda by himself and be the first to surrender in person to the nearest judicial authority when the Emergency was lifted. Like his previous letter, this one, too, got no response.

Relief for Malhotra

The second week of December brought good news for Malhotra. Following Justice Mishra's order that set aside Nagarwala's plea to make Malhotra a co-accused in the case, the director of prosecution and legal adviser examined the papers submitted by the team of investigators. On 12 December, the official concluded that the 'investigating staff have no evidence for the prosecution of Malhotra, who has to be discharged'.

Malhotra appeared in Kakkar's court on 18 December. The magistrate discharged him on the ground that there was 'no sufficient evidence to connect the accused with the offence punishable under Section 409 IPC'.

Malhotra was a free man again—only to run from pillar to post seeking justice and rehabilitation in the State Bank of India.

Notes

1. Nagarwala had met Indira Gandhi and later P.N. Haksar in December 1967 during the Vietnam War, urging the PM to mediate between south Vietnam, the US and north Vietnam. Usha Bhagat had facilitated the meeting through correspondence.

CHAPTER 10

DEATH OF INVESTIGATING OFFICER KASHYAP

Nearly six months had passed since that morning when a mysterious caller pulled a hoax on a seasoned banker and managed to do the unthinkable: con him into parting with a huge amount of bank cash. A trunkful of cash. The alleged self-confessed caller was now in jail and his purported victim had not yet been washed of the taint of collusion. Life had certainly changed for these two men.

But circumstances would alter—and inexorably so—for others too.

'Are you sure your son died in a car accident?' Union Minister Yashwantrao Balwantrao Chavan is said to have asked S.D. Kashyap, the father of the late ASP D.K. Kashyap, when the latter called on the politician one day.[4]

D.K. Kashyap, the chief investigator in the Nagarwala case, died in a road accident on 20 November 1971. His father had approached the minister for a job for his second son on compassionate grounds.

---

4   Y.B. Chavan refuted having made such a statement when he appeared before the Reddy Commission.

Death of Investigating Officer Kashyap

'God knows the truth,' the senior Kashyap told Chavan, who was the finance minister when the Nagarwala incident happened in May 1971.

In the Congress's internal politics, Chavan, a powerful leader from Maharashtra, was considered a rival of Indira Gandhi. Earlier, when Jawaharlal Nehru was the Prime Minister, Chavan had taken charge of the defence ministry after V.K. Krishna Menon, who was blamed for India's military unpreparedness, resigned in the middle of the 1962 war with China. Chavan would later serve as the Union minister for external affairs and even hold the post of deputy Prime Minister in the Charan Singh government in the late 1970s.

Coming from such a powerful figure, Chavan's purported query reflected the widespread scepticism about the whole Nagarwala affair. If disbelief was the initial response to the Rs 60-lakh heist, the unnatural death of the young officer, who had got married less than a month earlier, on 22 October 1971, added to the general air of suspicion. Understandably, there were questions about the official version that it was a road mishap. After all, it was a case in which the Prime Minister's name had come up, and someone had pretended to be her, giving coded instructions on the phone to the SBI to hand over money to Nagarwala. Kashyap had solved the case and the general refrain was that he knew too much, so he had been done away with.

The 1967-batch IPS officer Devinder Kumar Kashyap had become somewhat of a celebrity among his peers after he had cracked the sensational case in just a few hours and got the culprit convicted within days. A month and a half later, on 7 July, he was promoted to additional superintendent of police. The government later asserted that it was a regular promotion and that Kashyap's elevation to the higher post 'had nothing to do with the investigation of the Nagarwala episode'.

Thirty-one-year-old Kashyap, who had had a stint with Delhi Police's security wing before getting the field posting at the New Delhi district, got married in October to Ramesh Kumari, daughter of a businessman Bansi Lal Dhir. Kashyap's junior colleague, inspector A.K. Bose, SHO of the Tughlaq Road police station, had broached the marriage proposal. Bose knew the Dhir family well, and he and his wife were friendly with Dhir's eldest son, Jagdish Chand.

Ramesh had done a diploma in home science and taught at a school in south Delhi. The senior Dhir owned a poultry farm and his third son, Gopal, ran a restaurant in Gole Market. The family had a house in Malviya Nagar.

In April 1971, about a month before the news of the audacious bank heist broke on a lethargic summer afternoon, Kashyap had introduced the family of his would-be wife to his father. The police officer had met Ramesh and her parents at the Bose residence a few days earlier. The couple got engaged in May, soon after Kashyap's birthday on 4 May, at a ceremony held in Kashyap's ancestral place in Haryana, days before Nagarwala's purported telephone call to the SBI branch. The wedding was held in Delhi, at a venue opposite Chelmsford Club on Raisina Road.

Ever the meticulous policeman, Kashyap had planned everything to the last detail. In July he had got his thirty-day earned leave for October approved by his bosses so he could get married and take his wife on a honeymoon trip. He was to go on leave from 19 October, three days before the wedding.

After a small party at Kashyap's residence, 38-B Irwin Road, the couple had left for Shahbad Markanda, Kashyap's native village in Haryana, to spend two days with his father and other members of the family. The two had then proceeded to Dehradun and stayed with Ram Prakash, Ramesh's second brother, who was a chief engineer with the Oil and Natural Gas Commission (ONGC). After a few days there, they had come back to Delhi before heading to Nainital. They returned to the capital most likely on 17 November.

Kashyap's Mannat

Kashyap, apparently, had a mannat to keep, where one makes a wish and if it comes true, one has to visit the dargah. He had earlier in the year visited the mausoleum of the Sufi saint Salim Chishti at Fatehpur Sikri, near Agra, tied a string and made a vow that if he got married to the woman he wanted to, he and his wife would visit the shrine again to untie the string, as per popular custom.

The mausoleum had been built by the Mughal emperor Akbar between 1571 and 1580 as a mark of respect for the saint, a descendant of Khwaja Moinuddin Chishti, whose tomb is located in Ajmer, Rajasthan. Legend has it that Akbar had prayed to Salim Chishti for a male heir. When a son was born to him, the emperor named him Salim in the saint's honour. Prince Salim would later succeed Akbar as Emperor Jahangir.

After their marriage, Ramesh would recall later, Kashyap had told her that he intended to visit the shrine with her to 'untie the string'. She had no idea what the mannat was about. 'He had made some mannat. He wanted to untie the string and tie another string. I also wanted to tie a string,' Ramesh said.

Kashyap returned to work for a day after coming back to Delhi from Nainital and applied for a day's casual leave on 19 November with permission to avail himself of a gazetted holiday on 20 November. The next day, 21 November, was a Sunday. The application was sanctioned. He then asked his brother-in-law Jagdish's wife and Inspector Bose's wife whether they, too, wanted to visit the mausoleum with Ramesh and him, but both declined. Kashyap then asked his driver, Constable Vishwanath, to come along with them, and applied for the required leave. As a precaution for the journey, he secured a revolver from the 'malkhana', or the police storeroom.

Ramesh, Kashyap, his brother-in-law Gopal's wife Lalita and two children—Anupam, four, and Anju, two—along with Vishwanath, left for Agra by road to cover a distance of over 200 kilometres in a 1965-make Ambassador (DLJ 3679) that the driver had brought from Ramesh's brother in Gole Market. They spent the night at the residence of Lalita's uncle in Agra, but not before the newly married couple made a trip to the Taj Mahal in the evening.

The next day, the six of them started from Agra early in the morning. They reached Fatehpur Sikri, barely 36 kilometres from Agra, between 7 and 7.30 a.m. and performed their intended rituals at the shrine. The group then set off on their return journey to Delhi via Agra and Sikandra, halting on the bypass road for Mathura, where they had vegetarian food at the Open Sunshine roadside dhaba.

Kashyap was at the wheel when they resumed their journey. Ramesh and Lalita were with him in the front seat. Driver Vishwanath was in the rear seat, giving the two children company. Around 4 p.m., when the car had proceeded a short distance, maybe ten minutes from the dhaba, and reached Chhatikara Chowk, Lalita noticed three or four tongas (horse-driven carriages) carrying a wedding party coming from the opposite direction. The tongas were racing each other, she would later recall.

Flung on the Road

Before Lalita could understand what was happening, one of the tongas had hit their car and a pole had smashed through the windscreen. Kashyap lost control of the steering wheel as the car lurched over a pile of stones. Thrown off balance, Vishwanath, who was in the rear seat, leaned forward to check on Kashyap, but saw him missing from the car. Still in the rear seat, he hauled himself up, reached forward to catch hold of the steering wheel and managed to bring the car to a halt at the edge of a field. Kashyap, who had injuries in his right eye and temple, had been flung on the road. He was dead.

Among the first to reach the spot a few minutes later were passengers of an Uttar Pradesh Roadways bus heading towards Mathura from Delhi. The passengers got down and ran towards the car to rescue the victims, who were still inside. Among the passengers were Prakash Narain Deepak and Harish Chand Agarwala, both employees of a cooperative bank in Mathura.

The tonga driver, Komal, from Ajhari village under the Chaitta police station, was in bad shape. He was gasping for breath and was being attended to by a woman, a foreigner, who was also a passenger on the bus. The horse was dead. In a few minutes, the tonga driver died as well.

Kashyap's body lay 'near a heap of gitti [crushed stones]'. Near him sat his driver, Vishwanath.

Soon more people gathered at the spot. Among them were Balram, a constable at the Jet chowki of the Brindaban police station, Sub-Inspector Madan Gopal Shukla, the Chhatikara chowkidar Beeda Singh and eyewitnesses Keshav Dev Sharma and Chhagan Lal.

Most of the witnesses said the tonga drivers were from the Ajhari village and corroborated what Lalita would later say—that there were three or four tongas. The witnesses said the baraatis (wedding guests) were pushing their tonga drivers to move faster and overtake the other tongas. After the accident, the baraatis fled the spot.

Babu Lal, one of the first to reach the site, said 'people were saying' that the tonga race was the cause of the accident. Normally, he added, 'baraatis go on merry-making' and make a lot of 'mischief'. Babu Lal signed a panchnama, a police record of witness testimony, stating all of this.

When the passengers Prakash Narain Deepak and Harish Chand Agarwala checked on Ramesh, who was unconscious, they saw she had injuries on her 'forehead, above the eyes'. The two women, the two children and Vishwanath were taken to the Mathura district hospital by the same bus.

'I did not see Kashyap, and was told that he had died on the spot,' recalled Ramesh.

Ramesh was still unconscious when they arrived at the Mathura hospital. She and Lalita were both admitted and later shifted to a private ward. As soon as Vishwanath reached the hospital, he rang up Kashyap's brother-in-law, Jagdish Chand, and informed him about the accident. Jagdish, his father Bansi Lal and Magan Singh, Kashyap's personal orderly, left immediately in a car. Ramesh's sister, Dr Rajinder Gupta, and her husband followed in a separate car.

By then news of the accident had reached senior officials in Delhi Police. Ajit Singh Cheema, deputy superintendent of police (headquarters), Kashyap's two favourite inspectors Hari Dev and A.K. Bose, and police inspector Ashwini Kumar Puri then set off for Mathura by road, a distance of 180 kilometres.

When Bansi Lal and Jagdish reached the accident spot, they saw two bodies—of Kashyap and the tonga-wallah—wrapped in white cloth, but were not allowed to have a closer look. They were advised by the police to go to the hospital.

'Where Is He?'

Ramesh was still unconscious when her sister, Dr Rajinder Gupta, saw her. 'I pinched her and she responded,' Gupta would say later.

Around midnight, Ramesh asked her sister, 'Where is he?' She did not know yet that her husband was dead.

Late in the night, Bansi Lal and other members of the family, accompanied by some officials of Delhi Police, visited the office of the Mathura district magistrate-cum-collector A.P. Sinh to get the autopsy waived at the family's request. Earlier, in the evening, Sinh and Superintendent of Police S.N.P. Sinha had stopped at the accident site on their way to a social event.

Ramesh, who had been drifting in and out of consciousness, was brought to Delhi later in the night. She woke up the next morning at her husband's official Irwin Road residence and recalled seeing 'some faces of people from Malviya Nagar' (her parents' place in south Delhi). 'What are they doing here?' she asked her sister-in-law before losing consciousness again.

Kashyap's body was brought to Delhi under police escort and the last rites were performed at Nigambodh Ghat. His father and brother reached Kashyap's official residence the next morning.

There was more trouble in store for the young widow. Apparently, some of her in-laws had searched the house, emptied the jewellery boxes and then confronted Bansi Lal about the empty boxes. Bansi Lal said the contents of the boxes may have been kept in a bank locker. Ramesh would later complain that she was not allowed to operate the locker.

The following months would see bitter acrimony between the two families over property. Police officials had to intervene to bring about a rapprochement. Ramesh had to give in writing that she would not 'claim' her share of immovable property. The items given to her by her in-laws had to be returned.

Thirteen months later, Ramesh got married to an army official, a widower with two children.

Had Kashyap been alive, he would have certainly become the commissioner of Delhi Police. But destiny willed otherwise.

CHAPTER 11

MOTHER AND SON: NAGARWALA'S LETTERS FROM HOSPITAL

Police officer D.K. Kashyap died in November 1971, leaving behind a young widow and a cloud of unease over the manner of his death. Less than three-and-a-half months later, the man he had investigated, Rustom Nagarwala, would die too—from a heart attack following a brief illness while in custody. Ironically, illness would bring Nagarwala closer to his mother after years of infrequent communication and even rarer meetings.

Nagarwala had an uneasy equation with his mother Goolbai ever since he had been discharged from the Indian Army in 1951 following road mishaps. He had not had a regular job and not enough means to settle down either. His financial constraints meant he could not take care of his ageing mother, who shuttled between her nephew and sister, who lived in Bombay.

On 10 January 1972, Nagarwala suddenly developed chest pain and was rushed to the twenty-eight-bed Tihar Jail Hospital by his fellow inmates. The hospital lacked even basic X-ray facilities. Dr A.K. Ghosh, the chief medical officer, noted that the patient had fever and had been having pain for the past two days. Nagarwala was admitted and the doctor advised that half a litre of milk, one slice of bread and two eggs be added to his regular diet.

After two days Nagarwala felt slightly better. He was examined by another jail doctor, who prescribed Gelusil tablets, used to relieve acidity and other gastrointestinal issues, adding to the list of medicines already given by Dr Ghosh. The same day, Nagarwala wrote to his mother, informing her that he had caught the flu and was being treated at the hospital for the past 'five days'. He told her that he was being given Terramycin—a prescription medicine used to treat symptoms of a wide variety of bacterial infections—and said the hospital staff were taking excellent care of him. 'So please do not worry. Keep well and chin up,' he wrote.

Clearly, life in jail had changed Nagarwala. For someone who only wrote occasionally to his mother, he now maintained regular correspondence in a desperate attempt to cheer her up.

Dr Ghosh, however, found no improvement in Nagarwala's condition. He examined him on 12 January too, and within fifteen minutes, asked for the patient to be shifted to Irwin Hospital (now known as Lok Nayak Jaiprakash Narayan Hospital), the referral hospital for the jail's inmates.

The reference slip mentioned that the patient had been 'given tetracycline capsule and Gelusil tablets', that the fever was less but there had been 'no improvement in chest pain'. Nagarwala made the 16-kilometre journey to Irwin Hospital in a van, not an ambulance. The prestigious hospital complex in central Delhi also houses GB Pant Hospital and Maulana Azad Medical College (MAMC).

Myocardial Infarction

Associate professor Dr N.P.S. Verma, who examined Nagarwala, noted that the case was 'strongly suggestive of myocardial infarction'. An ECG done after two days confirmed the diagnosis. The infarction could not have been of more than 'three weeks' duration', the radiologist said.

Myocardial infarction happens when one or more parts of the heart don't get enough oxygen and blood flow is blocked. The blockage is mostly caused by a build-up of plaque in the arteries. When a plaque ruptures, a blood clot forms, which causes a heart attack. If the blood and oxygen supply are cut off, the muscle cells of the heart suffer damage and start to die. Irreversible damage begins within thirty minutes of blockage. Due to the lack of oxygen, the heart no longer works as it should.

The next day, 15 January, Nagarwala again wrote to his mother, saying, 'I have been admitted here last night from the Tihar Hospital. It was just as well … or my trouble would have been aggravated. Due to a severe chill in the chest area, my respiratory system was affected and I was in pain for a few days. Right now I am perfectly well and happy.'

After two days he wrote another letter, saying he felt a lot rested and better. 'Life is far more comfortable here than in Tihar Jail. Please don't worry too much about me as I shall be here for another two weeks, at least … I am bound to put on some weight, considering that I had lost over 20 kilos in the past few months …'

While Nagarwala was in hospital, Pandey, who worked as a driver for Delhi Race Club, called up Pudumjee and informed him that his friend had suffered a heart attack and was admitted in Irwin Hospital. Pandey, who was Pudumjee's driver when the latter visited the city, had been to Tihar Jail twice to deliver winter clothes to Nagarwala.

Pudumjee took the next available flight from Bombay to visit his friend in the hospital. Seeing Nagarwala's condition, Pudumjee said he could arrange bail for him. The bail amount was small and all his friends could easily pool in, he said. In fact, Pudumjee added, 'I can provide the entire amount.'

But Nagarwala seemed reluctant to get out on bail. Pudumjee would recall later that his friend believed that if he remained in custody, the police would have to produce him before a magistrate at periodic intervals, else they would just keep delaying his appeal.

Nagarwala then requested Pudumjee to pay 'Rs 300, not more', to his lawyer, Maheshwari. 'If you pay him more, he might lose interest in the case,' he told his friend.

Honouring his friend's wish, Pudumjee made a short trip to the lawyer's chamber in the Supreme Court complex and handed over Rs 300 to him. Maheshwari, who knew very little about his high-profile client's background, quizzed Pudumjee for nearly half an hour to elicit information about Nagarwala. The young lawyer was candid with Pudumjee. He told him that Nagarwala had refused to tell him anything and that he was finding it difficult to defend him in court.

On 28 January 1972, a Friday, Nagarwala was discharged from the hospital but was advised to attend the follow-up clinic on the coming Wednesday. Jail doctors were to follow the course prescribed by Irwin Hospital.

Before being shifted back to jail, Nagarwala wrote to his mother, informing her that he was going back to Tihar and that he would take bed rest for two weeks and be back for a check-up at Irwin on Wednesday for a day only for his ECG follow-up. 'So far, I have no pain,' he wrote. 'Progress is excellent.'

'Russi, My Son ...'

Nagarwala received a reply from his mother on 1 February. 'I wished so much that you would have remained in Irwin Hospital two weeks more, because going and coming from such a long distance is not good. So you could have at least stayed there, dear, till they again took your cardiogram (ECG). Anyway, please let me know as soon as you know what the doctor's opinions are. If possible and if allowed, would the doctor give you the ECG so that you may send it to me through Nusli [Pudumjee], or anybody who comes to see you?'

Goolbai also wrote that a person known to Jamshed S. Lilaoowala, a family friend, had left for Delhi the previous night and that Lilaoowala had requested him to meet Nagarwala and inquire about his health at the Irwin Hospital and contact his advocate too. 'Perhaps Mr Maheshwari will inform that you are not at Irwin,' Goolbai wrote.

Nagarwala's worried mother turned emotional. 'Russi, my son, this ailment is not to be neglected. Even in the case of a mild attack, four to six weeks' complete rest is essential. It matters not to anybody, but it concerns and worries your dearest ones a great deal. So it is up to you to take proper care of yourself and not to give the slightest reason to exaggerate [sic] yourself,' she wrote. 'Keep up the nourishment with Horlicks, Bournvita, honey and biscuits, which I have asked your advocate to provide for you. Honey and jaggery are very good for the heart … Use them instead of sugar. Ask Maheshwari to buy a box of any good oats.'

On 30 January, two days before the letter arrived, Nagarwala complained of breathlessness while walking inside the jail. He was advised not to exert himself or walk, except for going to the bathroom. The doctor recommended 'Pethidine injection, strict bed rest', and firmly told Nagarwala not to smoke.

On 2 February, Nagarwala returned to Irwin Hospital and reported for the follow-up check-up at the OPD. The doctor on duty examined him and sent him back to Tihar after prescribing medicines and bed rest for a week. 'If the patient gets pain, administer 1/6 morphea [morphine] stat,' he prescribed.

Exactly a week later, on 9 February, Nagarwala was back at Irwin Hospital, where he was sent to the male medical emergency ward. He was later shifted to Dr N.P.S. Verma's unit. The case sheet mentioned 'old myocardial infraction'. Nagarwala remained in hospital until 17 February. Pudumjee again visited him, this time in the public ward. When the two friends met, Pudumjee told Nagarwala he had met his mother in Bombay and that she was keen to visit him in hospital.

Pudumjee would later say that he found his friend quite depressed. For the first time, Nagarwala told his friend, 'I am not feeling well.' He also said he had reconsidered his earlier decision and wanted to 'come out on bail' and conduct his own court case.

Pudumjee told Nagarwala he was going to Australia to attend a conference and that he would be away for three weeks to a month. He assured his friend that bail would be arranged once he returned and again broached the topic of Goolbai's wish to visit her son in Delhi.

'Please do not allow her to come to Delhi,' Nagarwala begged his friend, urging him to use all his persuasive skills to stop his mother from making the trip.

Nagarwala seemed to have made up his mind to fight back. He told Pudumjee he wanted to meet D.F. Karka, editor of the *Current* magazine, as he 'wished to tell him something about the case', Pudumjee told the Reddy Commission later.

Nagarwala also made a strange request to his friend. Since Pudumjee knew many people in the film industry in Bombay because of his association with Delhi Race Club, could he introduce him to 'certain film directors, producers and actors'? When Pudumjee asked why, Nagarwala said he wanted a script for a movie on his escapade. Maheshwari would later recall how Nagarwala was keen to be introduced to actor Dilip Kumar.

When Pudumjee was about to leave, Nagarwala made a significant remark. 'He told me that he had to settle accounts with certain people who would be quite happy if he never left the hospital,' Pudumjee said.

Pudumjee was curious. He wanted Nagarwala to tell him everything in detail, but the latter remained cagey. Pudumjee thought that once his friend was out, he would tell him everything.

But that was to be their last meeting. Nagarwala was discharged from Irwin Hospital the next day and was back in the jail hospital on 18 February.

Back to Irwin

Nagarwala wrote to his mother again, soon after he was back at the jail hospital. 'I am much better now, though quite weak, as I cannot take food that may increase my weight. Nobody is quite sure as to what kind of heart trouble I have. The ECGs show some kind of infarction. Yesterday, after Nusli left, the heart specialist told me that he thinks it is angina, but that it is not too severe. It is definitely not thrombosis ... I am getting the best possible care at the Tihar Hospital,' he wrote.

Two days later, Nagarwala fell down in the bathroom. The jail doctor Y.P. Gupta found Nagarwala with 'severe' pain in the chest. He administered an injection of pethidine and referred him back to Irwin Hospital. From the casualty ward, Nagarwala was referred to the male medical ward under Dr H.K. Chuttani, professor of medicine at MAMC.

According to Nagarwala's case history at MAMC, the patient had 'severe pain in the left side of chest, which did not radiate. It was a crushing pain lasting two hours. No excessive sweating. The patient became unconscious for a few minutes and recovered fully after that.'

The ECG, done at MAMC, revealed 'fresh changes of myocardial infarction in [the] anterior septal [anteroseptal myocardial infarction] region', which the doctors there felt could have occurred between 14 January and 20 February. Dr Sindhwani, of the adjoining GB Pant Hospital, examined Nagarwala around 10.45 p.m. and recommended that the patient be shifted to the CCU of GB Pant Hospital. Nagarwala's condition deteriorated the next day (21 February). He did not respond to questions from the MAMC hospital staff, including doctors, and also vomited. The next day, on 22 February, he was shifted to GB Pant Hospital, where the eminent cardiologist Dr S.I. Padmavati examined him. The well-known doctor was a former director-principal of MAMC and associated with three hospitals.

Over the next few days several other doctors—Dr S.K. Gupta, registrar of cardiology, Dr M.P. Gupta, associate professor of cardiology, and Dr G.D. Gupta, professor of medicine—visited Nagarwala on their usual rounds.

A Mother's Appeal to a Mother

On 22 February 1972, worried about her son's health, Goolbai wrote a long and emotional letter to Prime Minister Indira Gandhi seeking her intervention. 'I live in an agony of fear and suspense,' she wrote, detailing a single mother's struggle to bring up her two children, and Nagarwala's series of misfortunes. 'My son has recently had a heart attack and been moved to the Irwin Hospital for treatment. He writes me cheerful postcards, yet I cannot but despair.'

She then sought the Prime Minister's intervention. 'Please forgive me, but somehow I feel that a broken-hearted old mother's appeal to another mother and a woman who has borne the burden of caring for 10 million hapless human beings will not be in vain,' she wrote, possibly referring to the refugees from East Pakistan who had fled persecution in their country.

There was no response from the Prime Minister or her office, just as there had been no response to the letters Nagarwala had written from jail.

On 23 February, Nagarwala again wrote to his mother. From the tone of the letter, he seemed to be in a better mood. 'The lady boss of the hospital, Miss Padmavati, who is also a top cardiologist, came on her round today instead of Thursday, and I had not even bothered to shave. She seemed to be a dolly-rolly-polly babe in her early forties. Anyhow, she seemed very capable in her work and told me not to worry too much and that they would give me the best care possible. I am quite happy here and already feel heaps better in the three days I have been here. So the rest is up to Allah …'

In keeping with Dr Padmavati's advice, a lecturer of neurology, Dr Jayaram, checked on Nagarwala following an 'episode of giddiness and unconsciousness', and gave his opinion on the case sheet on 24 February.

Out of CCU and Back

The same day, Dr M.P. Gupta, the associate professor of cardiology, sent a note to the medical superintendent, saying, 'He [Nagarwala] does not any more require to stay in the CCU. Kindly advise whether he should be shifted to the nursing home, general ward of the GB Pant Hospital or back to the Irwin Hospital from where he was transferred.' For reasons best known to the doctors, Nagarwala was shifted promptly to Irwin Hospital on 24 February.

On the morning of 25 February, a worried Dr Chuttani wrote an urgent note on the patient's case sheet and sent it to Dr G.D. Gupta and Dr M.P. Gupta of GB Pant Hospital. 'I shall be extremely grateful if you could kindly give your expert opinion on this patient,' he wrote in his note. The note resulted in Nagarwala's returning to the CCU of GB Pant Hospital in the afternoon, where he was first seen by Dr M.P. Gupta, the same doctor who had recommended that Nagarwala be shifted back to Irwin Hospital.

The case sheet of 26 February revealed that Nagarwala had severe chest pain for ten minutes and mild pain for about fifteen. He did not have any chest pain the next day, but complained of pain in his shoulder and was referred to a physiotherapist, Sarla Bhatt.

Last Visitor

Om Prakash Malhotra, the retired army official from Ranikhet, was probably the last person to visit Nagarwala from outside the hospital. After the previous year's bank episode of 24 May, Nagarwala had planned to visit Malhotra at his Ranikhet home, probably to return the money he owed him. Nagarwala had earlier helped Malhotra build a house in Delhi's Defence Colony. Malhotra had not only paid back the loan, but had also kept Nagarwala's request and continued to send him money orders when Nagarwala had fallen on hard times.

'He was very weak,' Malhotra would later say, recalling his visit to the hospital. While Malhotra sat with him, Nagarwala wrote to Goolbai. 'Om Prakash is sitting beside me. He came down just to wish me. I am very well taken care of and quite comfortable.'

That would be his last letter to his mother.

CHAPTER 12

DEATH ON HIS BIRTHDAY

Goolbai seemed happy—almost happy—as she neatly folded her clothes one by one and put them in a bag. It was 2 March 1972. She had finally got her way. She had managed to persuade Jassi (Jamshed S. Lilaoowala), a family friend for years, to accompany her to Delhi. Her daughter, Armaity, had tried to dissuade her. So had Pudumjee. But the seventy-five-year-old was adamant. She had made up her mind to visit Russi in Delhi.

She knew her son well and did not believe the apparently cheerful notes she had been receiving from him. She had to go and see him.

The desire to go to Delhi had become more intense after she had heard about her son's heart attack. How could she not go and visit her only son when he was battling for his life in a hospital in another city? Finally, S.B. Shroff, her son-in-law, had relented and booked a Bombay-to-Delhi flight ticket for the next day—Friday, 3 March.

It would have been better had Shroff booked the ticket for 2 March, Goolbai thought, as she rested for a while. She could then have been with her son the day he turned fifty, but she wasn't complaining. If there was anything that life had taught her, it was to not expect too much. The family had already sent birthday cards and a few gifts to Maheshwari's address, and she was certain that he would pass them on to Russi. Goolbai resumed packing her clothes for Friday's journey—at last she would get to see her son again.

In Delhi, over a thousand kilometres away, Nagarwala, too, seemed somewhat cheerful as he relaxed in his bed at the CCU in GB Pant Hospital. Doctors had examined him in the morning and, except for mild pain in his left shoulder, he had no complaints. On Wednesday, the doctors had told him that his condition was satisfactory. A physiotherapist had been requisitioned four days back, but she hadn't turned up yet.

A little before lunchtime, Maheshwari walked in. He found Nagarwala 'cheerful, happy and hopeful, though a little pale'. He wished him and handed over the greeting cards from his mother, sister Armaity, and his nephew and nieces. They chatted for about half an hour before the lawyer took leave as the hospital staff got ready to serve lunch to the patients.

Sudden Collapse

Nagarwala was served lunch on his hospital bed. He was eating when he suddenly collapsed. The hospital staff present in the CCU immediately alerted the on-duty doctors, who examined Nagarwala. His blood pressure was 'not recordable' and his pulse was running 'very fast'.

Nagarwala was immediately hooked to the ECG monitor, but the doctors noticed that there was no ECG activity. His heart had stopped.

'Code Red', 'Code Blue', 'Code Black'—people sometimes wonder what these terms mean. Technically, there is no formal definition for a code, but doctors in a hospital or clinic often use one of these terms when a patient goes into cardiopulmonary arrest and requires a team of providers (sometimes called a code team) to rush to the location and begin immediate resuscitative efforts.

Dr Padmavati, who, along with the other doctors, had examined Nagarwala in the morning, was checking on other patients at the Irwin Hospital when she received the message. She immediately rushed to GB Pant Hospital. So did Dr G.D. Gupta, the professor of medicine. They supervised the resuscitative measures that lasted 'over two hours'. Nagarwala was given intracardiac injections and doctors tried to revive him with mouth-to-mouth resuscitation.

At 1.30 p.m., the doctors observed ventricular fibrillation (irregular twitching of the heart) and an electric shock of 150 joules was given to restore the heart's normal rhythm, but the heartbeat did not come back.

External massage continued and another electric shock, this time of 300 joules, was given. An attempt was also made to revive Nagarwala by internal catheter (electrically driving the heart), but that, too, was unsuccessful.

In his statement before the Reddy Commission, Dr M.P. Gupta said that external pacing, a treatment that allows medical personnel to temporarily pace a heart by delivering controlled pulses of electric current, can produce a palpable pulse for a few minutes, but in this case Nagarwala could not be revived and was declared dead.

As the body lay in the CCU at GB Pant Hospital, the physiotherapist arrived with Nagarwala's case sheet, which she had 'just received'. Dr Gupta had referred the patient to her on 27 February. When she arrived, the physiotherapist saw 'his body was covered' in a white sheet.

The hospital authorities conveyed the news of Nagarwala's death to the Tihar Jail authorities. In keeping with the standard procedure followed when a jail inmate dies, Tihar Superintendent R.N. Sharma informed the hospital that a magistrate would conduct the mandatory probe. Sharma then contacted the Parsi dharamshala and informed Darius Bagli, the priest and manager, that Nagarwala had died. Nagarwala's brother-in-law S.B. Shroff was also contacted.

Bagli soon reached the first floor of the hospital, where the body had been kept. He offered prayers as officials completed the legal formalities.

In Tihar, it was a bad day for Rajendra Singh, the jail inmate who adored Nagarwala. He received news of his friend's death soon after a magistrate had convicted him in a case of murder. Rajendra later blamed Colonel Amrik Singh, another jail inmate, and the jail doctors for ruining Nagarwala's health and leading him to an early death.

In Bombay, Shroff could not believe the telegram he had received from the Tihar superintendent. Soon after the wire message, he received a telephone call from the jail authorities, probably to discuss the funeral arrangements. Goolbai, who had been busy packing her bags, slumped into a chair, shattered. Her son was gone—she would never see him again.

Nagarwala's closest friend, Pudumjee, was in Melbourne when he received the news through a wire message. His wife would later write to him quoting from a newspaper report that Hajee had wanted his friend to make the funeral arrangements. 'I was helpless,' Pudumjee would later say. He was attending a conference in Melbourne, thousands of miles away from India.

Different from a 'Normal Heart'

The subdivisional magistrate of Shahdara, P.N. Gupta, conducted the inquest. Dr Bishnu Kumar, head of forensic medicine at MAMC, assisted by Dr Yashpal Rana, performed the autopsy the next day, on 3 March, at the GB Pant Hospital mortuary. Apart from Shroff and Bagli, Nagarwala's lawyer Maheshwari and inspector Hari Dev, who was now the SHO of the Kotwali area, were present at the time of the inquest.

Dr Kumar showed Nagarwala's heart to the people present. At Maheshwari's insistence, he explained the difference between a 'normal heart' and Nagarwala's, which would be preserved for academic purposes. 'I did not find any sign suggestive of poisoning,' Dr Kumar later said.

After the autopsy, the body was stitched from the neck to the stomach by an employee at the mortuary and handed over to Shroff. It was embalmed and taken to Palam airport, where Bagli and Nagarwala's friends B.N. Italia and Dadi Eruch Shaw Mistry were present. On the night of 3 March, Nagarwala's body was cremated at the Chandanwadi Electric Crematorium in Marine Lines, Bombay, in the presence of his friends and his mother Goolbai.

Nearly a week later, the senior prosecutor in the Nagarwala case informed the trial court of Nagarwala's death. Magistrate N.L. Kakkar went through all the documents and ordered that the records be 'consigned', since the trial had 'abated' on the death of the accused. It was 9 March 1972, less than a year since the summer-day bank episode that sent ripples through Delhi's streets and officialdom.

Now that the case had been closed, the magistrate cancelled the superdarinama related to the cash amount of Rs 59,94,300 and the Rs 2,600 seized from N.B. Captain, *The Statesman* employee from whose house the police had retrieved the cash-stuffed bags. The money was released to the SBI for use, along with the bank's car (DLK 760), which was also covered under the superdarinama. The cash trunk in which the money had been shifted from the vault was also returned to the bank. The court ordered that the briefcase, tyre, tube, felt cap and keys—properties related to the case—were to be confiscated by the State. They would be sent to the court's custodian of property for disposal. The 'remaining articles' were to be released in Goolbai's favour, as Nagarwala's counsel had petitioned.

What was interesting—rather, intriguing—was the court's observation on the money being released to the SBI. 'In view of legal provisions, the court had thought it fit for the delivery of the money to the SBI claiming to be entitled to possession thereof,' it said.

No application had ever been presented by Nagarwala that he was interested in the delivery of the money. There was never any suggestion, either in applications by Nagarwala's relatives or during the cross-examination of witnesses, that the money belonged to the deceased person.

Despite the court's order, Goolbai had a tough time getting her son's 'personal belongings' from Delhi Police. Pudumjee had to seek the intervention of Yezdi Gundevia, an Indian Civil Service officer who had served as the foreign secretary under Jawaharlal Nehru and Lal Bahadur Shastri, to get Nagarwala's personal belongings released. Russi's friend, Captain, would eventually collect them and hand them over to Pudumjee. After several months, Nagarwala's personal belongings finally reached his mother in Bombay.

Notes

1. There was a controversial write-up by Maheshwari in *The Illustrated Weekly of India* on 9 April before he left for the US. He did not cooperate with the Reddy Commission and the veracity of Maheshwari's conversations with Nagarwala received severe criticism from the inquiry panel.

SECTION II

PROFILES: NAGARWALA AND MALHOTRA

CHAPTER 13

NAGARWALA: PERFORMER, PLAYER OR A VICTIM OF CIRCUMSTANCES?

Until the evening of 24 May 1971, Rustom Sohrab Nagarwala was a mysterious figure without a name. All that the police knew about him, before they came across his biographical details in his rented dharamshala room, was that he was tall, fair and well built. And that he carried a revolver with him.

More details emerged after his arrest, but to know Nagarwala the person, especially the character behind the alleged bank con, it is necessary to go back to his past. This chapter takes a look at Nagarwala's life, from his early youth and student days to his later years, as a person who would often walk the thin line between acceptable behaviour and the morally debatable—even as a kid—before it would all eventually unravel.

Rustom, Russi to his friends, always had a knack for spotting opportunities to make a quick buck. There are many glimpses from Nagarwala's life—spread over several cities in India and outside—that bear this out, from accounts given by his childhood friends, colleagues, extended family and acquaintances, all of which hint at financial vulnerability and his love for easy money. Little did they realize that one day this trait would cost him dearly.

When Russi was barely eight or nine years old and studying at St. Vincent High School in Pune, he had approached Gustap Rashid, a boy from a batch junior to him, asking if he would like to buy his old textbooks. 'They are of no use to me,' Gustap recalled Nagarwala as saying.

But Gustap's parents had already bought him a new set of books at the beginning of the academic session, and he didn't need Nagarwala's books. But the latter continued to pester him with the same request at the beginning of each session, and Gustap politely declined all of them.

'Russi was dogged by misfortune,' Goolbai said, with a tinge of regret and sympathy, talking about her son's early childhood. Gool Sohrab Nagarwala had lost her husband early, within four-and-a-half years of their marriage. Her husband was barely twenty-eight when he died. The young widow moved in with her brother and later left Bombay with her two children—Russi, barely three-and-a-half years old then, and Armaity, two—and shifted to Pune to start a new life. She had 'very little money' and struggled to raise Russi and Armaity. The only support was from Goolbai's brother, ICS officer Sir Ardeshir Dalal, the first Indian to become the municipal commissioner of Bombay, who later joined the house of Tatas. Sir Ardeshir Dalal was part of the executive council of Viceroy Lord Wavell in 1944. Knighted in 1939, he would eventually resign from the executive council and go back to the Tatas as resident director of the Tata Iron and Steel Company, as Tata Steel Limited was known then.

St. Vincent School, where Nagarwala studied, had been founded in 1867 by the Society of St. Vincent de Paul, an international Catholic voluntary organization, under the presidency of an eminent Catholic, T.C. Loughnan, Esq. The school would admit boys from many underprivileged families in its initial years at a monthly fee of Re 1, but the quality of education remained high throughout. Russi subsequently matriculated from Esplanade High School in Bombay and joined the Nowrosjee Wadia College in Pune. Throughout his education, Nagarwala kept shuttling between Pune and Bombay due to family reasons.

It was at St. Vincent that he got the nickname Hajee. Nagarwala was considered an 'extrovert'. He was interested in music, would sing and was a tad adventurous as well. A glimpse of the adventurous streak came from Gustap, who recalled the day Nagarwala crashed his new racing cycle.

Gustap had at first refused to let Nagarwala ride the cycle, but the latter kept pestering him till Gustap relented. To 'my horror', Gustap would recall, Nagarwala met with an accident and smashed the cycle, but was fortunate enough to not suffer any injuries.

Gustap had followed Nagarwala to college and become a 'bagpiper' in the University Training Corps (UTC) band section, where Nagarwala was a brass drummer who took part in dramatic activities. Nagarwala was quite popular and had a big circle of friends.

N.B. Grant, who went on to become a brigadier in the Indian Army, knew the Nagarwala family from his schooldays. Grant was studying for an engineering degree in Pune when Nagarwala joined the college. 'He was very popular and was invariably invited to all social functions. Russi consistently became the life of all parties. Fond of music, he would entertain people with his singing,' Grant would say later. 'He had a deep bass voice.'

In Grant's assessment, Nagarwala was a spirited student, more inclined towards sports and physical activities than academics. Nagarwala would soon become the chief physical instructor for the college sports team. His college mate Nusli Pudumjee, who came from a prominent family in Pune and would play a major role in Nagarwala's life later, was a fellow instructor. At the UTC, Nagarwala was a corporal and Nusli a lance corporal, and the two spent four years in the college together. Pudumjee, too, joined the army and was posted with the Army Salvage Depot.

Nagarwala was eighteen when he had a 'near fatal attack of typhoid', which brought his studies to an 'abrupt end'. But as soon as he was able to, he joined the army, fulfilling an ambition he had always nurtured. That was sometime in 1940–41, his mother recalled. As a junior commissioned officer, Nagarwala was posted in Jabalpur in 1941. The Ordnance Corps at Jabalpur had an operational as well as a logistical role within the defence forces. The logistical role of the Ordnance Corps was to provide technical support to the forces for procurement, storage, distribution, inspection, maintenance, repair and disposal of all ordnance-related equipment.

Russi joined the Indian Military Academy in 1943 and was commissioned as an officer the next year. He was attached to 1 Ordnance Corps and was posted in places such as Harbanspur, Quetta, Lahore, Jabalpur, Dehu Road and Kirkee.

While Nagarwala had joined the Ordnance Corps, his friend Grant was in the Corps of Engineers. The two would meet again in 1943–44 in Lahore when Nagarwala was posted in Harbanspur in undivided Punjab, barely 10 kilometres from Lahore city. He was a 'happy-go-lucky' kind of person, Grant said.

Nagarwala was posted in Punjab when India was partitioned in August 1947. The violence that preceded the Partition led to the displacement of about 15 million people (Hindus, Muslims and Sikhs) on either side of the border. The abrupt division of the country also stunned smaller minority communities such as the Pakistani Goans, Christian Mangaloreans, Parsis and Bene-Israel Jews, who were early migrants to Bombay and Karachi in the seventeenth and eighteenth centuries. Some Parsis who had stayed back in Karachi would later come to India in the wake of growing intolerance and overt Islamization of the Pakistan state.

In 1971, while he was being tried, Nagarwala told the court that the Partition, especially the suffering of the people, had affected him deeply, the reason he wanted to do something twenty-four years later for the people of Bangladesh, who were then reeling from the onslaught of a genocidal regime. But a 1947 episode, if true, sheds a different light on Nagarwala's personality.

Sometime that year, on one of his visits to Pune where his mother stayed, Nagarwala conned A.M. Surveyor, a resident of the same building, into parting with a substantial amount of money. Nagarwala had apparently told Surveyor, with whom he often played cards at the Parsi Gymkhana Club, that he had hidden money collected from refugees.

He told Surveyor that he and another officer had collected the money during the Partition from 'refugees desiring assistance to go from one side of the border to the other'. Nagarwala said he had buried the cash in the compound of the officers' mess in Ambala, but had not been able to 'recover' it because the other officer was keeping an eye on it.

He asked Surveyor to give him Rs 25,000, saying that once he had recovered the money, he would pay him double the amount—Rs 50,000. Surveyor agreed and Nagarwala even gave him a promissory note to that effect. Surveyor had paid Nagarwala by cheque from his account (A 256) in the Bank of India, Bombay on 28 July 1948. His daughter had preserved her father's passbook and account statement, and submitted these to the Reddy Commission.

Pudumjee also refused to help Surveyor when he wanted his money back. Instead, he asked Surveyor to keep his mouth shut, lest he be 'ridiculed for his stupidity' and for believing a 'cock and bull story'.

'Hajee also tried this story on me a few months back, and knowing him as well as I did, I laughed in his face and he laughed with me,' Pudumjee would later recall.

Motorbike Accident

In 1949, Nagarwala was home on leave when he collided with two stationary lorries while riding his motorbike one evening. The lorries had no parking lights on and Nagarwala nearly had a leg torn off on impact. For four days he remained critical. Then, after months of pain and suffering, just as the injury was healing, he had another accident and broke the same leg. This time an amputation seemed inevitable, but thanks to the army surgeon's skill and his own tenacity, the leg was saved.

'He spent two years in different hospitals and underwent twenty-six operations, but throughout this period, he was bright and cheerful. His liveliness and courage endeared him to the doctors and hospital staff, and the former continued to take a very kindly interest in his welfare,' Goolbai wrote in her letter to Indira Gandhi.

According to Goolbai, Nagarwala's leg was spared but he had a foot drop and limped. 'Moreover, he was in constant pain. Discharge from the army was inevitable. Russi was disabled and jobless. He had no qualifications and no special ability, but he had a great zest for life and always managed to find work.'

While convalescing in Pune, Nagarwala was a regular visitor to the Parsi Gymkhana, where he played cards. He also visited the race course. In 1951, Nagarwala was discharged from the army after being in hospital for nearly two years. After leaving the hospital, Nagarwala got involved in a bitter battle with the Indian government over his future prospects. He made several trips to Delhi, making the rounds of defence establishments seeking compensation and pension. On one such trip, he stayed with J.D. Kapadia, Pudumjee's brother-in-law and a joint secretary in the Ministry of Defence. Kapadia helped Nagarwala, who started drawing a monthly pension of Rs 35, but told him not to expect any more. Nagarwala, Pudumjee would recall later, 'drifted around' after his benefactor died of cancer.

The American Connection

After his discharge from the armed forces, Nagarwala shuttled between Pune, Bombay and Delhi, and appears to have started a taxi business in the national capital. As mentioned earlier, Nagarwala had become a 'sleeping partner' in the Marina Taxi Service. He had invested Rs 10,000 in the venture, started by his friend Rajinder, and was now earning up to Rs 500 a month from Rajinder's son, Mohinder Singh.

Sometimes he would hire a cab from the taxi service to tour Delhi and its surrounding areas with a friend, Jeanette Spears, who worked as a personal secretary in the US embassy in Delhi. Nagarwala's friend Lieutenant Colonel S.R. Jokhi, who was in the Corps of Electronics and Mechanical Engineers (EME) (the engineering service of the armed forces), had introduced Jeanette to Nagarwala when he was posted in Delhi. Jokhi and Nagarwala were together in Jabalpur when the former was with the ordnance factory in 1942–43.

At times, Nagarwala would take a taxi and drive himself. Jeanette, his 'American girlfriend', lived in the US embassy staff quarters and Nagarwala was 'financially well off and used to pay regularly', Mohinder, owner of the Marina Taxi Service, told the Reddy Commission. 'They were very deeply in love.'

Nagarwala's college friend, N.J. Ardeshir, managing partner of the Bolton Fine Art Litho Works, recalled Jeanette as 'a very homely sort of person'. She and Nagarwala went on a motor tour of India and 'stayed with us in Bombay for a few days' in 1951–52, Ardeshir told the commission. Ardeshir's printing business would often bring him to Delhi, where he would stay in posh hotels such as The Imperial or The Oberoi. 'I used to hold parties for my friends and business acquaintances. Sometimes, I would invite Nagarwala to my parties and also Jeanette Spears, and once in a while I would visit them in her quarters at the American hostel,' he recalled. The hostel was close to The Imperial in Janpath.

Did Jeanette and Nagarwala think of getting married?

According to Ardeshir, 'they could not get married'. She would have lost her job if they had. 'Once, she was reprimanded [by embassy officials] for being involved with an Indian,' he added.

Jamshed S. Lilaoowala, Nagarwala's classmate in college, recalled visiting Jeanette at her Delhi apartment with Nagarwala. 'It was a Christmas dinner,' he said. Nagarwala was staying at the Parsi dharamshala then. Nagarwala and Jeanette had visited Lilaoowala and his wife in Bombay when they were touring the country in his old Mercedes-Benz.

Pudumjee, too, knew that Nagarwala had become 'very friendly' with Jeanette, but the latter had assiduously avoided introducing her to him in Bombay at that time. 'Russi used to be in possession of foreign cigarettes, tinned foods, etc. I doubt he ever paid for those, but got them as presents from this friend of his,' Pudumjee said.

However, Jeanette was transferred to America and later posted in Japan.

Off to Japan

Despite Mohinder's statement that Nagarwala was financially well off, the former army officer was not doing too well in Delhi after his discharge from the force. Always short of money, Nagarwala had no permanent source of income except for the paltry sum of Rs 35 that he drew as monthly pension and negligible returns from the taxi service. During this difficult phase, he approached Lilaoowala to 'stand guarantee' for his passport, which his friend willingly did. In 1959 Nagarwala flew to Japan from Delhi.

His friends later learnt that Jeanette was posted in Nagoya then. 'Hajee followed her there. On a few occasions, we corresponded and Hajee informed me that he was eking out an existence as a teacher of English to the Japanese. He was earning the equivalent of

Rs 1,800, which is hardly a salary on which one could live in Japan, but he had assistance from Jeanette, and so he was able to pull on,' Pudumjee said.

Nagarwala had learnt Japanese and taught 'conversational English' in Japan, where he was associated with a university and the American Cultural Center. Foreigners living in Japan then had to leave the country periodically before they could get a visa to re-enter. Nagarwala would either make a trip to India or to Hong Kong.

It was clear to Pudumjee that his friend was using these trips to 'augment his income'. Nagarwala would bring with him foreign articles such as tape recorders, watches and cameras, and sell them at inflated prices in India. With the remaining money he would buy Indian articles and jewellery, and sell them at higher prices in Japan. Nagarwala would stay with Pudumjee in Bombay on these trips.

Pudumjee had once asked Nagarwala to bring for him 'some object' (he could not recall what) from Japan. Nagarwala, he said, told him that it was a 'very small object' and that he could write to his friends at the Sitlani Silk Stores in Hong Kong and ask them to send it by post. Considering how hard-up Hajee was, Pudumjee immediately suspected that Nagarwala was buying goods from the store and clearing his dues to it by selling the items in India.

During one of Nagarwala's trips to India, Pudumjee introduced him to a wealthy businessman, Bansi Dhar Gupta, who lived in Delhi's Civil Lines area. Gupta was planning to visit Japan in 1965 and Pudumjee felt that if the two were acquainted, it could benefit his friend, who could act as a tour guide to the businessman and his family. But instead of meeting the family and taking them around, Nagarwala gave them the addresses of some people in Hong Kong and requested Gupta to carry back some articles, including 'two IBM typewriters and two cameras', to India. Gupta was aware that these items would invite penal duties and cause unnecessary harassment, so he refused.

A few days after Gupta's return, Nagarwala called him. He expressed his displeasure and asked him to compensate him for his loss in India. Gupta again politely refused. He did not know the ordeal he would have to go through for turning down Nagarwala's request.

In 1966, Nagarwala came to India on another visit. Jeanette had by then been transferred to Oslo, but Nagarwala had stayed on in Japan to continue his teaching job. After arriving in India, Nagarwala had a brush with customs authorities, who refused to clear the items he had brought with him and insisted that they be re-exported. It was 'a great blow' to Nagarwala, as this source of income was now closed to him and he could never afford to go back to Japan, Pudumjee said.

Car Accident in Pune

Nagarwala stayed with Pudumjee in Bombay, but soon got bored and borrowed a car from his other friend, Lilaoowala, to make a trip to Pune. He promised to return the next Sunday morning and requested Pudumjee to leave a pass for him so that he could meet him at the 'box' at the race course in Bombay.

While driving to Pune, Lilaoowala was later told, Nagarwala had 'given a lift to a hitchhiker'. The car met with an accident near Dehu Road and 'turned over'. The hitchhiker, who escaped unhurt, 'robbed Nagarwala of his watch and wallet', and fled the spot. Nagarwala was badly hurt. An army officer passing by picked him up and took him to the Dehu Cantonment Hospital, where doctors put him in an ambulance and shifted him to Sassoon Hospital in Pune.

Dr S.M.S. Mody, a prominent cardiologist in Pune who knew Nagarwala well through social circuits, got him shifted to Jehangir Nursing Home in the city. According to Pudumjee, Nagarwala had a fractured skull. Many of his teeth had been knocked out, his jaw was broken and he had hurt himself on the upper part of the body.

When Nagarwala was eventually discharged, one of his eyes was enlarged and he had lost control of his upper lip movement, which would slump over his lower lip. So he wore a 'band around his forehead, from which a hook was suspended to keep his lip in place', Pudumjee said.

Dr Mody, who had struck up a friendship of sorts with Nagarwala, found his patient to be a clever operator, fond of racing and cards, and one who wanted to make 'quick money', a trait that would be highlighted again and again in recollections about the main protagonist of the Rs 60-lakh heist. He enjoyed betting at the races and was a 'likeable person', Mody would tell the Reddy Commission.

Jeanette visited him in hospital after hearing about his accident. She was then posted in Ceylon (now Sri Lanka). After his discharge, Nagarwala shifted to a former college mate N.H. Watchmaker's house in Pune, where he stayed for almost a year. He would later make a trip to Ceylon to visit Jeanette.

Jeanette stayed at Pudumjee's house in Pune with Nagarwala for a week. She was around forty then. Pudumjee would remember her as a 'very decent lady', genuinely interested in Nagarwala's well-being.

Nagarwala told his friends he and his girlfriend had purchased two adjoining burial plots in the US and that he was expecting a 'heavy price' on them, Pudumjee recalled.

After his recovery, Nagarwala visited his mother in Bombay. Goolbai was then staying with Sir Ardeshir Dalal's son, Rustom Dalal. 'He never asked for any financial help from me,' Dalal said.

Nagarwala's mother had no idea what her son did for a living. Apparently, Nagarwala had taken exception to Rustom once asking his aunt about his cousin and his activities. 'He was an adventurous person, who would prefer all kinds of challenging jobs. Perhaps he had inherited these qualities from his father,' Rustom Dalal said.

At Watchmaker's home, where Nagarwala stayed for almost a year, his daily routine was to get up 'late in the morning and then go out after lunch', according to Watchmaker. 'In the evenings, he would go to the Gymkhana Club and play cards. He also used to visit his friends for cards, where they would play with stakes. He was very fond of racing, but he was not doing well at this sport.' He would spend 'heavily on races and entertainment', Watchmaker added, saying he did not know what Nagarwala's 'sources of income' were at that time. He was a 'secretive man' and had a 'flair for making quick money', he recalled. After spending a year at Watchmaker's house, Nagarwala moved to Bombay, saying he would not return to Pune.

Habitual Borrower

After Nagarwala's death, all his friends who spoke about him recalled two primary traits in his character: his love for cards and horse racing, and his habit of borrowing money. To some he returned what he had borrowed, but not to others. This is what Brigadier N.B. Grant had to say about Nagarwala, whom he had met in 1970 at the Parsi dharamshala. Nagarwala had told him he ran a private taxi service. He was no longer the 'jovial' person he had been, Grant recalled. 'What I could gather, he was in the habit of borrowing money from friends which he could not return; as a result, he lost many friends.'

On one occasion, Nagarwala had approached Grant's father-in-law to stand surety for a loan from the SBI, but the older man had refused. Nagarwala had also asked Grant for money. 'He was not hard-working and was interested in earning a living without much effort. He seemed to be angry with the world and society, which he felt owed him a living,' Grant said.

Even Gustap Rashid, his schoolmate from Pune, recalled that Nagarwala had 'grandiose ideas about making money but was never interested in a job'. Gustap, too, had heard about the Surveyor episode. Surveyor had represented to the Cantonment authorities how Nagarwala had duped him by promising to double the Rs 25,000, which he had taken from his mother's neighbour. Nagarwala was 'prohibited from coming to Poona by the police' as he was an 'unsavoury character', the Reddy Commission's report quotes Gustap as saying. Nagarwala had, however, visited the city subsequently.

Nagarwala's love for cards and betting also led to a temporary break in his friendship with Pudumjee. Once, while playing bridge in Bombay, Nagarwala and another person had agreed on a high-stakes game of Rs 15 per point, much higher than what Pudumjee was playing for—'eight annas' a point. Despite Pudumjee's warnings, Nagarwala played, and lost.

'He asked me to clear his debt,' Pudumjee recalled. But when he refused, Nagarwala took offence and cleared out of his house the same evening. For a very long time, he didn't speak to Pudumjee.

Nagarwala's mother Goolbai tried to intervene. She took Pudumjee to the Navy Hospital, where Nagarwala was being seen by a doctor for his leg problem. He was rather 'offhand' with his friend and Goolbai had to apologize to Pudumjee for Nagarwala's behaviour. For a year and a half after Goolbai took Pudumjee to visit Nagarwala, the latter did not speak to Pudumjee. The ice was broken during a visit to Pune, where one day Nagarwala came across Pudumjee's wife. She 'berated' him and told him that her husband was the one person who had stood by him through all the 'vicissitudes' of life and such behaviour was 'shameful'. Later, when Pudumjee and his wife were preparing to go to Japan, Nagarwala called up, shared with his friend his experiences there and behaved as if there had never been any rift in their friendship. The two friends would later meet on odd occasions.

Lilaoowala, too, knew that Nagarwala was fond of the 'races' and bridge, and occasionally lent money to his friend, who did pay him back. Nagarwala later shifted to Delhi, where he worked as a tourist guide. In 1970, Nagarwala wrote to Lilaoowala saying he was searching for a job.

He was 'bitter about life, but all the same he did not show his bitterness and took life as it comes', but he was 'very secretive and did not disclose his movements even to his friends', Lilaoowala said. Nagarwala came across as a 'good man at heart, always jovial and considerate for the downtrodden', he added.

On several occasions, Nagarwala had also borrowed money—'Rs 1,000 to Rs 2,000 at a time'—from Ardeshir, his college friend. Later, when the two met in Delhi, Ardeshir felt a 'change in Nagarwala's personality'. He had begun to feel that he had been 'ill-treated by society', but he was never 'vicious' and never exhibited any 'criminal tendencies', Ardeshir remarked, adding that 'he did not want to be dependent on anyone and that, I think, is why he did not get married, since he was not in a position to set up a home of his own'.

B.N. Italia, who studied with Nagarwala in college, had a similar impression. Italia had met his old friend in 1968–69, after nearly three decades, at the Parsi dharamshala in Delhi. At that time, Italia was staying in his mother-in-law's house as a paying guest. His impression was that Nagarwala then believed in simple living.

After his accident in Pune, Nagarwala, his friend would recall, had developed a feeling of frustration. 'He was a bachelor and an independent type of man. He didn't want to take any obligation from anyone and wanted to lead an independent life,' Italia is quoted as saying in the commission's report.

Another friend who felt that Nagarwala was secretive by nature was Dadi Eruch Shaw Mistry. The two had known each other from their days in Poona since the early 1960s, when Mistry worked for JN Marshall & Co. When Mistry was transferred to Delhi, Nagarwala had given him company and the two of them had travelled from Pune to Delhi in Mistry's car. At that time Nagarwala's sister, Armaity, and his brother-in-law lived in Delhi, which gave him an opportunity to meet them.

Later, in 1969, Nagarwala asked Mistry if he could stay with him as a paying guest in Delhi. Nagarwala was without a regular job then and would contribute Rs 200 towards monthly kitchen expenses. What Mistry had then gathered was that Nagarwala used to draw a pension, apart from 'money orders' he received from Ranikhet from Om Prakash Malhotra.

Nagarwala had also asked Mistry's permission to use his Defence Colony address on his visiting card as a tourist guide. Apart from that, he taught English to a few Japanese students in Delhi. Mistry also remembers Nagarwala playing bridge with high stakes.

In his statement to the commission, Mistry said that Nagarwala would visit the US embassy and was known to an American in the commissary department. Occasionally, he would take Mistry's car during these trips to the embassy, from where he would bring back 'tinned food and some other items' for personal consumption. Nagarwala would maintain this contact with the US embassy as long as he stayed with him, Mistry told the commission.

Nagarwala shifted to the dharamshala after an argument with Mistry over a 'petty matter concerning the household'. He packed his bags and left in a huff.

O.P. Malhotra of Ranikhet was a retired major who knew Nagarwala through another army official. Nagarwala had planned to meet Malhotra in Ranikhet and had booked an air-conditioned taxi for the journey on 25 May 1971, but was taken into custody by Delhi Police the evening before the trip.

Their relationship dates back to 1957, when Nagarwala had lent Rs 5,000 in three instalments to Malhotra to build his house in Defence Colony. By 1970, Malhotra had paid him back through regular money orders. Nagarwala had requested him to continue the money orders, saying he would repay him later. In all, Malhotra had paid Nagarwala Rs 6,900. In fact, when Nagarwala was staying at the Parsi dharamshala, Malhotra had come to meet him. While in jail,

Nagarwala had once written a letter to Goolbai at O.P. Malhotra's Ranikhet address.

Different Facets

Nagarwala was not new at the dharamshala. He knew the people who managed the guest house, including Bagli, the priest cum manager, from his earlier visits. 'He was a man of simple habits. I never saw him drinking liquor. But he was a smoker,' Bagli would recall about the controversial guest who had arrived in November 1970. Nagarwala, he added, would visit the fire temple on the premises. He was also in the habit of playing billiards.

At the dharamshala, Nagarwala shared Room No. 3, a twin room with an attached bath, with Homi C. Gotla, who worked with Indian Explosives. Gotla later moved to a house in New Rajinder Nagar, from where Nagarwala had borrowed the bags to shift the Rs 60 lakh from the bank's cash trunk. 'He was a voracious reader and knowledgeable about several subjects. He could convincingly talk [about] anything from classical music to philosophy,' Gotla said, revealing another side to Nagarwala's personality.

Nagarwala also built a good rapport with Nashir B. Captain, who, too, had initially stayed at the dharamshala after being transferred from *The Statesman's* Calcutta office to Delhi, before shifting to his Defence Colony residence, from where the police had recovered the stolen cash. Nagarwala, who had a tourist guide identity card, taught Captain how to play bridge. In his testimony, Captain also recalled seeing a 'revolver' in Nagarwala's possession.

Dinyar Kolaji—Nagarwala's dharamshala roommate at the time of his arrest—remembered Nagarwala as someone 'busy with reading books and newspapers'. He never wore a sacred thread, as Parsis are supposed to, Kolaji said, adding that once he had even told Nagarwala that smoking was 'against their religion'.

Mohinder Singh, the owner of Marina Taxi Service, knew Nagarwala since 1955 when his father ran the service. Nagarwala, Mohinder recalled, knew many languages. He would write to them from Japan. One day, Nagarwala had told him that he had lent Rs 30,000 or so to one Mr Ahuja and that he would go back to Japan after he got the money back.

Mohinder also recalled an incident involving Nagarwala and his teenage brother that he had disapproved of. That was when Nagarwala had taken his brother, Harbhajan, to a place in Tagore Garden in west Delhi, nearly 17 kilometres from Connaught Circus, to settle scores with a boy who owed Nagarwala some money following dollar transactions between the two.

Bansi Dhar Gupta, Pudumjee's industrialist friend who had tried to help Nagarwala, also had a bitter experience to narrate before the Reddy Commission. After four or five months of Gupta's visit to Japan, Nagarwala called up and asked the industrialist to meet him at Janpath Hotel, saying he had 'very important documents' from Pudumjee and that he should come and collect them. Gupta had not realized that Nagarwala still held a grudge against him because he had refused to bring certain high-value electronic items from Japan to India with him.

To his horror, when Gupta reached the hotel, Nagarwala pointed a revolver at him and called him a 'very bad' man. 'He said I had to pay him, or he would shoot me with the revolver,' Gupta told the commission.

A frightened Gupta put up a brave front and promised to give Nagarwala 'some money'. Before leaving, he told Nagarwala that his actions were 'foolish' and 'could cause him trouble'. When Pudumjee came to know about what had happened, he apologized to Gupta over the telephone. The three later met and a repentant Nagarwala also apologized to Gupta.

Pudumjee warned Nagarwala, saying that if he continued to behave this way, he would one day have only himself to blame 'if his funds were cut off'. Pudumjee would occasionally help his friend, who was 'chronically broke'. Nagarwala's biggest need was money to pay for his room at the dharamshala so he would not be evicted.

The true friend that he was, Pudumjee also told Gupta that Nagarwala was in a 'very tight position, having no means of livelihood', and requested the industrialist to help out his former college mate with a monthly amount of 'Rs 100 or Rs 150 till he gets a job'. Gupta reluctantly agreed but stopped sending money after a few months.

Gupta, prodded by Pudumjee, also gave Nagarwala letters of recommendation to help him find a job in Delhi. Nagarwala knew English, French, German and Japanese. He also spoke Punjabi well and could converse in broken Hindi. But the recommendation letters to Claridges, the Ashoka and the Oberoi hotels, and the Handicraft Corporation did not help him find a decent job.

Again, for a few years, Nagarwala just 'drifted' around, staying with friends to save on room rent. His mother stayed with his sister's family, but Nagarwala was 'not on speaking terms' with his sister and brother-in-law, a fact stated by Pudumjee.

That, in a nutshell, sums up Nagarwala the person—a versatile drifter bitter with the world; a committed lover, but one who had no qualms about pulling a fast one where money was concerned; distrusted by some but could command loyalty from friends, although they were aware of his not-so-stellar qualities.

A damning comment would, however, came from someone not even affected by Nagarwala's shenanigans—Mahabir Pandey, the driver who worked for Delhi Race Club and Pudumjee's part-time chauffeur when he was in Delhi.

Pandey was at the wheel when his passenger, Nagarwala, who was using Pudumjee's car that day, asked him to say something in his native Bhojpuri. After Pandey had obliged the unusual request, Nagarwala 'copied his voice in Bhojpuri exactly in the same tone'.

Pandey told the commission of inquiry that Nagarwala was a cheat and that he alone, without any help, could have pulled off the 'bank fraud'.

CHAPTER 14

MALHOTRA: SINCERE, SOUND SENSE, INEXPLICABLY NAIVE

The horrors of the Partition had affected Rustom Nagarwala so much that a quarter of a century later, the Bangladesh genocide prompted him to do something sensational, he claimed. The searing event, however, had a telling impact on another man too—Ved Prakash Malhotra, the other key character in the Nagarwala saga.

Malhotra, himself a victim of the 1947 division of the country that would displace millions along religious lines, dreamt of doing something for his nation. So, when a purported call from Prime Minister Indira Gandhi informed him that Rs 60 lakh was urgently required for a secret mission, Malhotra felt it was an opportunity he couldn't miss.

On the one hand, where Nagarwala was smart and even lied to get what he wanted, on the other, the sequence of events that unfolded after the telephone call Malhotra received on the morning of 24 May exposed the SBI cashier's naiveté. He probably thought his swift and extraordinary response would bring him closer to the most powerful leader in the country, but it was a brain fade hardly expected of a forty-six-year-old seasoned banker.

'A spell was created in my mind after hearing the purported voice of the Prime Minister, and in a zeal of patriotism, I thought it was for a national cause and that my country should not be let down because of me. There should not be a bad name associated with my institution,' Malhotra said in his thirty-seven-page statement before the Reddy Commission.

It would be a costly error of judgement. After twenty-seven years at the bank, Malhotra was dismissed from service following a departmental probe that held him guilty of violating the bank's norms in handing over the cash to Nagarwala.

In 1978, a few years after his dismissal, Malhotra appeared before the Reddy Commission that the then Janata Party-led Morarji Desai government had set up to probe the scam, at that time the biggest political-financial controversy in independent India.

Had he ever seen a cheque signed by the Prime Minister? Malhotra was asked.

No, he hadn't, Malhotra replied. But he believed that since the demand came from the Prime Minister (to hand over the cash to her purported courier), he would be given a bank draft or a government draft against the payment.

Does the Prime Minister generally sign government cheques?

'I don't know', he replied.

Asked from which account, or to which account he could have got the draft or cheque from the Prime Minister realized, Malhotra said that a 'government draft can be realized' as the amount of Rs 60 lakh had been given to the government.

Did Indira Gandhi have an account with the bank?

'She was the PM and she was in charge of all affairs,' Malhotra replied.

Did you try to ascertain on telephone whether the call was really from the Prime Minister?

'As the amount demanded was very heavy, I was firmly convinced that it could be nobody else other than the Prime Minister who wanted to help the other nation [Bangladesh] in a big way. So I did not think it fit to ascertain if Haksar or Mrs Gandhi herself really made the telephone call,' Malhotra told the commission.

Early Struggle

Malhotra was born in Lyallpur in west Pakistan, later known as Faisalabad, in July 1925. A school dropout, forced to discontinue his studies because of circumstances, he was barely twenty when he joined the Imperial Bank of India as a cashier on a monthly salary of Rs 30. The Imperial Bank would later become the State Bank of India in 1955.

Malhotra was barely twelve or thirteen when he lost his father, Gokal Chand, who worked as a munshi (agent of an advocate) in his native Lyallpur, named after Sir James Lyall, who served as the lieutenant-governor of Punjab between 1887 and 1892.

The teenage Malhotra had studied up to Class X at the local Sanatan Dharam High School when the burden of a joint family fell upon his young shoulders. They were four brothers and four sisters. The families of his father's two brothers were also part of the extended household. His eldest brother, who had studied up to FA (the equivalent of Class XII today) and had started working, separated from the family soon after Gokal Chand's death.

In 1943, when he was eighteen, Malhotra joined a textile mill in his hometown. Then, in February 1945, he managed to get the job of a cashier at the Imperial Bank, Lyallpur. Two-and-a-half years later, in August 1947, British India was divided into two independent nations: India and Pakistan. Malhotra's entire family migrated to

Delhi the same year, leaving behind their native Lyallpur, which was now part of Pakistan.

Malhotra's employer, The Imperial Bank, first sent him to Patna, Bihar. After a year's posting there, he was transferred to the Chandni Chowk branch of the bank in Delhi. In 1956, Malhotra was promoted to assistant head cashier and, the following year, transferred to the Parliament Street branch as deputy head cashier.

His next promotion—to head cashier—sent him to Rewari in Haryana. Although an under-matriculate, Malhotra had caught the eye of his seniors as a hard-working and loyal employee and, in three months, returned to Delhi as the head cashier at the Tis Hazari branch in 1958. In 1960, he was back at the Parliament Street branch as special grade head cashier. This was a busy branch that catered to VIPs in New Delhi.

Malhotra's superiors considered him an efficient officer and, according to his service record, he had good knowledge of the local conditions, maintained close contact with the business community and had the capacity to assess the soundness of business propositions. Malhotra was later designated as chief cashier, a post created especially for him by the bank.

If his superiors valued his service, his peers respected the man who had risen through the ranks. Malhotra was the vice president of the employees' union and had 'quite a control' over the bank. This was commendable for someone who had to drop out of school after his father's death.

In his personal life too, the difficulties of the initial years seemed to have eased. The family was more or less well settled. His estranged elder brother was in Rohtak, employed with the local municipality. Malhotra's other two brothers were employees of the New Delhi Municipal Committee—one a health inspector and the other a pharmacist. His sister-in-law, wife of Malhotra's younger brother, worked as a teller at an SBI branch in Delhi. Malhotra's eldest son, Pravin, was a Grade I SBI officer and based in Delhi. His only daughter was married to a civil engineer. Among his material possessions was a house in Naya Mohalla in north Delhi that Malhotra had got as 'compensation' after his family's displacement from Pakistan. He owned a car too.

Everything seemed to be going fine—before a ringing telephone destroyed his equilibrium one morning. But what was it that made a person considered efficient and capable of sound judgement fall for such a trick, that, too, over the phone? For that it's perhaps necessary to take a deeper look at the man himself.

Patriotic Zeal

A typical migrant, Malhotra was full of patriotic zeal and had always desired to do something for the country. During the Sino-Indian War, he was one of the SBI's first employees to come forward and donate a day's salary for it. Later, in 1965, when war broke out with Pakistan, Malhotra and one of his colleagues, B.K. Gupta, attended public meetings held by the then Prime Minister Lal Bahadur Shastri.

During the war, he worked at the Prime Minister's residence at 1, Janpath, and recalled with pride an interaction with Shastri himself. 'All of a sudden, along with the staff, PM Lal Bahadur Shastri came to our room and inquired if people working there would come the next day in view of the Diwali celebrations,' Malhotra, who was actively involved in collections for the National Defence Fund and the National Defence Gold Bonds, told the Reddy Commission.

'If my country lives, we will have thousands of Diwalis. We will come and we will work,' Malhotra, then forty years old, had told the Prime Minister.

'He [Shastri] then kissed me and told me that the country needed young men like us. So the national spirit is [strong] in me,' Malhotra told the commission.

The bank's job was to collect cash, cheques and gold ornaments donated by visitors to the Prime Minister's residence, prepare records and deposit them at the Parliament Street branch. Malhotra was fond of collecting letters of appreciation from customers and important persons. One such letter, dated 2 January 1966, was from the principal secretary to Prime Minister Shastri appreciating his services in collecting donations for the National Defence Fund. Malhotra had also visited the residence of Indira Gandhi, who was then the information and broadcasting minister in Shastri's Cabinet.

His nationalistic feelings were in evidence again in 1969, when Malhotra was part of an employees' union delegation that met the then deputy Prime Minister Morarji Desai, who held the finance portfolio in the Indira Gandhi government, with a charter of demands. Desai refused to meet their demands to increase salaries and appealed to them to not go on strike. His appeal had an effect on Malhotra, who resigned from the union vice president's post and did not participate in the strike that followed.

Malhotra was then working with the Tis Hazari branch. His confidential service record showed that he 'exercised effective supervision' and that his 'current post' (of chief cashier) had been 'specially created' for him. According to the confidential record, Malhotra was also associated with the sports council of the SBI, was a 'sympathizer of the employees' union' and 'it was generally believed that he would not ordinarily let go of any opportunity to make himself effective'.

His colleagues, including the four who had assisted him in withdrawing Rs 60 lakh from the bank, had good words to say about Malhotra when they appeared before the commission—about his work, sincerity and dedication. No one could question his loyalty to the bank, they insisted.

In fact, nothing could affect Malhotra's loyalty to his former employer, not even termination of service. When Malhotra, then fifty-two, appeared before the Reddy Commission, six years after his dismissal, he defended the bank's decision to ask him to make up for the shortfall of Rs 3,100, the amount missing from the Rs 60-lakh heist that the police could not trace when they recovered the bulk of the stolen cash. 'As per my service agreement, I am liable to replenish the loss,' Malhotra told the commission.

He confirmed that Nagarwala's voice on the telephone, recorded by the police team led by ASP Kashyap, matched Indira Gandhi's. Malhotra had received the call at the district SP's office. About the discrepancies in the code words he and Nagarwala had exchanged before the cash changed hands, Malhotra, in his statement to the police and later to the bank, said he was 'under a spell' and could not immediately recall the exact code words.

Suspended, Dismissed, Benefits Denied

Suspended by the SBI after his arrest, Malhotra was not allowed to rejoin even after he had been set free by the court. H.C. Sarkar, secretary and treasurer of the bank, told the commission that an internal probe had been delayed because of the court proceedings. On 26 July 1972, in his report to the bank, Sarkar found Malhotra guilty 'despite the fact that the court had exonerated him for criminal action'.

The bank's local board considered the report and recommended Malhotra's dismissal from service. The executive committee of the central board of the bank later called for an explanation from Malhotra and, on 10 November 1972, decided to dismiss him. It was conveyed to him by the bank's managing director the next day.

The authorities also stopped Malhotra's pension, and he didn't get his provident fund dues. It was an ignominious exit for someone who had worked hard all his life. This bitterness would come out later in an interview with *Hindustan Times* in 1986. 'Okay, don't take me back in service, but which law stops my provident fund and pension?' Malhotra told the interviewer.

There was 'no corruption' or evidence of malafide intention in his case, he said, but he had still been treated as a pariah. 'Why was I thrown out like a leper?' he asked while asserting that 'the thief Nagarwala became a hero. And nothing happened to the man from whose house the money was recovered. Why?'

Malhotra added that four of his colleagues were also found 'guilty of identical charges—only I was suspended. Two officials were let off with stoppage of increments alone and all of them worked till their retirement.' His twenty-seven years of service, he said, had gone down the drain.

Malhotra had begun with a monthly salary of Rs 30 and the bank would deduct 14 annas and 2 pies as his provident fund contribution. After twenty-seven years of service, the accumulated provident fund amount due to him would have been substantial, around Rs 16,000.

After his dismissal from service, Malhotra assisted a cousin, H.L. Malhotra, in his transport business.

If the loss of retirement benefits was a blow, there was more trouble in store. Malhotra's younger son Ashwini's appointment as a clerk in the bank also triggered a lot of questions as the young man was hired when his father was under suspension. However, thankfully, the bank officials maintained that there was nothing illegal about Ashwini's appointment. They said the post had been advertised and Ashwini had qualified through a written test conducted by the National Institute of Bank Management, Bombay, ranking high in the quota meant for family members of bank employees. Subsequent investigations by the Reddy Commission revealed that Ashwini's selection was proper and based on the prevailing bank recruitment policy.

Questions were also raised about a loan that was sanctioned for Malhotra's brother 'in a day's time'. The bank again said there was nothing illegal about the transaction and cited before the commission several cases in which loans had been sanctioned the same day or the very day they had been applied for.

A Political Jab

Malhotra maintained before the commission that he had no political affiliations. But a Jana Sangh leader alleged before the commission that Malhotra had worked for the Congress during elections in the capital while still in service.

Dharam Yash Dev, an author and a former diplomat, while deposing before the Reddy Commission, suggested that Malhotra would 'unofficially' help senior Congress leader Uma Shankar Dixit, chairman of the *National Herald* newspaper, 'to keep the accounts of the money collected by Indira Gandhi'.

Charan Singh, the Union home minister then, told Parliament that Malhotra, after his dismissal from the bank, was given a job in Maruti, where Indira Gandhi's son Sanjay Gandhi was the managing director. The company denied the claim before the commission.

In his interview with *Hindustan Times* in 1986, an embittered Malhotra asserted that his grandchildren would know 'their dada [grandfather] never sold his soul despite horrible mental torture since that day. ... The Opposition leaders wanted me to get out of this by just uttering that it was Mrs Gandhi's money ... but I did not oblige,' he said.

According to the commission's report, Malhotra was helpful by nature and considerate towards everybody. It was also said that he was a man who would help any needy person and that he had helped arrange the marriage of a peon.

SECTION III

THE REDDY COMMISSION

CHAPTER 15

THE POLITICAL LANDSCAPE (1966–71)

The Nagarwala saga altered the lives of two men—profiles in contrast and unknown to each other until then, but inextricably linked afterwards, both sucked into the heart of the turbulence that would set in. But life had already been an extended period of churn for another person, Prime Minister Indira Gandhi, whose supposed voice over the phone would open the locks of even the most heavily guarded bank vault in the country.

For Indira Gandhi, the Nagarwala episode was the latest in a series of contentious developments. The scam broke at a time when a war with Pakistan appeared imminent. Politically, the Congress appeared to be invincible, and, in the economic sphere, Indira Gandhi had already antagonized powerful business groups with her move to nationalize fourteen leading banks.

Bigger developments would eventually overtake the scam, but it coincided with a testing time for the Prime Minister and even succeeded in dragging her name into the controversy. Here's a look back at that era, not for any subterranean link to the scandal, but to provide a glimpse of what those years were like—before the scam unfolded and immediately after.

Some readers might wonder what purpose this backdrop serves. It's a valid question, but a retrospective look, especially with a long-forgotten account of this type, where the plot threads its way through intrigue and insinuations, does help give some perspective before the narrative picks up again in the book's next section.

Eventful Years

The period between the 1966 and the 1971 parliamentary elections was one of endless turmoil for Indira Gandhi, who was still learning to navigate the tricky terrain of politics. Her father, Jawaharlal Nehru, independent India's first Prime Minister, had died two years earlier, unhappy and disillusioned after the Indian Army's defeat in the 1962 war with China.

According to Marie Seton, a British actress, art, theatre and film critic and biographer, Nehru had an air of desolation about him. The issue of his successor was in the air, but, contrary to present-day perceptions, Indira was not the obvious successor. In fact, in 1963, she had toyed with the idea of living in England, where her sons Rajiv and Sanjay were studying. In a letter to her friend Dorothy Norman, nineteen days before Nehru's death, Indira wrote that she had to settle down outside India for at least a year and was looking for ways of earning foreign currency to do so.

Nehru himself was not grooming Indira to be his successor, supporting her rejection of offers to contest parliamentary elections and making no plans for her future. When Indira became the Congress president in February 1959, Nehru's detractors alleged that the Prime Minister had used his influence to secure the coveted post for his daughter. However, a large section of the Congress's leaders felt that Indira had earned the post through merit.

Indira was the fourth woman to head the party and quickly proved her mettle by tackling the Kerala crisis, where the E.M.S. Namboodiripad government's sweeping land reforms and education bill controlling private schools in the state had so upset powerful sections of society that they demanded his removal. She also recommended the creation of Maharashtra and Gujarat to end the linguistic troubles in what was then the Bombay state.

When her one-year term came to an end in February 1960, the Congress Working Committee tried to persuade her to stand for re-election, but Indira firmly declined, paving the way for K. Kamaraj to be elected president. Subsequently, she avoided assuming any formal political role, but continued to protect her father from people she thought were fair-weather friends. She was also careful not to let her political and social work affect her bond with her children.

Destiny, however, willed otherwise. Nehru died on 27 May 1964. Within hours of Nehru's death, the Congress's old guard, informally known as the Syndicate, closed ranks to elect Lal Bahadur Shastri as Nehru's successor. Kamaraj, a politician among politicians, preferred Shastri to the hardliner Morarji Desai.

According to Pupul Jayakar, Indira's adviser and close friend, Shastri had called on Indira before taking the oath of office and secrecy, offering her the Prime Ministership. 'Indira Gandhi refused,' Jayakar wrote in her biography of Indira Gandhi, because 'she felt if she had become Prime Minister at that time, she would have been destroyed'.[5]

Shastri had then offered her a ministerial assignment, insisting that without Indira's presence he would not have a stable government. Indira relented and took up the information and broadcasting portfolio.

---

5 Pupul Jayakar, *Indira Gandhi: A Biography*, Penguin India, 1992.

In September 1965, Pakistan launched Operation Grand Slam in the Chamb sector of Akhnoor in Jammu and Kashmir. Indian troops quickly crossed into West Pakistan at three points, aiming for Lahore. The United Nations brokered a ceasefire agreement on 22 September, with both sides holding some of the other's territories at the end of the war.

In January 1966, Soviet Prime Minister Alexei Kosygin invited both Shastri and Pakistan President General Ayub Khan to Tashkent, Uzbekistan, to work out a settlement. The night Shastri and Ayub Khan signed a treaty, the Indian Prime Minister suffered a massive heart attack and died.

General elections were due early next year and Kamaraj moved swiftly, projecting Indira as Shastri's successor. A number of senior Congress leaders led by Morarji Desai raised objections, but Kamaraj had seen a quality in Indira that, according to him, the others did not have. Kamaraj, considered a crafty politician, felt that Indira's lack of experience and acceptability within the Congress would make her compliant and dependent upon him. Party leader and future Prime Minister P.V. Narasimha Rao would later say that Indira was supposed to be merely a 'vote-catching device', who, after the 1967 polls, would be forced to take a back seat, with an experienced person chosen to lead the country.[6]

Desai forced a leadership contest within the Congress Parliamentary Party. Nine days after Shastri's death, a vote was held among the Congress's elected members. At 3 p.m., the presiding officer handed over the result to Kamaraj in the Central Hall of Parliament. Kamaraj announced the winner in chaste Tamil. Few members of Parliament or the All India Congress Committee (AICC) office-bearers could understand what the Congress chief had said.

---

6 Rasheed Kidwai, *Ballot: Ten Episodes That Have Shaped India's Democracy*, Hachette India, 2022, pp. 6–7.

The suspense did not last long, as someone excitedly declared that Indira had won 355 votes to Desai's 169.

Indira was sworn in as Prime Minister on 24 January 1966, facing a sandstone statue of the Buddha at Rashtrapati Bhavan, which had the words 'Be without Fear' inscribed on it.

Indira rose in stature and many of the Congress's old guard who had thought of manipulating her to their advantage were left in shock. Kamaraj, who had played a huge role in shaping her career, was also disappointed when he realized that Indira had a mind of her own and an independent style of functioning. At one point, Kamaraj was heard describing her rather ruefully as 'a big man's daughter, a little man's mistake', referring to himself as 'a little man'.

But storm clouds were about to darken the blue sky of success. On 7 November 1966, thousands of gau rakshaks (cow protectors), with sadhus and other religious leaders among them, marched on Parliament demanding a law banning cow slaughter across the country. Led by the Bharatiya Jana Sangh Member of Parliament from Karnal, Swami Rameshwaranand, a huge crowd of sadhus marched menacingly towards the Parliament House complex, clearly intending to storm it. There was little security to protect Parliament, so the guards on duty hurriedly closed the gates. The agitators went berserk and attacked government buildings on Parliament Street. The police opened fire, killing eight sadhus, triggering widespread condemnation of the police action and the government's inept handling of the situation. The Prime Minister, sensing the disquiet, sacked veteran politician Gulzarilal Nanda, who was the home minister then.

This was Indira's first year in office and she was already battling on several fronts. The cow-slaughter issue forced her to set up a panel under a retired judge, former Supreme Court chief justice A.K. Sarkar, to see if a nationwide ban on cow slaughter was feasible. In a daring move she made the Rashtriya Swayamsevak Sangh (RSS) chief M.S. Golwalkar a member of the panel, along with the Shankaracharya of Puri. Verghese Kurien, of the National Dairy Development Board, and the economist Ashok Mitra were also part of the panel.

Kurien later wrote that Golwalkar had admitted to him in as many words that the RSS had launched the November 1966 campaign to embarrass the government and with definite political objectives in mind. The committee's initial mandate was to submit a report in six months but it kept delaying, until it was dismissed in 1979 by the Morarji Desai government.[7]

Indira's Rising Popularity

In 1967, Indira Gandhi turned fifty. Earlier that year, general elections were held to elect members of the fourth Lok Sabha, and Indira, for the first time, contested a direct election, choosing her late husband Feroze Gandhi's parliamentary constituency, Raebareli. While Indira's popularity ratings were high, the country was struggling on multiple fronts. The 1966 famine and drought were so severe that they led to food riots in some parts of the country; Mizo tribals were rebelling; and a linguistic agitation was brewing in Punjab. To make matters worse, a series of scurrilous posters surfaced in Delhi and elsewhere, insinuating that Indira was inauspicious for the country. The posters sought to remind people that the day she had taken oath as Prime Minister, an earthquake had struck in New Delhi and an Air India plane carrying the scientist Dr Homi Bhabha had crashed. It was also mentioned that she was a widow and therefore inauspicious. That was decades before the arrival of internet-savvy social media trolls, but the content was similar.

On the political front, the socialist movement was gaining ground in India, with 'backward castes' such as the Yadavs, the Jats,

---

7 Ibid.

the Reddys, the Patels and the Marathas becoming disillusioned with the Congress. Ram Manohar Lohia, a former Congressman, felt that the elections of 1952, 1957 and 1962, which the Congress had won with ease, had made voters believe that the party could not be defeated. To counter this, Lohia urged the fragmented Opposition to field a single candidate against each Congress nominee.

The 'Lohia formula' proved to be a success in the 1967 general elections, making a dent in the Congress's seat tally, although Indira's party managed to retain the Centre, winning 283 out of 520 seats. It also led to the formation of non-Congress governments in multiple states. The politically influential Uttar Pradesh slipped out of the party's hands within a month when Charan Singh left the Congress with a large number of legislators to become the state's chief minister, backed by a non-Congress coalition.

The Socialist Party would manifest itself as the key Opposition in its different avatars, such as the Janata Party and the Janata Dal. Lohia and the socialists felt that like Nehru, Indira was not seriously committed to socialism and, although both talked a great deal about it, they had done little to empower the working class. The socialists also felt that big public-sector institutions had merely created another set of bureaucrats and industrialists with no grounding in the socialist ethos.

With the battle lines drawn, Indira, too, went on the offensive. At a public meeting in Jaipur, Rajasthan, she hit out at former royals and took on Maharani Gayatri Devi, who fancied herself Indira's rival. The glamorous royal had won the 1962 Lok Sabha elections from the constituency by a mammoth margin and worked hard to bring the Swatantra Party, which believed in free enterprise and closer ties with the West, close to the right-wing Jana Sangh.

At the public rally, Indira asked the voters to go and ask the maharajas and maharanis how much they had done for the people in their states when they ruled them and what they had done to fight the British 'while they lived in luxury at the cost of the people'.

According to V. Krishna Ananth,[8] the 1967 elections exposed the fractures in the nation's social and political edifice. What emerged in 1967 was the fragmented sociopolitical reality of India as a nation, which had been stitched together in 1947. The 'experiments in alliances, coalitions and vote appeal on the lines of caste, region, etc.' would have a far-reaching impact, and continue to influence politics even today.

Nationalization of Banks

Indira preferred to answer these developments with surprise countermoves. She announced some far-reaching populist measures, such as the abolition of privy purses and the nationalization of banks. The July 1969 move to nationalize fourteen leading banks won the nation's heart and mind. The 'Shoe-Shine Boys Union' offered to shine for free the shoes of all AICC delegates as a show of gratitude towards the party.

The biggest bank that was nationalized at that time was the Central Bank, controlled by the Tatas, which had deposits of more than Rs 4 billion; the smallest was the Bank of Maharashtra, which had deposits totalling Rs 700 million. Indira had struck a severe blow to other big business houses too, such as the Birlas, who ran the United Commercial Bank, the Dalmia–Jains, who controlled the Bharat Bank and its 292 branch offices, and some Gujarati entrepreneurs who had big stakes in the Dena Bank. The Punjab National Bank, set up by Dyal Singh Majithia, Lala Harkishan Lal, Lala Lajpat Rai and others, was nationalized as well.

---

8 V. Krishna Ananth, 'Why 1967 General Election Was a Watershed in Indian Politics and the Lessons It Has Left Behind', *DNA*, 22 February 2017, https://www.dnaindia.com/analysis/column-1967-poll-that-changed-india-2330738

An economic survey of twenty leading banks of that era showed that 188 people who served as directors were also directors of 1,452 companies. The large funds that they had used to acquire private profit and privileges were now open for public welfare—for measures such as financing the rural sector and lending money to cab drivers to buy taxis.

Politically, Indira had slowly begun to tighten her grip on the Congress and the government against Desai's group of conservative right-wingers, as she sought to get rid of the old guard. The unbridgeable rift widened, with Indira emerging as a messiah of the poor. Eventually the party split in November 1969. Indira managed to retain power with a thin majority and took the Opposition by surprise, forcing general elections nearly a year ahead of schedule.

She returned to power in the elections held early in 1971, powered by the slogan 'Garibi Hatao', an emotive call to eradicate the deep-rooted malaise of poverty. For Indira, the March 1971 polls were a personal triumph, which proved her growing popularity. The election had brought Desai's Congress (O), the Bharatiya Jana Sangh, Swatantra Party and the Samyukta Socialist Party (SSP) together on one platform—the National Democratic Front—but Indira's Congress romped home with 352 of the 518 Lok Sabha seats that went to the polls. The results were notified on 15 March and Indira was sworn in on 16 March 1971.

Crackdown in East Pakistan

While the Congress was celebrating Indira's victory, trouble was brewing across the border in Pakistan. In March 1971, General Yahya Khan, President and chief martial law administrator, ordered a military crackdown in East Pakistan, about four months after Sheikh Mujibur Rahman's Awami League had swept the elections in the eastern region and secured a majority in Pakistan's Parliament. The balance of power had, for the first time, shifted to East Pakistan.

Khan had Rahman arrested and flown to West Pakistan. By April 1971, Indira had started weighing the options of getting involved in a war and, by all accounts, the Indian Army had started collaborating with the Mukti Bahini, the eastern region's resistance movement, in its struggle against the Pakistan federation's dictatorial regime. That was around May—the same month the Nagarwala scandal broke.

The day Nagarwala was roaming the streets of Delhi with Rs 60 lakh in cash, the Bharatiya Jana Sangh was demonstrating outside Parliament House demanding India's intervention in East Pakistan. The Prime Minister's secretary, P.N. Haksar, would later tell the Reddy Commission that they were preoccupied with the unfolding crisis in Bangladesh and had ignored the Nagarwala episode as a simple case of cheating.

Indira maintained complete silence in public after the scam broke, baffling everyone, including the media. On 26 May, when the issue came up for discussion in the Lok Sabha, she quietly walked out of the House, prompting a Jana Sangh member, Omkar Lal Berwa from Kota, Rajasthan, to remark, 'I find something fishy about this matter because the Prime Minister left the House before the notice (calling attention) came up. She should have remained in the House.'

In August, India and the then USSR concluded the Treaty of Peace, Friendship and Cooperation, prompting the Jana Sangh to hold a rally in Delhi, and party leader Atal Bihari Vajpayee to call it 'a conspiracy between Delhi and Moscow to deny recognition to Bangladesh'. The party would launch a satyagraha between 1 and 11 August, seeking recognition for Bangladesh.

Rash of Theories

In the absence of credible information on the Nagarwala controversy, Delhi's media had a field day from the moment the news of the 'robbery in the government bank' broke. Below are some of the theories that swirled around as newspapers fed the curiosity of readers:

- The Rs 60 lakh was unaccounted money that belonged to Indira, who had kept the amount in the bank and could order transactions over the phone.
- The money was meant for her younger son Sanjay Gandhi for his dream Maruti project. Sanjay, according to this theory, was to take the money abroad or pay the Haryana government towards the cost of the land for the project.
- The amount was meant for Bangladeshi freedom fighters, but could not be sent because of a last-minute goof-up by Malhotra, as the chief cashier had informed the police.
- Nagarwala was a crook and could mimic the voice of the Prime Minister.
- Both Nagarwala and Malhotra were known to Indira Gandhi.
- Nagarwala outsmarted Indira's courier, obtained the code words and ran away with the money before her actual agents could arrive at the SBI branch.
- Nagarwala was forced to make the confession to save Indira Gandhi from embarrassment and was promised that he would be let off quietly.
- Nagarwala did not die and was hiding in Italy, the country of Indira Gandhi's daughter-in-law Sonia.
- Nagarwala was an intelligence agent and worked for the MI6, the foreign intelligence service of the United Kingdom.
- Principal investigator Kashyap knew everything, and so was done away with. His death was made to appear like an accident.

- All officers associated with the investigation, including the magistrate who had tried Nagarwala, were shifted out of Delhi.
- Nagarwala's uncle, a retired commissioner of police of Hyderabad, was murdered because he knew the true story behind the case.

Among politicians, veteran leaders such as Morarji Desai and S.K. Patil penned articles in newspapers and periodicals, casting aspersions on Indira, even as *Motherland*, a newspaper owned by the Jana Sangh, carried story after story with juicy details.

The Nagarwala controversy would get overshadowed towards the end of 1971, much before the death of the alleged conman and main protagonist of the saga, as events of greater importance—such as the formation of Bangladesh and subsequent elections to assemblies in the major states of India—would divert attention from the scam.

On 13 June 1974, a fire in the Tis Hazari court complex destroyed the records of many criminal cases, including certain papers related to the Nagarwala case. These papers, including those pertaining to the strongroom from where the Rs 60 lakh was withdrawn, had been seized from the bank.

The blaze, described as a 'medium fire', had broken out around 5.40 p.m. and engulfed the entire record room (criminal) on the third floor in the western wing of the court complex. Three officials were suspended over the incident, later probed by an additional district and sessions judge, Muni Lal Jain.

Seething Seventies

The 1971 Bangladesh war was arguably Indira's greatest moment of glory. The surrender of thousands of Pakistani troops and the creation of Bangladesh, splitting Pakistan into two countries, capped her electoral triumph earlier that year. But it was not entirely smooth-sailing for the leader described as 'Durga' by someone no less than Vajpayee. There were other problems to grapple with. The economy had started showing a downward trend, and inflation, unemployment and industrial unrest had led to strikes in different parts of the country. In Uttar Pradesh, Congress Chief Minister Kamlapati Tripathi had to bow out of office following a mutiny by the Provincial Armed Constabulary (PAC).

'The press, which had overall turned hostile to the government and Mrs Gandhi, regularly regaled its readers with rumours and tales of bribery in high places, sale of licences, collection of black money by politicians and other financial scandals,' historian Bipan Chandra would later recall in his book *In the Name of Democracy*.[9]

The period also saw the emergence of Indira's younger son Sanjay Gandhi, then in his early twenties, as a power centre, and his efforts to circumvent the process in securing land and licence for his Maruti project. Then, Railway Minister L.N. Mishra's death in a January 1975 bomb blast in Samastipur, Bihar, provided enough material for the Opposition and the media to keep up their attack on Indira's leadership.

'The desperation of Opposition parties in the seventies also contributed to the political turmoil. [The years] 1974 and 1975 witnessed the strange spectacle of conservative and right wing political parties going for massive, extra-legal agitational politics to remove duly constituted governments,' Bipan Chandra wrote.

A protest by students of LD Engineering College in Gujarat against an increase in their monthly mess charges spread all over the state. The Navnirman Yuvak Samiti, spearheading the agitation, demanded the ouster of the Congress government in Gujarat.

---

9 Bipan Chandra, *In the Name of Democracy: JP Movement and the Emergency*, Penguin Books, 2017.

Chief Minister Chimanbhai Patel stepped down, but Morarji Desai, not satisfied with the resignation, went on an indefinite fast seeking fresh elections in his home state. Indira conceded the demand, but Desai went on another fast to press for immediate elections.

Veteran freedom fighter Jayaprakash Narayan, popularly known as JP, emerged from political hibernation to lead an agitation by students and youths across northern and eastern India against the Indira regime. Railway employees, under the leadership of firebrand socialist George Fernandes, went on strike. JP, who drew massive crowds, went to the extent of urging the armed forces not to obey illegal orders of the government.

The final blow to Indira's moral authority came from the Allahabad High Court on 12 June 1975, when Justice Jagmohanlal Sinha set aside her election from Raebareli on the election petition of socialist leader Raj Narain. The Supreme Court gave Congress MPs a conditional stay of twenty days to elect a new leader. The same day, assembly election results in Gujarat signalled the exit of the Congress, although no single party or alliance, including the Janata Front, got the required majority. To form the government, the Janata Front had to seek the support of Chimanbhai Patel, the very person whose removal they had agitated for. Patel had by then left the Congress party.

Then, on the night of 25 June, the Indira Gandhi government imposed the Emergency. In the twenty-one-month period that followed, Indira's key opponents were jailed and the media silenced through widespread censorship. Indira got the term of the fifth Lok Sabha, scheduled to end in March 1976, extended twice. On 8 January 1977, eighteen months before the extended term was to end, Indira took the nation by surprise, lifted the Emergency and announced general elections.

In the elections held in March 1977, the Congress was routed. The Janata Party, comprising the Bharatiya Lok Dal, Congress (O),

Bharatiya Jana Sangh, the Socialist Party and the Congress for Democracy (CFD) won 295 of the 544 seats in the Lok Sabha. Its allies secured nearly 50 more seats, ensuring a comfortable majority against the Congress's 154.

Commission of Inquiry

Desai became the Prime Minister and, keeping his party's electoral promise to expose the misdeeds of Indira, the Janata Party government appointed Justice Pingle Jaganmohan Reddy, a retired Supreme Court judge, to probe the Nagarwala case. The Home ministry issued the notification on 9 June 1977, announcing that a commission of inquiry had been set up under Reddy.

The commission's mandate was to probe:

- Chief Cashier V.P. Malhotra's withdrawal of Rs 60 lakh from the SBI's Parliament Street branch on 24 May 1971.
    - The manner and the circumstances in which the amount was taken out.
    - The source and ownership of the said amount.
    - Accounts, if any, from which the said sum was taken out.
    - The manner in which the said sum was accounted for in the books of the SBI branch before it was taken out.
    - The subsequent return of the amount to the SBI branch.
- The transfer of the aforesaid sum by Malhotra to another person alleged to be one Shri R.S. Nagarwala, son of Shri S. Nagarwala.
- The complaint filed with the Parliament Street police station by officers of the said SBI branch relating to the withdrawal and the subsequent police investigation.

- Nagarwala's arrest, recovery of the whole or part of the said sum from him and the subsequent criminal proceedings against him.
- The involvement, if any, of other persons with Malhotra or Nagarwala in any of the aforesaid transactions.
- Nagarwala's death during the pendency of the criminal proceedings against him.
- The death of investigating officer D.K. Kashyap.

Born on 23 January 1910, the Cambridge-educated Justice Reddy had practised in the high courts of Hyderabad, Madras and Bombay before becoming a judge. In 1966, he became the chief justice of Andhra Pradesh High Court, and was elevated to the top court in 1969. Justice Reddy was one of the judges who had inquired into communal disturbances in Gujarat in 1969 and authored, among other works, *The Revolutions I Have Lived Through*.

In all, the commission examined 245 persons, including Indira Gandhi, Y.B. Chavan, Morarji Desai and L.K. Advani, between 10 April and 14 September 1978. The first person to be examined was Dr S.M.S. Mody, medical director of the NM Wadia Institute of Cardiology, who had treated Nagarwala after his car accident in Pune. The last to be examined was Irfan Ullah Khan, who then worked for the *Current Weekly*, a tabloid magazine.

Notes

1. Chimanbhai Patel, whose government's very dismissal was the demand of the students' agitation, was out of the Congress. His new party joined the Janata Front to form the government in Gujarat.

CHAPTER 16

INDIRA APPEARS BEFORE THE COMMISSION

'A section of the people were occupied in manufacturing this kind of propaganda day in and day out, and I did not pay it much attention.'

This was Indira Gandhi's response to the Justice Reddy Commission when asked why she did not consider it necessary to hold a public inquiry into the episode in which her name was sullied.

The former Prime Minister was at her aggressive best before the commission on 12 June 1978. Her party had been voted out of power. She had suffered a humiliating defeat from her Raebareli Lok Sabha seat in UP. The Janata Party government was out to punish her for her 'misdeeds'.

She had already spent a night in Tihar Jail on 3 October 1977 when the CBI arrested her for the alleged involvement in what was called the 'Jeep scam'. Out of power and short on public sympathy, Indira had effectively used the Janata regime's bid to arrest her as a route for a great comeback. Sonia Gandhi was preparing tea for her mother-in-law on 3 October 1977 around 5 p.m. when the CBI superintendent of police N.K. Singh knocked on their door.

'Handcuff me!' Indira had shrieked at N.K. Singh. 'I will not go unless I am handcuffed!' she had roared. Even as Sonia stoically watched the proceedings, Sanjay made frantic telephone calls to Congress supporters, and from another phone, R.K. Dhawan called upon the local media. Reporters of that era remember getting calls from Maneka Gandhi, who was then part of the *Surya* magazine, telling them that if they rushed to Indira's house, they would get a great story.

Until the media arrived in great numbers, Indira kept delaying her arrest. 'Where is the warrant of arrest and the FIR report?' she asked N.K. Singh. When the CBI officer struggled to produce the relevant documents, Indira's lawyer Frank Anthony chipped in, 'Is that Charan Singh's [then the Union home minister] new law?'

'I'll not budge until you handcuff me,' Indira kept repeating. 'Bring the handcuffs and take me.'

The next day, Indira was released on technical grounds. It prompted Rajiv Gandhi, who was maintaining an apolitical profile then, to comment, 'Even Mummy herself couldn't have written a better scenario.'[10]

'Political prisoners,' commented *Le Monde*, 'are often regarded as martyrs in India, where prison, as was once the case for the majority of members of [Morarji] Desai's government, can be an antechamber of power.'[11]

Indira was jailed on another occasion in December 1978, when Desai managed to pass legislation to set up special courts to try Indira and Sanjay Gandhi. Soon after her expulsion and dramatic exit from

---

10 Rasheed Kidwai, *24 Akbar Road: A Short History of the People behind the Fall and Rise of the Congress*, Hachette Books India, 2013.
11 Rasheed Kidwai, 'Will Rahul Gandhi's Disqualification Trigger an Opposition Onslaught?', *India Today*, 24 March 2023, https://www.indiatoday.in/news-analysis/story/will-rahul-gandhi-disqualification-trigger-an-opposition-onslaught-2351025-2023-03-24

Parliament, Indira was arrested and taken to Tihar Jail, where she was put in a barracks of her own—in the same cell complex that George Fernandes had occupied during the Emergency. Sonia used to bring Indira meals three times a day from home.

Indira also had the experience of running a legal feud with the J.C. Shah Commission since 1977 on various charges. Two of its interim reports damning her and her acolytes are in the public domain since March 1978.

Not deterred by the Janata government's onslaughts, Indira started making whirlwind tours of the country. She seemed to have sensed that the political wind had begun blowing in her favour.

Accompanied by her team of lawyers led by Vikram Mahajan, Indira appeared before the Reddy Commission and got her two-page statement recorded before Dwarka Nath, SP, attached to the commission, before subjecting herself to cross-questioning.

Recalling her statement that to any such crimes 'if the name of a national leader is added, it becomes sensational news', she was asked why she did not consider instituting a public inquiry into the episode. She said, 'Frankly, it did not strike me.' There were 'competent officers' in the home ministry and in her secretariat. Once they knew of the matter, 'I thought they would take necessary action', she said.

To the question whether holding a full inquiry into the episode would have 'embarrassed' Bangladesh because there were reports that the money was meant for her government's secret operations in East Pakistan, her reply was, 'It did not strike me one way or the other.'

Did the Nagarwala episode embarrass her? 'Certainly not, since I had nothing to do with it. I did not know any of the persons concerned,' she asserted.

Her instant reaction to the incident, she explained, was 'extreme bewilderment as to how such a thing could happen; that a person who was in such a job for such a long time [Malhotra] should have taken away the money like this, or that he should imagine that the

Prime Minister would ring herself. That was itself a big assumption. It is extremely unlikely. I did not know that money could be taken out so easily. And the whole thing had a fictional quality to it.'

She recollected that her erstwhile private secretary, N.K. Seshan, had informed her of the incident and that she had mentioned this to her secretary P.N. Haksar, who had taken the incident as a prank played on the bank. She could not remember having ever met Nagarwala or 'having seen any letter addressed to her or to her office'. The letters, if any were received from Nagarwala or his relatives, may have been 'sent to the concerned departments'.

She also made it clear that there was no relation between her Parsi husband Feroze Gandhi and Nagarwala. Family members of Nagarwala, his mother Goolbai and her sister, too, made similar assertions before the commission to scotch rumours about possible Parsi connections between the two families.

Indira Gandhi maintained that she did not know Malhotra and did not remember having seen him. If he had ever visited the Prime Minister's house on behalf of the State Bank of India, he might have greeted her along with the others.

Making it clear that she never spoke to Malhotra over telephone, she said that all her telephone calls were put through by her private secretary and that she never dealt directly with the bank authorities regarding any operation of her accounts.

The commission also questioned Delhi Telephones officials, who had categorically refuted allegations appearing in a section of the press that there was a hotline between the Prime Minister's Office and the chief cashier of SBI.

She said many people visited the Prime Minister's residence with their grievances and Nagarwala 'might have seen her', but he was 'not employed by her in any job'.

Indira Gandhi admitted that she had asked then Union Home Secretary Govind Narain about 'certain details' of the case.

'Since the matter came up in Parliament and my name was mentioned and I did not know who Nagarwala was or who Malhotra was, I must have asked about them.'

Y.B. Chavan, who was the finance minister when the scam broke and had replied on behalf of the government in both the Houses of Parliament about the scam, also supported Indira Gandhi's contention. Chavan said that when he had told her about the episode, she had observed that it was 'fantastic' and 'absurd' for a bank official to have behaved in that manner. 'She of her own never inquired or expressed any anxiety to me with regard to this issue,' Chavan said. He never felt 'the Nagarwala affair was a matter of public importance'.

Did Indira Know Nagarwala?

In her deposition Indira Gandhi did not rule out the possibility that Nagarwala might have met her, because many people used to meet her seeking help.

The commission had the proof. Her social and cultural secretary, Usha Bhagat, who operated from the Prime Minister's house, had written two letters to Nagarwala. The letters, dated 29 November 1966 and 19 November 1968, handed over by the CBI, were in the commission's possession. The letters conclusively established that Nagarwala had met Indira Gandhi at least once.

In the first letter, Bhagat had thanked Nagarwala for writing to the Prime Minister and said, 'When you pass through Delhi, please get in touch with me.' The second letter was in the form of an acknowledgement. Bhagat had written, 'The Prime Minister is extremely busy, so you can convey to Mr P.N. Haksar, secretary to the Prime Minister, whatever you wish to tell the Prime Minister.'

Nagarwala had met Haksar and written another letter to Bhagat, thanking her for having 'seen him' and 'arranged' a meeting to see the Prime Minister. Nagarwala had met the Prime Minister on

16 December 1967, when she had directed him to meet Haksar, which he did on 18 December.

In this letter, Nagarwala had enclosed another letter addressed to the Prime Minister regarding the talk that he had had with her. 'I shall be grateful to you, Miss Bhagat, if you kindly hand over this letter to Mrs Gandhi personally.'

The letter from Nagarwala referred to the ongoing Vietnam War in 1966. When the war was on, two months after becoming Prime Minister, Indira Gandhi had gone to Washington seeking financial assistance and food for India's millions. Her close advisers had counselled her to tell the then US President Lyndon Baines Johnson that India 'shared America's agony over Vietnam'. She refused to draw American hostility.

Amid all this, Nagarwala, in his letter to Indira Gandhi, said that he was unable to 'sound convincing to you or your secretary P.N. Haksar' during the meeting with them, and appealed to her to mediate between Washington, Hanoi and Saigon. Nagarwala, who was living in Japan at that time, had claimed that he had gathered certain information from there about the need for a third party to intervene and diffuse the crisis, and wanted Indira Gandhi to take on the role of mediator.

Asserting that such an initiative would enhance her 'prestige', Nagarwala volunteered to be her messenger (to different leaders) in this endeavour.

Bhagat confirmed having written the letters to Nagarwala, but these were matters of routine, she said. 'Many a time I used to acknowledge letters from the public in a routine manner,' Bhagat explained to the commission.

When Indira Gandhi was confronted with these facts during the cross-examination by the commission, she said she generally gave the public an hour and a half for interviews in the morning, and in that interview if something serious was mentioned, she made notes and passed on whatever they had said to the relevant office, unless she felt it was a request of special importance. Then she took it seriously and followed up on it.

'How could I believe that Nagarwala was going to be a mediator [between me, Washington and Hanoi], bringing me into the picture about Vietnam War?' Indira Gandhi retorted.

The two letters that Nagarwala wrote from jail and the emotional appeal from Goolbai seeking 'a mother to mother' response, too, evoked a guarded response from Indira Gandhi. She said she had not seen the letters and that they must have been routinely forwarded to the departments concerned.

In her cross-examination, Bhagat was evasive in her replies. She said she had seen the letters but had not placed them before Indira Gandhi. But the joint secretary in the Prime Minister's Office, B.N. Tandon, who was by then the chief secretary of Delhi, confirmed that he had seen those letters and had endorsed that the letters 'need not be shown' to the Prime Minister. He had suggested to Private Secretary N.K. Seshan that 'no notice be taken of these letters. If Nagarwala has personal grievances, he should approach the jail authorities.'

Asked whether he had communicated this to Nagarwala, Tandon replied in the negative. On the letter from Nagarwala's mother seeking Indira Gandhi's intervention after her son was admitted to hospital, Tandon said he had 'marked it to Deputy Secretary M. Malhoutra on 4 February 1972'. He disposed of it by saying that 'no action was called for'.

In fact, Tandon, who later became the principal secretary to Prime Minister Atal Bihari Vajpayee during his thirteen-day tenure in 1996, came in for severe criticism by the commission for his evasive and noncommittal replies.

Indira Gandhi denied having shown any interest in the investigation of the case, but the commission had enough evidence to establish Tandon's interest in the case. He had visited the Parliament Street police station at least twice on 24 May, the day the incident occurred, and was also part of official meetings where the Nagarwala issue was discussed.

Initially, Tandon claimed that he had visited the police station once, along with his brother G.N. Tandon, who was working with BHEL, after the money was recovered. They were going to Connaught Place for a post-dinner cup of coffee when they saw a number of cars and scooters outside the police station. Since during the day the case had 'aroused a lot of curiosity', they had dropped in to find out what the latest position was.

Tandon claimed that he had met district SP Rajpal outside the police station for 'eight to ten minutes', while his brother G.N. Tandon, who later became the special assistant to Information and Broadcasting Minister L.K. Advani in 1977, had gone inside the police station at Rajpal's suggestion to take a look at the cash seized by the police.

But DIG Rosha went on record saying that Tandon had also visited the police station in the afternoon and had told them—the IG, Rajpal and him—that the Prime Minister 'was anxious that the culprit must be traced and money extracted, especially when her name has been used'.

Confronted with this fact, Tandon had to concede. He said he would not 'rule out [the second meeting], since senior police officers are saying so'.

Tandon had feigned ignorance about certain meetings at the Parliament House office attended by then Minister of State for Home Affairs K.C. Pant and Home Secretary Govind Narain to discuss the Nagarwala issue, but had changed his statement when presented with the versions of other officials and certain official communication.

However, Tandon maintained all along that he had 'no instructions' from Indira Gandhi on the matter, although 'ordinarily' he dealt with the Nagarwala case from the Prime Minister's Secretariat—he never carried any message on her behalf and nor did he instruct any official on the case.

Indira Gandhi, too, told the commission that 'as far as I can remember', she had not discussed the matter with Tandon.

It was natural for Justice Reddy to feel otherwise. 'I find no difficulty in holding that this message was in fact conveyed and must have had the authority of Smt Indira Gandhi,' Justice Reddy remarked in the report. He was convinced that Indira Gandhi was 'fully informed' about the developments 'at every stage', because Home Secretary Govind Narain, who later became the governor of Karnataka, had admitted that he had discussed these matters with her 'once or twice'.

During the cross-interrogation, as mentioned earlier, Indira Gandhi said that since this matter had come up in Parliament and her name was mentioned, and she did not know who Nagarwala or Malhotra were, she must have asked about them.

Indira Gandhi feigned ignorance about the home secretary's letter to Delhi Police on 29 May 1971 to investigate if there was a conspiracy to 'tarnish' the image of the Prime Minister, and also to find out Nagarwala's antecedents and political affiliations. She said someone may have 'mentioned' the inquiry to her. The commission refused to believe her.

The Intelligence Bureau (IB) and the Research and Analysis Wing (R&AW), which were under the Prime Minister, were hardly 'likely to inquire' into this. The Prime Minister or any member of the government did not consider it proper to institute any inquiry to settle the dust of 'doubt' and controversy that was being 'raised all the time and which came to thicken all the more as time passed', the commission noted.

A wider inquiry was restricted in view of these instructions. The commission believed the then New Delhi District SP Rajpal's statement to this effect. The commission was of the opinion that a wider inquiry was 'restricted' by the home secretary with the knowledge of Indira Gandhi. 'A fuller inquiry would have revealed much more and could have thrown light on the people who did not want Nagarwala to come out of jail,' it said.

But the commission held the view that 'though it would appear that Nagarwala had met Smt Indira Gandhi in or around 1954 or 1955 seeking assistance to get interim relief or compensation when he was boarded out of the Army and again on 15 December 1967, in connection with the Vietnam War, it is not possible to hold that Nagarwala was well-known to her as to make her employ him as a courier to discharge secret duties purported to be entrusted by her to such couriers'.

B.N. Tandon, joint secretary in the PMO, was not alone in causing embarrassment to Indira Gandhi. The presence of her first cousin Gautam Kaul, an IPS officer, at the Parliament Street police station on the day of the arrest, too, became a subject of controversy.

Rajpal, who had become a DIG and was with Delhi Police, told the commission that Kaul had almost 'become a nuisance hovering around and impeding the investigation'.

'He was free to investigate—he is a senior officer to me,' Kaul had retorted at the time of cross-examination.

But Rajpal did not think it to be 'prudent' to pursue the matter as Kaul was the cousin of the Prime Minister.

Kaul, a 1969-batch IPS officer, who was also the PM's cousin, did not take kindly to the remarks. 'I was a police officer not related to the case, but was the staff officer to the IG. [Delhi Police used to be headed by the IG.] I was well within my jurisdiction to know the facts for the information of the IG and if the district SP wished that I not be there, he could have ordered me out of the parameters of the inquiry.'

Kaul, who was the assistant inspector general, also had the additional charge of being the press relations officer, a job that entailed him to interact with the media on a daily basis.

'Quite often I had to be present at the scene of occurrence [crime] to assist correspondents of daily newspapers in their efforts to collect relevant information,' Kaul added.

In the evening, he had arranged the press conference at the police station for senior officials to brief the media.

Kaul said he never had 'the occasion to talk to or see Nagarwala or Malhotra', and had seen Nagarwala only at the press conference. He was associated with the affair for the 'next two days' only to brief newspapers.

The commission held the view that Tandon, Kaul and the bank officials were all in the police station during Nagarwala's interrogation.

Among the police officers, Rajpal was quite forthcoming in parting with information to the commission, unlike his colleagues. He stated that during his interrogation of Nagarwala, the latter had 'repeatedly said that if he was taken to the Prime Minister, he would reveal the whereabouts of the money. He was willing to do so if he was taken to the Chief of Army Staff General Sam Manekshaw or Director General of Border Security Force K.F. Rustomji.'

Rajpal alleged that Rustomji had subsequently rung up DIG Rosha to examine the possibility of releasing Nagarwala on bail. Rosha denied the charge. So did Rustomji.

Rustomji said, 'Surely I would know that, in a case like this, bail would not be granted. Also as he was a Parsi, I wanted to keep away from the case completely. Officers who know me will bear me out, that I would not interfere in a case of this type as it would affect my reputation.'

At the same time, Rustomji admitted that he knew the fellow Parsi Nagarwala from his army days through social gatherings.

Rajpal also told the commission that it was felt by the home ministry that Finance Minister Y.B. Chavan was deliberately trying to put the ministry (headed by Indira Gandhi) in an embarrassing situation. Rajpal, who had supervised the investigation as the district SP, had doubted Nagarwala's ability to mimic Indira Gandhi's voice. The tape-recorded conversation 'to my mind did not indicate if this was a faithful imitation of Smt. Gandhi's voice'.

Rajpal also told the commission that Malhotra had told him during his interrogation that there was a 'precedent of taking money to VIPs' residence(s) and thereafter taking the cheque, etc., from the VIP', but had refused to name the VIPs. But he admitted that he had not disclosed this to the investigating officer during his interrogation. 'It was apparent that Malhotra had personal regard for Mrs Gandhi,' he told the commission.

Even Markandey Singh, SP (CID), who had become the DIG, CISF, Calcutta, provided certain information to Justice Reddy on 21 July 1978, which was recorded. It was to 'not be made available' without his permission, Justice Reddy had ordered. The file is now available at the National Archives.

The IPS officer had said that 'rumours had come to me that the money was to be taken out in a plane, which could not leave and was cancelled because the money could not reach the airport at the appropriate time'. He also said that there were 'rumours that Nagarwala was an army intelligence man, but it could not be verified'.

'It was reported that V.P. Malhotra had campaigned for the Congress in the Ramnagar area of Delhi when he had been either suspended or dismissed, and that his services had been enlisted by Shri Yashpal Kapoor [a key political aide of Indira Gandhi]. It was also rumoured that V.P. Malhotra's son had been employed by the SBI either when he was under suspension or had been dismissed.'

Role of P.N. Haksar

Justice Reddy did not appear to have taken kindly to the remarks of Haksar during his interrogation. 'As far as rumours go, with no disrespect to our public life, our public life is full of rumours and if one were to chase them, every bureaucrat would be chasing rumours and not doing anything else,' Haksar had once said.

Referring to the rumours to the Reddy Commission, he had remarked, 'Frankly I have grown as a hardened bureaucrat. I do not pick up rumours, nor am I moved by the kind of atmosphere that prevails where any kind of allegation is made. This is a great country and if all these anonymous letters and rumours are to be gone into, we would be wasting our time.'

It was natural for the commission to shoot back if it was 'also wasting its time' by holding the inquiry.

To this, Haksar was at his best as a fine bureaucrat. He said 'No, I don't think so. I hope it is not wasting its time, since it is in the hands of a very distinguished judge.'

Haksar had maintained that he had not taken an interest in the case because of his preoccupation with the affairs of Bangladesh, and felt 'what had happened was in the hands of the authorities; that it will be investigated and maybe we will come to know the truth'.

Justice Reddy was not convinced that the matter was dealt with properly, nor 'do I generalize that 650 million people are all rumour mongers' and that the issue was 'not a matter of public importance'.

There were a number of circumstances that lent plausibility to the feeling that there 'was more to the incident' than had been allowed to come out either by the police investigations or the hurried manner in which the Nagarwala case was sought to be buried, the commission felt.

Nagarwala Alive: An Italian Angle

Rattan Singh Razda, MP from south Bombay and a former Congress leader close to Morarji Desai, raised a red herring. Nagarwala was 'alive' and living in Italy, he said.

The commission took cognizance of the statement and asked the CBI to probe the information. CBI director John Lobo informed the commission that Razda had divulged his sources, and after questioning them, the CBI had contacted Interpol about whether Nagarwala was alive and staying with the in-laws of Rajiv Gandhi, Indira Gandhi's eldest son.

'It was ascertained that no such person was living there, nor was any person by that name alive and living in Italy,' Lobo said.

Razda was not alone in thinking that Nagarwala was alive. K.L. Gauba, author of the book titled *The Mystery of Nagarwala Case* published in June 1977 by Hind Pocket Books, dedicated it to Rustom Sohrab Nagarwala 'Dead or Alive'!

He, too, told the commission that 'Nagarwala was alive and is living under a different name'.

The jail inmate Colonel Amrik Singh told the commission, 'I am not sure if the same Nagarwala died.' In his view, 'they had set up a double of Nagarwala about whom I have heard subsequently from different sources. Only about two months back I was given the information that a man of the same name was visiting Delhi from Japan and was trying to make inquiries about the pending proceedings.'

Justice Jaganmohan Reddy refused to believe the statements of the police, Nagarwala and Malhotra, except for the fact that Rs 60 lakh was taken out in contravention of bank rules. To him, the statements were unreliable. The investigation was confined to the recovery of money and, thereafter, there was manipulation of facts because the police felt Indira Gandhi was somehow involved

Indira Appears before the Commission

in the whole affair. 'The attitude of the police may be described as that of a person sweeping everything under the carpet and feeling that they have done the cleaning,' he said.

He was not convinced with the statements of Indira Gandhi, P.N. Haksar or, for that matter, Finance Minister Y.B. Chavan that the government had more important tasks such as the Bangladesh crisis on its plate than to 'chase rumours' and waste their energy.

He seemed to have given credence to Prime Minister Morarji Desai's charge that Indira Gandhi avoided the issue in Parliament 'deliberately' as she had something to hide.

CHAPTER 17

THE SANJAY STORY

As the Nagarwala saga played out before the Reddy Commission with all its intriguing twists and turns seven years after the incident, one person's name repeatedly came up in the to and fro of allegations and counter-allegations. That person was Sanjay Gandhi, Indira Gandhi's younger son. According to one theory, among the many that swirled around, the money that was withdrawn from the SBI was meant for Sanjay, a claim the commission did not accept.

But why did Sanjay's name crop up in connection with the controversy? Here's an attempt to reconstruct the picture from around 1969, when Sanjay was an ambitious young man of about twenty-three, intent on coming up with a new car that middle-class Indians could afford, a revolutionary idea at a time when automobile was a protected industry.

Educated at St. Columba's School in Delhi, Welham Boys' School in Dehradun and then Doon School, Sanjay was a university dropout. He had done a three-year apprenticeship at the Rolls-Royce factory in Crewe, UK, but did not complete the course. He had not yet dabbled in politics, but had enough friends and admirers among politicians and others who encouraged him to turn his idea into reality. After all, he was the Prime Minister's son.

The first step was to seek a licence to manufacture a small and cheap car in India, which Sanjay did, one of several applicants to do so. In 1970, he was the lone applicant to have been granted the licence. The Haryana government, under Bansi Lal, handed over 300 acres in Gurgaon (now Gurugram) for Sanjay's Maruti factory. About 15,000 farmers were evicted to free the land that was offered at a throwaway price.[12]

The Opposition accused Indira Gandhi of nepotism and the Prime Minister made little effort to deny the charge. Each time the matter was raised in Parliament, she would purse her lips and shrug off the criticism.

Sanjay started working on his pet project and got a huge boost in 1971 when the Indira government awarded a contract to Maruti Motors Limited, where Sanjay was the managing director, to build 50,000 'people's cars'. Neither the company, incorporated in 1971, nor Sanjay had any previous experience in building a cheap and fuel-efficient car. The company also did not have a tie-up with any other company that had the technical know-how.

This was the beginning of Indira's efforts to groom Sanjay as her successor, and he slowly emerged as a decisive power centre with a coterie around him—enough fodder for the Prime Minister's opponents to see her son's hand in all her deeds and alleged misdeeds. It was in this atmosphere that the Nagarwala controversy broke.

Even IPS officer Y. Rajpal, who was part of the investigation into the case as the superintendent of police of New Delhi district, submitted to the Reddy Commission that 'someone had told him' much later, after he had left Delhi Police, that Sanjay was 'familiar' with Nagarwala and used to call him 'Uncle'.

---

12 Rasheed Kidwai, *24 Akbar Road: A Short History of the People behind the Fall and Rise of the Congress*, Hachette Books India, 2013, p. 41.

The writ petition before the Delhi High Court, filed by Urmilesh Jha, private secretary to the socialist leader Raj Narain, had specifically alleged that Sanjay needed money to pay the Haryana government for the land required for the Maruti project. That was the buzz in political circles at the time. The commission considered the contents of the petition.

Former diplomat Dharam Yash Dev, author of *The Nagarwala Mystery: The Sixty Lakhs State Bank Robbery Story*, had a pointed query: Was it arranged for Sanjay Gandhi and another friend to leave India the same evening (24 May 1971) and were their bookings ready on one of the international flights?

The Blitz, in an article on 4 March 1977, came up with a similar question for the public to ponder and the authorities to answer: Was Sanjay Gandhi's flight to Mauritius on the night of the alleged theft (24 May) just a coincidence?

The Reddy Commission had called Yash Dev to tell them what he knew about Sanjay's involvement in the scam. From where had he learnt that Sanjay was scheduled to fly abroad on 24 May, it asked the former diplomat? Yash Dev claimed that it was from 'somebody in the Air India office', but added that he didn't know if the records were changed or could have been changed. Sanjay's trip, he claimed, might have been cancelled because of the tamasha (drama) that took place on 24 May.

Yash Dev cited a report *The Statesman* had carried on 29 June 1971, from Stuttgart. Titled 'Sanjay Gandhi's German Visit', the report said, 'Mr Sanjay Gandhi had made a secret visit to the Volkswagen plant in West Germany. The visit was made several weeks ago but it is an indication of the hush-hush nature of the visit that Mr Sanjay Gandhi did not call at the Indian Embassy in Bonn during his stay in West Germany.'

Yash Dev told the commission, 'Our information about Sanjay's holidays in May 1971 may have been correct or may not have been correct, but that was the information that was available to us from reliable sources. Sometimes, it is difficult for us to name the party that gives us such information.'

He said he had also heard that Sanjay was to go to Mauritius, but because of the 'fiasco' on 24 May, did not. 'Nagarwala was to meet somebody, but that somebody did not turn up, therefore everything went wrong.' Asked by the commission if he could back up his claims with facts, Yash Dev's lengthy answer suggested that records could have been tampered with.

When Indira Gandhi deposed before the commission, she was specifically asked by Justice Reddy whether Sanjay was to leave for Mauritius 'about that time'. She replied in the negative. Asked whether Sanjay was in Delhi then, she said, 'He must have been, but certainly he had not gone to Mauritius.'

Malhotra's statement, too, suggested as much. While he was waiting for the Prime Minister at her official residence on 24 May 1971, he told the commission that a person had got down from a car. Assuming that it could be P.N. Haksar, he had asked the officer at the reception who the person was. The officer, he said, had told him that it was Indira Gandhi's younger son.

Maruti and Malhotra

The commission also explored the claim that Maruti had employed Malhotra after he had been dismissed by the SBI. Charan Singh, a senior minister in the Morarji Desai government, asserted in the Lok Sabha that the company had hired Malhotra. The claim implied that Malhotra knew the Gandhi family and had acted at their behest to deliver the cash to Nagarwala.

The commission examined three senior Maruti executives—Wing Commander R.H. Chowdhury, who worked as the company's chief executive between 1971 and 1974; Jagdish Pahuja, the accounts officer; and A.D. Kolhatkar, the personnel manager. Malhotra was present at the hearing when the three executives were asked if he had ever worked with the company. They had a close look at him and were categorical in their response—they had not seen him working for the company during their tenures. Pahuja went to the extent of saying that the man 'has never worked as V.P. Malhotra or under any assumed name' in the finance unit of the company.

Asked by Malhotra's counsel during cross-examination, Indira Gandhi had made it clear that she did not know the former SBI cashier. She recalled that when Charan Singh had made a statement in Parliament alleging that Malhotra had been employed by Maruti, she had inquired and found out that Malhotra had 'no connection whatsoever' with the company.

The Reddy Commission had approached the Justice A.C. Gupta Commission, which had already been probing the Maruti project, to examine the veracity of the claim that the Rs 60 lakh withdrawn from the SBI branch could have been meant for the car factory. The secretary of the Justice A.C. Gupta Commission informed the Reddy Commission that the land allotted to Maruti for its car factory was acquired by the Haryana government, which bore the entire cost of the land—Rs 35,32,826 (Rs 35.32 lakh).

According to the Gupta Commission, Sanjay had taken possession of the land on behalf of Maruti after submitting a cheque for Rs 3,53,289 (the first instalment payable under the special agreement entered into with the company). This amount was raised by the company from the issue of share capital to a company controlled by one of the then directors of Maruti Ltd. The cheque was encashed on 20 August 1971. The next payment was made on 13 March 1974, amounting to Rs 6,21,790.

The Gupta Commission also informed the Reddy Commission that the company came into being on 4 June 1971—eleven days after the 24 May bank episode—and obtained a certificate of commencement of business from August the same year.

'It is apparent from the information furnished by the Maruti Commission that the suspicion existing at the time in the minds of some people who were actuated to file the petition, that the exact amount, which was taken from the State Bank on 24 May 1971, was needed about that time by Sanjay Gandhi to pay as compensation for the land acquired by the Haryana government, is not substantiated,' Justice Reddy said in his report.

'I do not find any evidence before me to justify the suspicion of Sanjay Gandhi being involved in the episode,' Justice Reddy remarked, citing the statements of Indira Gandhi and Malhotra before the commission.

Sanjay had all along alleged conspiracy theories against him. 'How long can I leave it to Mummy to defend me? I want to answer these charges myself,' he had once said, justifying his decision to enter politics.

Indira Gandhi, too, spoke in the same vein while talking to Congress volunteers on 23 December 1976, at the conclusion of a training camp. 'In fact, I think, Sanjay would never have come to politics if there had not been a tremendous attack on him in Parliament even before the Emergency, because he was not interested in any of these things,' she told the volunteers. 'But when there was that attack, he did feel that nobody was speaking for him. This is what urged him to join politics. The greater the attack on him, the greater his determination to do what he can. One thing he inherits from me is that when we are under attack, we fight back. I can say this because I know his psychology, his nature and my own nature.'

Mohammad Yunus, who had loaned his house to Indira Gandhi after the Congress's 1977 electoral rout, also felt that Sanjay had been treated unfairly. 'He was accused of every conceivable vice and mischief, and held responsible for everything going wrong,' Yunus, who had been a close associate of Jawaharlal Nehru, said.

Haksar's Exit

Sanjay's growing influence on Indira Gandhi, Congress politics and his alleged interference in the official functioning of the PMO had a direct bearing on a key figure in his mother's immediate circle. Haksar, the Prime Minister's principal secretary, considered the most powerful civil servant in independent India, was abruptly dropped from his post.

Haksar was Indira's main adviser on several tricky issues, including the move to nationalize banks, the decision to support the liberation struggle in what would become Bangladesh and even the taming of the Congress old guard. Indira had once remarked that the Prime Minister's secretary was as important as a Cabinet minister and most of the time knew more about the government than any Cabinet minister did. Yet, after the Nagarwala episode, Haksar was removed in 1973, ostensibly for opposing Sanjay's Maruti car project.

In a 1998 article, Indira's press adviser, H.Y. Sharada Prasad, had said the reason behind the principal secretary's fall from grace and exit from the PMO could be summed up in two words—Sanjay Gandhi. Prasad, who had a way with words, recalled the 'growing friction between sovereign and chamberlain over the doings of the prince'. Haksar, he said, had remarked that 'Indira Gandhi's will to power was not, alas, matched by her will to greatness'.

Haksar, who was not part of Indira's decision to impose the Emergency, later joined the Planning Commission as deputy chairman, but Sanjay and his team had their own way of getting back at him. It may have just been a coincidence, but Haksar's eighty-year-old uncle, who owned Pandit Brothers, a textile shop in

Connaught Place, had to spend a day in police custody during the Emergency. The reason? Apparently, the towels and napkins at his shop did not carry individual price tags, although the bundles did.

'Simple, Sincere Boy'

After the Congress's defeat in 1977, writer and filmmaker Khwaja Ahmad Abbas met Indira and cited specific instances of excesses during the Emergency, ranging from forced sterilizations to violence. Indira defended her son. 'Sanjay is a very simple, sincere boy,' she kept repeating. 'He does not drink or smoke, and does not take tea or coffee.' Abbas would later say he had noticed a tremor in her voice, as if Indira was pleading for her son.

Indira blamed her party's chief ministers, the Congress Working Committee and the AICC office-bearers for the entire 'Sanjay build-up'. Apparently, as Prime Minister, Indira had written numerous letters to the chief ministers of party-ruled states, asking them not to accord state receptions for Sanjay, but they had continued to do so.

Indira had described Sanjay as a doer. 'You see, he isn't a thinker. He is a doer. I mean a cent per cent doer. When he wants something done, he gets it done,' she told her biographer, Dom Moraes.

Maneka Gandhi, a senior Bharatiya Janata Party MP now, continues to defend her husband and the Emergency. According to her, the Emergency was something that brought order and discipline to the country. 'There were no power failures, no strikes or lockouts, citizens went about without the fear of being mugged, robbed or raped, everything was available at reasonable prices, the slums had been cleared, the stench of open sewers abolished and, instead, clean, wholesome and cheap housing complexes were raised in the suburbs, the arid desert of sand and rock turned into lush green parks and woodland. These were only some of the things that Sanjay did for his city.'

Notes

1. The Maruti Commission, headed by Justice A.C. Gupta, gave its 471-page report in May 1979, nearly two months before Morarji Desai was ousted from power by Charan Singh with the support of Indira Gandhi's Congress. The report indicted Indira Gandhi, Sanjay Gandhi and former Haryana Chief Minister Bansi Lal, among others, for the blatant violation of norms while promoting the Maruti company. The report was virtually consigned to the dustbin.

CHAPTER 18

ODD CHARACTERS

Many people, among them a host of public figures and senior government officials, appeared before the Reddy Commission as it sought to unravel the mystery of the Nagarwala case. Whether they helped clear the air or deepened the fog further will be dealt with in the next sections of this book. But among those who testified before the panel were some who clearly wasted the commission's time with their claims that bordered on the ludicrous. For the purpose of this book, they have been clubbed in this chapter. We'll start with one such character, a former wing commander of the Indian Air Force, before moving on to others, one of them a habitual litigant.

S.N. Rampal, a retired wing commander, dropped a bombshell on the commission when he said he had 'scripted' the entire drama to expose how easily money could be taken out of a bank and passed on to unworthy 'political persons'.

'It was a practical joke planned by me,' Rampal told the commission, adding that he had 'mimicked the voice of P.N. Haksar while Nagarwala spoke to the bank in the voice of Prime Minister Indira Gandhi'.

Rampal claimed that Nagarwala was a mere puppet in his play and had gone along with the script until he chickened out at the last minute. The drama flopped because Nagarwala's 'intention changed' during the execution of the plan, Rampal said.

Rampal approached the commission in June 1978, four months before it was to submit its report, and demanded 'full immunity as an approver'. Rampal, author of eight books, said he had taken voluntary retirement in 1974 after the Indian Air Force had levelled 'false charges' against him for not seeking permission to write articles.

According to his version of the story, he was working as a deputy director at Air Headquarters and had gone to the Armed Forces Club for a glass of beer when Nagarwala had approached him. Apparently, Nagarwala had told Rampal that he had met him earlier when he was convalescing at a military hospital after being injured in an air crash in the 1950s and that he considered Rampal a 'hero' for his daredevil acts.

At the Armed Forces Club, Nagarwala had narrated his supposed misfortune of working in a 'cloak-and-dagger organization' directly under Prime Minister Indira Gandhi. Rampal said Nagarwala told him he was sick and tired of being used as a 'domestic servant' and a 'messenger' to do a 'thankless job', which was to 'collect money' from the bank and pass it on to the 'most undesirable political persons'.

Nagarwala, he said, told him that his conscience was 'revolting' as large sums of money from the public exchequer 'were being made available to him', merely on Indira Gandhi's and Sanjay Gandhi's 'telephonic instructions' to the bank. Rampal said he decided to help Nagarwala 'out of the mess', and the two met later to hatch the plan, aided by the 'code number' through which Nagarwala used to operate.

On 24 May 1971, the day of the bank incident, Rampal and Nagarwala met at the INS India Officers' Mess, Dhaula Kuan, between 10 a.m. and 11.30 a.m. (Malhotra, as mentioned earlier, had received the call around 11.45 a.m.) The plan, according to

Rampal, was to call up the bank cashier, give him the impression that Haksar and Indira Gandhi were on the line, take him into confidence about the immediate need for Rs 60 lakh and then tell him the code phrase—'which country do you belong to'—that he was to ask the courier when he met Nagarwala with the money. Nagarwala was to reply, 'Bangladesh.'

Rampal said he had asked Nagarwala if he was familiar with Indira Gandhi's voice. 'It's very easy—half male, half female, and a shrill tone,' Nagarwala had replied, expressing confidence that he could mimic the Prime Minister's voice.

After he had collected the amount from Malhotra, Nagarwala was to meet him with the cash at Defence Colony in the afternoon or at the Parsi dharamshala, depending on the execution of the plan. They were to then take the money to the office of *The Indian Express* newspaper, barely 200 yards from the dharamshala, and get the entire incident published.

After the two had finalized their plan, they made a telephone call from the mess to the SBI branch. Rampal spoke to Malhotra, giving the impression that he was Haksar, asked the cashier to withdraw Rs 60 lakh, required for urgent work of national importance, and then passed the receiver on to Nagarwala.

Nagarwala's voice was 'nowhere near' Indira Gandhi's, but Rampal said the Prime Minister's name had such a hypnotic effect on the man at the other end of the line that he could hear him repeating the words 'Mataji, Mataji'.

Rampal then drove to the SBI's Parliament Street branch and dropped Nagarwala there. Later, as decided, he went to Defence Colony. Unable to find Nagarwala there, Rampal said he visited the Parsi dharamshala, but couldn't find Nagarwala there either.

Rampal said he thought that Nagarwala had turned traitor. He then approached the Chanakyapuri police station and *The Indian Express* office to inform them about the 'practical joke'.

Why had he remained silent till June 1978?

Rampal said he had 'erased' the episode from his memory through his 'yogic ways'. Those who didn't believe in certain concepts would never be able to understand the reasons he had given, he told the Reddy Commission, which heard him in disbelief.

After years of practice, Rampal claimed, he had activated his kundalini, a yogic power that could help him erase certain memories. He could relegate memories to the 'unconscious part of his mind', he told the commission.

What had made him recall this memory now?

Rampal said his memory got triggered when he was speaking to the dead during one of his sessions. His tape recorder was on and he had concentrated and called the spirits, as guided by the Latvian author and parapsychologist Konstantin Raudive in his book *Breakthrough*.

Rampal said he heard Nagarwala's voice on the tape recorder. 'Sir …' the voice had said, before trailing off.

After a pause, the voice had returned again, introducing itself from the world of the dead. 'Rustom Sohrab Nagarwala …' it said. 'Have you forgotten me, sir?'

That triggered the memory, the retired IAF officer said, adding that he had come before the commission now to share the important facts of the case.

The commission needed corroboration of the events, but there was none. The military hospital's records of 1959 had no evidence of Rampal and Nagarwala being together at the hospital during the period mentioned. An officer of the rank of major general who deposed before the commission asserted that no person by the name of Nagarwala was at the hospital when Rampal was admitted there.

That wasn't all. More evidence against Rampal's claims was yet to come. Rampal had claimed that he and Nagarwala had met at the INS Delhi Officers' Mess on 24 May and finalized their plan over a glass of beer. But officer after officer, including the commanding officer of *INS Delhi*, maintained that the mess was meant for naval officers and under no circumstances could the two have ever entered the mess, let alone use the bar. Retired officers, unless they were on a list of VIPs, could not visit the mess, they said. Nagarwala and Rampal were certainly not VIPs. Moreover, the bar opened at lunchtime, not between 10 a.m. and 11.30 a.m., when Rampal claimed to have had beer there, the officers said. Nor could they have accessed the telephone at the naval mess, from where they supposedly made the call to the bank.

People at *The Indian Express* and officials at the Chanakyapuri police station, too, denied Rampal's assertions that he had informed them about the 24 May incident. Rampal's thirty-three-page statement fell flat.

The commission dismissed Rampal's claims as improbable. 'I have no hesitation in holding that Rampal's version receives absolutely no corroboration from anyone and appears to be a pure figment of his imagination and a creation of his fantasy, a child of his own brain,' Justice Reddy said.

'There is absolutely no credence in the story,' the commission remarked, rejecting the former wing commander's claims on the grounds of 'untenability and inherent improbability'.

Rampal, who has supposedly authored eight books—*Unknown Visitor*, *India Wins the War*, *Unknown Skyjacker*, *Air War*, *Frustration in India*, *Bharat Ki Vijay*, *Indian Women and Sex* and *Moonlight Mystery* (then at the binding stage)—was not prepared to accept defeat. He shot off another petition to the court, saying, 'I do not expect fairness or justice from the commission.' This was because the commission's counsel had made a 'derogatory reference' at his statement and laughed jeeringly out of 'lack of knowledge of the advancement of occult science'.

He wanted to examine the witnesses appearing before the commission. Justice Reddy was not willing to entertain the request, for obvious reasons.

Man with Multiple Aliases

Rampal was not the only one who came up with strange claims before the commission. Another such person was Colonel Amrik Singh, alias K.S. Sahi alias General Amrik Singh Chindit alias General B.P. Phantom, Gen. Ombudsman C/O Marina Arcade, Connaught Circle. Whatever his real name, this person was an inmate of Tihar, jailed in a contempt-of-court case, when Nagarwala was lodged there.

Here's the backstory first, which shows the mystery person. One day, in May 1971, a warden told Baldev Das Makhija, a jail doctor, that a Colonel Amrik Singh, who claimed to know the doctor quite well, was now in the prison and wanted to meet him. Makhija tried to recall the name but couldn't, and told the warden he did not know anybody by that name.

After a few days, when this person was brought before the doctor, along with a few others, Makhija found the face familiar. He was an old acquaintance who was a chief engineer with the Nepal government and whom he had met at the residence of the Indian ambassador in Kathmandu in the 1950s. Makhija had met this person again at a government dispensary on Pusa Road in New Delhi, but his name was K.S. Sahi, not Colonel Amrik Singh.

Amrik would later write to the Reddy Commission, saying he feared for his life. He submitted annexures, including a copy of a letter Nagarwala is alleged to have written on 22 May, two days before the bank episode, to someone. He claimed that the annexures were faithful copies of the original in Nagarwala's handwriting.

Deputy superintendent of police Ajmer Singh Chauhan, a seasoned Delhi Police officer who was attached to the commission, had made an internal inquiry into Amrik Singh's background after the 'colonel' approached the Reddy Commission saying he wanted to assist in the Nagarwala investigation.

Amrik's real name, Chauhan found out, was Khalsa Singh Sahi, and in 1955 he had secured a job as a project engineer at the Durgapur Steel Plant in West Bengal. A year later, he was suspended by the government of India when it was detected that the certificate he had submitted claiming that he had a civil engineering degree from the University of Edinburgh was fake.

Chauhan suspected that Sahi was not Amrik, who was wanted in a case in Ambala in 1949. It gets more complicated here. Sahi faced two cases in Delhi. But he had the habit of taking most cases against Amrik on himself and had been making references to different cases filed in different courts at different times, said Chauhan, adding, 'He has been interposing in most of the important cases being tried, such as the Dalmia Jain case, the Karol Bagh murder case, the petition against V.V. Giri and the Paharganj murder case. He has developed a habit of interposing in important cases, just to delay the proceedings, prejudice the courts and intermingle his own cases.'

In a landlord–tenant dispute in a local court, Amrik alleged that 'one of the suspected call girls' and 'her pimp' were the same persons 'who were participants in the conspiracy of the offences committed by R.S. Nagarwala' in the bank-fraud case. Amrik, who held the power of attorney on behalf of the landlord, had allegedly described the tenant as a 'call girl'.

The commission wanted Amrik to authenticate the documents he had submitted with original ones, but he didn't do that. Instead, in one of his several letters to the commission, Amrik said he wanted to collect documentary evidence from distant places and urged the commission to grant him 'sufficient actual expenses'. He said he wanted to travel by air to places such as Amritsar, Bangalore (now Bengaluru) and Cochin (now Kochi). As for the other places he wanted to visit, he asked for a staff car with a driver; if that wasn't possible, he wanted to be allowed to hire a private car.

One of the so-called documents he submitted, which all along he refused to authenticate, said there was a plan related to the requirement of Rs 60 lakh in four days, 'otherwise Bachtels or Snam may credit a/c PPP in USA or Italy'. This document not only mentions the name of Malhotra but also a person described as NTY going out of Delhi for some time.

The contents of the above document were 'typically related to Amrik Singh's pet topics', Justice Reddy said in his report. 'It mentions the Takru Commission, about D.P. Mishra's election appeal in the Supreme Court, some FIRs of the Paharganj police station, Bennett Coleman & Co., Jayanti Shipping Corporation, Dharam Teja, etc. ... It is surprising that he had not made reference to his involvement in the Radcliffe Award and Lord Mountbatten's part in the boundary dispute,' he added.

The iodine copy and the letters were addressed to one Bachhiter Singh, who died in 1971. Bachhiter's lawyer, B.R. Malik, described Amrik as a 'court bird' and said he saw him practically every day in court. The lawyer expressed doubts about the claim that Bachhiter knew Nagarwala or Amrik.

In its report, the Reddy panel would note, 'It has become difficult for the commission to hold the letters, particularly the iodine copy, as a genuine letter written by Nagarwala, because the text of it could have been typed on a blank paper containing Nagarwala's signatures given for some other purpose, or the signatures could have been superimposed from other documents.'

Amrik refused to admit that he had known Nagarwala for a long time, well before the bank episode, contrary to evidence that they were probably acquainted in the 1950s. Amrik was close to the owner of the Marina Taxi Service, which Nagarwala had invested in, and used to frequent his office.

Amrik also refused to reveal his background in the armed forces on the plea that the matter was 'pending before a court'. Neither would he divulge the number of cases pending against him. His stock reply was that 'many manipulated and false cases' had been foisted upon him for his crusade against 'corruption and other maladies' afflicting the country. 'Some are pending in Delhi and some are outside,' he said.

The commission was scathing in its remarks about Amrik. 'By adopting dubious methods, Amrik Singh has clearly wasted the time of the commission,' Justice Reddy remarked, adding that his hesitation to produce the originals and to admit that they were in his possession could be well understood. 'Because if he had produced these in original, he might have exposed himself to action and landed himself in difficulties,' Justice Reddy said.

Others Who Wasted the Panel's Time

Among those who came up with egregious claims was a person named Kailash Nath from Kanpur, who worked in a clinic. Nath wrote to the commission alleging that Yashpal Kapoor had 'mimicked the voice of Indira Gandhi'. Efforts to trace him did not yield any results.

An anonymous complaint the commission received took up quite a bit of its time. The person who filed the complaint claimed that a well-known surgeon, Dr M. Khalilullah, had administered an injection at the behest of Dr Padmavati, which had resulted in Nagarwala's death at GB Pant Hospital.

According to the complaint, the injection bottle was procured by a nursing orderly, Mahendra Singh, who was subsequently given three out-of-turn promotions; and a nurse who was present when the injection was administered was sent abroad within seven days. The complainant also said that Nagarwala's heart, which had been preserved by Dr Bishnu Kumar, who did the autopsy, was destroyed by another employee.

The Reddy Commission ordered a probe and examined all the officials named in the complaint. In its report, the commission said the anonymous petition 'has absolutely no basis and is written by someone who is actuated with malice and enmity towards Dr Padmavati and others. It is one of the tragedies that malicious, disgruntled and unbalanced persons who are consumed by envy, jealously and hatred of persons in authority make unjustified, sinister and serious allegations which they know will land them in difficulties if they make them openly and for which reason these individuals resort to anonymous and scurrilous attacks in this cowardly fashion.'

The allegation that 'an injection was given, as a consequence of which Nagarwala died, is preposterous and without any truth whatsoever', Justice Reddy said.

Matter of the Heart

After the postmortem, conducted at Maulana Azad Medical College, Nagarwala's heart had been preserved in the Forensic Medical Department Laboratory for academic purposes. There was nothing unusual in that, although, for ethical reasons, the authorities concerned ensure that the identities of the deceased persons, from whose bodies the specimens have been taken, are not revealed.

Dr Bishnu Kumar told the commission that Nagarwala's heart had been preserved for 'academic purposes as a museum specimen', but in the process of demonstration to students over a few years, the specimen got spoilt. 'The jar [in which the specimen was preserved] broke and the heart got putrefied,' he said.

Commissions of Inquiry Act

These episodes offer a telling commentary on the limitations that commissions of inquiry often face. The idea behind appointing such commissions is to collect information and ascertain facts so that if any malpractice or problem is revealed, corrective legislative or administrative action may be taken by the government.

The Indian Parliament had enacted the Commissions of Inquiry Act in 1952, which authorized the Central and state governments to appoint inquiry commissions to make inquiries into matters of public importance. According to the law, the notification had to state the period of duration of a commission; if it didn't, the defect could be cured by issuing another notification.

The Act, modelled on a British statute—the Tribunals of Inquiry (Evidence) Act, 1921—was enacted because experience had shown that parliamentary committees of inquiry tended to split along party lines. Some of the more famous tribunals of inquiry were the Budget Leak Tribunal (1936), the Lynskey Tribunal (1948), the Bank Rate Tribunal (1957) and the Vassall Tribunal (1962).

However, investigations conducted under the Commissions of Inquiry Act can face many limitations. First, the initiative to appoint a commission of inquiry rests with the executive. Second, it is open to the executive in such a manner so as to define the terms of reference of a commission in such a manner as to defeat, to the maximum extent possible, the purpose of the inquiry. Further, under the Commissions of Inquiry Act, the executive is not obliged to make public the findings of inquiry commissions and such panels can be used as an instrument of the government to divert attention from the real issue.

A commission's report is not binding and the executive's response can vary from outright rejection to slack corrective action. A commission, on its own, cannot impose a penalty. That is for the courts to do after a trial. Moreover, the setting up of a commission of inquiry is no bar to launching prosecution proceedings.

India has had a trial-and-error record with past inquiry commissions. For instance, the track record of various judicial commissions that probed communal disturbances in the country is pathetic. So far, forty such commissions have been appointed. Among the reports submitted, thirteen are missing.[13]

---

13 'Inquiry Reports on 13 Communal Riots Since 1961 "Not Available", CIC Asks MHA for Status', *The Economic Times*, 30 December 2018, https://economictimes.indiatimes.com/news/politics-and-nation/inquiry-reports-on-13-communal-riots-since-1961-not-available-cic-asks-mha-for-status/articleshow/67310258.cms

CHAPTER 19

THE LAWYER'S STORY: NAGARWALA'S LAST WORDS

Another person who, in Justice Reddy's words, led the commission 'down the garden path' was Rajendra Kumar Maheshwari, Nagarwala's young lawyer. Maheshwari had claimed in a letter that he had something important to convey, but by the time he sent his delayed affidavit, after several reminders, the Reddy Commission had already submitted its report to the government. The following is an account of what happened in the interim and how a potential opportunity to get to the bottom of the Nagarwala mystery was lost.

Shortly after Nagarwala's death, Maheshwari migrated to the US, but not before causing a sensation in the media through a write-up in the Bombay-based *Illustrated Weekly of India*. In the article, published in the magazine's April 1972 issue, Maheshwari said he had met Nagarwala on 2 March 1972. The day also happened to be Nagarwala's birthday, and the lawyer said his client was 'cheerful, happy and hopeful, though a little pale' when he wished him and handed over greeting cards sent by his mother, sister, nephew and nieces from Bombay. Barely half an hour later, Nagarwala suddenly collapsed in his hospital bed, leaving behind a host of unanswered questions.

Although he seemed outwardly cheerful, Nagarwala was becoming increasingly impatient. In the affidavit that Maheshwari sent to the Reddy Commission, the lawyer recalled their conversation shortly before his client's death. Nagarwala, he said, had asked him to move the courts so that his trial could be held 'in the jail or the nursing home'.

'Mr Maheshwari, I have waited enough, but now I am going to unmask everybody. You have never asked me who are those persons, and by now I know you are not a political man. I am therefore telling you, whether you believe it or not. I cannot change my voice. The medical record of Jehangir Nursing Home, Poona, will prove that I am unable to talk comfortably, what to talk of changing my voice to that of a sweet lady,' Nagarwala had told him, the lawyer said.

Nagarwala had retracted his earlier version that he had mimicked the voice of Indira Gandhi. In a petition filed before the Delhi sessions judge R.N. Aggarwal on 21 June 1971, Maheshwari claimed that Nagarwala was 'induced' by police officials to make the confession as 'dictated by them'.

Maheshwari said Nagarwala also told him that 'the Prime Minister is not involved in the case'.

Nagarwala's comment to his lawyer, that he wanted to 'unmask everybody' connected to the case, was not an isolated expression of a frustrated man. A fortnight earlier, his parting words to Nusli Pudumjee, his childhood friend who had visited him in hospital on 17 February, were on similar lines. As Pudumjee was about to leave, Nagarwala told him that he had 'to settle accounts with certain people who would be quite happy if he never left the hospital'.

Nagarwala had also expressed a desire to meet D.F. Karaka, editor of the Bombay-based *Current* magazine, as he wanted to 'tell him something about the case', Pudumjee had told the Reddy Commission.

These statements were bound to agitate the commission. Nagarwala probably wanted to divulge something he had not so far. But Maheshwari played truant with the commission.

Letter to the Minister

The Morarji Desai government had appointed the Reddy Commission on 9 June 1977, about two-and-a-half months after it came to power at the Centre. On 14 August that year, Maheshwari sent a 'confidential' handwritten letter to the then home minister, Charan Singh, offering to make a statement before the commission. 'It may amount to breaking the client-attorney privilege, but for bringing the truth out about the said financial transaction to the public, I have decided to take the risk. In fact, I have some documents in India to substantiate the truth. Meanwhile, I am trying to get a licence to practise in the US as a lawyer. Perhaps a testimonial from you, stating that I was a good practising lawyer in New Delhi, will help me a lot,' Maheshwari's letter urged the home minister, whose antipathy towards Indira Gandhi at the time was well known.

The home ministry had forwarded the letter to the commission, which had tried to locate Maheshwari. The Indian Embassy in the US was told to reach out to Maheshwari at the address he had given. But the ministry was told Maheshwari no longer lived there and was staying with his friends at an 'unknown address'.

The embassy's efforts continued without much success until 28 April 1978, when, through a cable, Maheshwari informed the commission that he would file an affidavit and become a witness in the case. The commission sent two cables asking Maheshwari to file his affidavits by 31 July.

On that date Maheshwari replied that he would send his affidavit through the embassy or the consul general in Chicago. He also disclosed that he would be in India in the first week of September and appear before the commission in person.

On 14 September, the consul general said that Maheshwari had contacted him and promised to file an affidavit within the week. The commission got its term extended from 30 September to 31 October, following the assurance given by Maheshwari through the consul general. Then, on 5 October, the commission got a letter from the Chicago mission that said it was yet to receive any affidavit from Maheshwari in spite of repeated reminders. 'Presumably, he is not prepared to submit his affidavit,' the consul general suggested in the letter.

Maheshwari's delay in filing the affidavit was bound to 'disappoint' Justice Reddy. 'It may be that he does not know anything that will be of assistance … as evidence. Perhaps that is why he is fighting shy of either filing an affidavit or appearing before [the commission] to depose, as promised,' Justice Reddy observed.

There seems to be no other reason, since Maheshwari had 'given an interview to *The Illustrated Weekly of India,* in which he appears to have stated what Nagarwala is alleged to have told him just half an hour before his death', Justice Reddy said, adding that the lawyer 'should have at least confirmed that statement'.

'When a person dies, people can impute anything to him and one has to be careful in assessing the statement of such persons imputing to deceased persons what they are alleged to have stated,' Justice Reddy observed, stressing that Maheshwari's statement, published in *The Illustrated Weekly of India* in April 1972, 'cannot be relied upon'.

'I hope I am not being too harsh if I were to say that this young lawyer has tried to lead the commission down the garden path,' Justice Reddy said, while agreeing with Pudumjee's assessment of the lawyer.

His statement of what Nagarwala said before his death 'would have to, even if deposed on affidavit, be subjected to cross-examination and severe scrutiny because after a person is dead, there is always a tendency to attribute statements or actions to him which he may or may not have said or done', the commission remarked.

What Pudumjee Said

When Pudumjee appeared before the commission, he was shown Maheshwari's letter offering to provide information. 'I do not know whether he has got any information to give, because Maheshwari told me he was relying on me,' Pudumjee told the commission.

Did Nagarwala have confidence in his lawyer?

'It was mutual,' Pudumjee said. 'The lawyer had no confidence in him either. Nagarwala had not told his lawyer who he was, what his family background was, etc., and in view of this, how could the lawyer prepare his case for defending Nagarwala, unless he got something out of Nagarwala?'

Pudumjee had earlier met Maheshwari at his friend's request and given the lawyer some money. Later, when he appeared before the commission after Nagarwala's death, Pudumjee said his friend had told him when they had met for the last time that Maheshwari had 'lost interest in his case because he knew that he [Nagarwala] had no money to pay, and, therefore, it was better if he could come out of jail on bail and fight his own case'.

Another deponent who seemed to share Pudumjee's view was veteran journalist Virender Kapoor, who worked with *The Motherland*. Kapoor said he had the 'distinct impression that Maheshwari was out for publicity, which he rightly thought would further his career as a lawyer', and that he was 'positive that Nagarwala did not take Maheshwari into confidence', and had parted with merely the information necessary for the court.

Kapoor said Maheshwari did not substantiate 'certain innuendos' mentioned in the article that appeared in *The Illustrated Weekly of India*.

The Lawyer's Affidavit

Maheshwari, however, kept his word, although late. His affidavit, sent through the US embassy, reached the commission on 6 November, but the exasperated commission had already come to the conclusion that Maheshwari wouldn't cooperate and submitted its report to the government on 23 October. The affidavit, dated 28 October, is among the home ministry's files lying in the National Archives.

Maheshwari's affidavit claimed that Nagarwala was apparently 'on the payroll of the government or any other persons' and was not happy with the treatment he was receiving at the hospital. The lawyer claimed that Nagarwala was a 'captain of military intelligence' and the money (Rs 60 lakh) was to be handed over by 'both of them' (Nagarwala and Malhotra) to a 'courier'. Malhotra and Nagarwala had waited at the agreed place, but around 3.30 p.m., when the courier had still not turned up, Nagarwala asked Malhotra to take the money back to the bank. By then, news of the withdrawal of the amount had already been leaked, 'probably by the coolies' who had helped shift the cash trunk from the vault.

According to Maheshwari's affidavit, Nagarwala had told Malhotra 'both of us are doing the same job and one must plead guilty'. Since Malhotra had a regular job and was due for a promotion, Nagarwala had to hide the money. The plan was that they would meet in the evening at the Parsi dharamshala to work out something for the 'benefit of both of them', but Malhotra could not handle the situation. So Nagarwala was 'made to agree to become the scapegoat' in the entire transaction. Interestingly, the affidavit, however, did not make it explicit who had made Nagarwala agree to becoming the scapegoat.

Maheshwari claimed that the 'whole money' (Rs 60 lakh) had been recovered from the Defence Colony house, but that the police showed 'some shortage to complete the investigation'. The affidavit said that Nagarwala was promised that he would be transferred to a prison in Bombay and then released, just as the navy commander K.M. Nanavati, convicted in a sensational 1959 murder case, had been freed after only four years in jail despite being sentenced to life imprisonment for killing his wife's lover, businessman Prem Ahuja.

As nothing was done and Nagarwala was not given the money that was 'agreed upon', he decided to go for an appeal. Maheshwari also claimed in his affidavit that his client had told him that the money (withdrawn from the bank) was 'unaccounted' and that the bank had no means of knowing the contents of the box.

The affidavit tried to link the bank money to Indira Gandhi's earlier move to nationalize fourteen leading private banks. It observed, 'The said money was of the same nature, as the money was lying in the banks when bank nationalization was done by Indira Gandhi. The Supreme Court had stayed the operation of the ordinance. There was "sufficient time" for industrialists to remove their "unaccounted valuables",' the affidavit claimed.

Maheshwari explained why he had made the statement that 'Indira Gandhi had nothing to do with the money' in the report that appeared in *The Illustrated Weekly of India*. He claimed that he had made the statement for his personal safety, as Nagarwala had advised him to do. He quoted Nagarwala to explain why his client had decided to make Malhotra a co-accused in the case: 'I do not divulge secrets of my friends even at the cost of my life, but if somebody tries to cheat me, I fight until my last breath,' Maheshwari recalled Nagarwala as saying.

Maheshwari's affidavit also said Nagarwala had asked him to meet film actor Dilip Kumar, as Nagarwala was planning to make a movie on his great escape after his release.

Notes

1. Nagarwala had wanted to meet D.F. Karaka, editor of the *Current* magazine. Pudumjee had met Karaka in Bombay and told him about his friend's wish. Karaka had expressed his inability to go to Delhi because of his heart ailment, but promised to ask a correspondent in Delhi to do the needful. After a few days, Pudumjee had received a sealed envelope meant for Karaka, which he promptly forwarded to the editor. Pudumjee had later asked Karaka about the contents of the envelope, and the veteran editor had told him that it contained a poem that 'did not make any sense' to him, so he had sent it to his correspondent in Delhi.

SECTION IV

WHODUNIT

CHAPTER 20

PRIME MINISTER MORARJI DESAI MAKES AN ALLEGATION

The palatial house at 5, Dupleix Road in Lutyens' Delhi, where the Reddy Commission worked from, reverberated with an explosive allegation not long after an eighty-two-year-old walked in to depose before the panel in connection with the Nagarwala probe. Prime Minister Morarji Desai was in a confrontational mood. His assertive attitude had a combination of belligerence and calculated bellicosity. Whether interacting with journalists, politicians or even visiting dignitaries, including heads of government and state, Desai seldom minced words, irrespective of the fallout, which at times was considerable.

Desai was no stranger to the bungalow. He had lived in the very house for many years before shifting to the Prime Minister's official residence.

Desai held many firsts. He was the first non-Congress Prime Minister of India. He is the lone recipient of the two highest civilian awards in two countries—the Nishan-e-Pakistan, from Pakistan, and the Bharat Ratna, from India. A strong protagonist of prohibition and yoga, he caused discomfiture to millions of Indians when, as Prime Minister, he propounded the efficiency of urine-drinking. He attributed his longevity to drinking urine—which he called the 'water of life'—at least twice every day.[14] Desai regarded abstinence as the only proper method of birth control; he renounced sex after his fifth child was born. In his autobiography *The Story of My Life*, Desai summed up his beliefs: 'I do not consider anyone inferior to me or myself superior to anybody. Ever since I became an adult, I have been convinced that one should form no habits except the habit of telling the truth. All other habits enslave one and make one dependent and weak.'[15]

Born in Gujarat, Desai was a strict disciplinarian and Gandhian who humbled the might of Indira Gandhi in 1977. Desai was always a prime ministerial candidate, losing out to Lal Bahadur Shastri after Jawaharlal Nehru's death in 1964 and then to Indira in 1965.

Deposing before the Reddy Commission as Prime Minister on the Nagarwala issue, Desai was as argumentative and assertive as a lawyer. 'It was Prime Minister Indira Gandhi's money from which Rs 60 lakh was given to Nagarwala on her telephonic instructions.'

Desai, a former Congressman-turned-Janata Party leader, who had written an article in *The Motherland* newspaper soon after Nagarwala's conviction in 1971, was categorical that 'the money taken out of the bank' on 24 May that year did not belong to the bank. 'In this particular case, Rs 60 lakh was in a trunk that was locked and sealed, and the money was not even counted,' he said in reply to a question

---

14 Lucy Karsten, 'Taking the Piss: A Brief History of Athletes Drinking Their Own Urine', *The Guardian*, 22 August 2015, https://www.theguardian.com/sport/2015/aug/22/taking-the-piss-a-brief-history-of-athletes-drinking-their-own-urine

15 Morarji Desai, *The Story of My Life*, Pergamon Press, 1979.

from Justice Reddy. 'That trunk was removed and, therefore, the money could not belong to the bank. That is my inference.'

'[What if] the money was taken out of the bank and put in a trunk?' Justice Reddy asked.

Prompt came the reply from the country's fourth Prime Minister: 'It is never done like that, as far as I know. I have inspected these chests sometimes and never found trunks like that.'

Desai was certainly not unfamiliar with banking rules and regulations. As the finance minister under Jawaharlal Nehru and then Indira Gandhi, Desai had presented ten Union budgets, still a record for India's finance ministers. A believer in free economy, Desai had been critical of Indira Gandhi's economic policies and quit her government after she divested him of the finance portfolio in July 1969. Three days later, on 19 July, she announced her decision to nationalize fourteen leading private-sector banks, a move Desai severely criticized.

The SBI was already a public-sector bank when the Nagarwala incident happened. But for those interested in the bank's history, until 1 July 1955, when it was nationalized, it had been a private lender with 80 per cent private holding in its earlier avatar as the Imperial Bank of India, formed in 1921 by the merger of three Presidency banks the East India Company had established in Bengal, Bombay and Madras.

Desai, whose guiding principle was that one should 'act in life according to truth and one's faith', insisted that the money taken from the SBI's Parliament Street branch could not have belonged to the bank. 'In this case, as the facts are, the head cashier had taken out the money on a supposed telephone call from the Prime Minister, and the Prime Minister asked him to make the payment. The Prime Minister can never ask a cashier to make a payment ... therefore, the money could not belong to the bank. This is my inference,' Desai reiterated before the commission.

The point Desai was trying to make was that if the money did not belong to Indira Gandhi, she would not have asked Malhotra, the SBI cashier, to withdraw the amount from the bank. Moreover, money cannot be given to anybody without a draft or a cheque and a valid receipt, he argued.

The Prime Minister's arguments before the commission were based on several premises: Indira Gandhi had deliberately avoided answering questions from Members of Parliament on the controversy; the case had been disposed of in just three days by three different magistrates; and the money was shifted as per a telephone call, kept in a trunk and not even counted before it was removed from the bank. That the trunk was removed, Desai insisted, meant that the money could not have belonged to the bank.

The conclusions that Desai drew, particularly about the removal of the cash trunk from the bank's premises, were not entirely correct. The bank did have arrangements with the US embassy in New Delhi and Indian Airlines to deliver money in trunks 'at their doorsteps'. There was, of course, an elaborate procedure the bank had to follow in such cases.

Commission's View

About the money not being counted, the commission in its report pointed out that 'money bundles are made through established procedures' before they are stacked in chests. In fact, Justice Reddy had inspected the bank and seen not only the 'manner in which the notes are packed in bundles, [but] also packed in the trunks', in a bid to familiarize himself with banking operations.

While he disagreed with Desai, Justice Reddy came up with a carefully worded comment. 'It is possible,' he said, 'that the matters noticed on the inspection of treasuries might be slightly different, and it is equally possible that since the time Shri Desai inspected the treasuries, the procedures may have changed. I cannot say.'

Justice Reddy disagreed with Desai that the money belonged to Indira Gandhi. However, the independent-minded judge, who believed that trials should start early and conclude soon, did not give Indira Gandhi a clean chit either. He said there was enough evidence to believe that while in power during the Nagarwala case, she did not ensure a proper investigation and that some officers in her secretariat had even tried to hamper the probe.

The bank wasn't absolved entirely either regarding the possibility of 'unaccounted' boxes being kept in its safe custody. Whether the boxes contained 'stationery', 'old newspapers' or 'miscellaneous cash belonging to the bank', Justice Reddy said he could not rule out the possibility that the bank kept such 'unaccounted boxes' in 'view of the fact that such unaccounted boxes had been kept as late as till 1978 ... before the commission was appointed'.

'If that could be done in 1978, it could have been done in 1971, where there was no such apprehension of any inquiry,' he remarked.

Justice Reddy's remarks were based on the feedback he had received from an expert. D.N. Ranjan, manager of the Reserve Bank of India (RBI), had inspected the bank at the behest of the commission in 1978, and come across a box lying in the strongroom. There was no proper entry in the bank's records about the presence of the box, which contained some 'balances' of the SBI's Agra branch.

Ranjan had also found that the vault room, apart from keeping money and valuables, was being 'used as a junk room to dump things which have no right to be there'. The bank had denied the allegations and claimed that Ranjan's comments were 'not warranted by facts'. But Justice Reddy was not convinced.

The commission, during its inspection, also came across a senior bank official keeping two boxes containing personal items in the strongroom area. It found something else too—a 'small packet' V.P. Malhotra had kept in the safe custody of the bank.

What Justice Rangarajan Saw

Another controversy arose when the chairman of the Monopolies and Restrictive Trade Practices (MRTP) Commission, Justice S. Rangarajan, told the Reddy Commission as a witness that he had seen a 'very big box' lying outside the currency cage but inside the strongroom. He also found a 'label or board' that had the words 'PM's House' on it.

Justice Rangarajan had visited the bank in 1975 to retrieve his own box that he had kept in the bank's custody. As a Delhi High Court judge earlier, he had dealt with the case pertaining to the SBI's dismissal of Malhotra and was, therefore, aware of the Nagarwala controversy. Justice Rangarajan, however, faced embarrassing moments after Indira Gandhi's counsel sought to impute a motive to his statement.

Earlier, in September 1975, when the Emergency was in force, the judge had delivered the judgment in *Bharti Nayar vs Union of India*. Eminent journalist Kuldip Nayar had been detained under the controversial Maintenance of Internal Security Act (MISA) and his wife, Bharti, had filed a habeas corpus petition in the Delhi High Court. Justice Rangarajan had heard the case and reserved the judgment. In the meantime, the government revoked Nayar's detention and released him.

That, however, did not stop Justice Rangarajan from delivering his judgment on 15 September. Not only that, he also added a postscript saying the habeas corpus writ was a public remedy. Therefore, after the judgment was reserved, the bench should have been told what action the authorities planned to take as a matter of 'courtesy'.

'Courtesy to the court demanded that we were apprised of the intended action before actually it was taken,' the judge said. Justice Rangarajan was subsequently transferred to the Gauhati High Court.

The counsel who appeared on behalf of Indira Gandhi asked Justice Rangarajan whether 'he gave a judgment in the

Kuldip Nayar case and whether, as a consequence of that judgment, he was transferred from the Delhi High Court'.

Justice Rangarajan said he 'did not know that the transfer [to Guwahati] was on account of that judgment'.

Justice Reddy took exception to the insinuations made by the counsel. 'The question appears to suggest motivation for the learned judge [Justice Rangarajan] giving evidence. I do not think this was a worthy suggestion when the judge was discharging a public duty of assisting the commission,' he said. 'I have no hesitation in saying that Shri Justice Rangarajan displayed a high sense of public duty and gave his evidence fairly and objectively.'

Coming back to Justice Rangarajan's claims about what he had seen inside the SBI strongroom, the bank maintained that it had prepared a wooden board as bank officials used to visit the Prime Minister's residence to collect donations (cash, gold and silver ornaments, and cheques). The bank said it would put such items in a box, maintain proper records of the donations and store the items in the strongroom in an almirah allotted for the purpose. A photograph of the box taken at the Prime Minister's residence was produced as evidence. When shown the wooden board, Justice Rangarajan remarked that 'it could be the same, but I am not too certain'.

The commission observed that 'the currency cage also does not show that there has been a daily tally of the balances and the stock in the currency chest, which, according to rules, they have to do'.

In his report, Justice Reddy remarked that 'while two facts that have been established show that it is possible that unaccounted money could be kept in the bank's vault, there is no direct evidence to show in fact any such amount was being kept'.

Indira's Assertions

When Indira Gandhi was asked if she had deposited any box with the SBI on or before 24 May 1971, the former Prime Minister was categorical in her assertion. 'I did not deposit then, neither before nor after the period, any box with the SBI,' she said.

In 1971, she had one current account at the Parliament Street branch of the bank (36/90202) in the name of 'Indira Nehru Gandhi'. On the day of the offence, the account had a balance of Rs 150.20. Neither did she have a fixed deposit in her account, nor a securities account as of 24 May 1971. The current account was closed on 9 February 1972 and a fresh account opened in the name of 'Indira Gandhi'.

Indira Gandhi was associated with another account, which was a joint account in the name of the holding trustees of the Jawaharlal Nehru Memorial Fund. Any two of the seven holding trustees could operate the account, which had fixed deposits.

Nagarwala did not have any account with the State Bank of India.

P.N. Haksar, Indira's former principal secretary, and N.K. Seshan, her former private secretary, both maintained that Indira Gandhi, as Prime Minister, had never handled her bank matters directly with the bank. The PM, too, in her written two-page statement, had made that clear, saying, 'My personal accounts in the banks were also being maintained and attended to by my private secretary, Shri N.K. Seshan. I had no occasion to draw cash from the bank personally.'

The SBI and the RBI made detailed presentations before the commission to assert that the Rs 60 lakh in cash that Malhotra had withdrawn was the bank's legitimate money. They explained that money kept in the vault belonged to the RBI and that the SBI was its custodian. Once cash is drawn from the vault, through a well-laid-down procedure, it belongs to the SBI. The account is maintained in different registers to maintain transparency. All its account books clearly indicated that the money was its legitimate money, the bank argued.

CHAPTER 21

WAS IT A CIA OPERATION?

It was inevitable. This question was bound to arise. And it did. Was theirs only a simple love story—a couple so deeply smitten that they followed each other to different countries just to be together? Or was there something more to this relationship between a jobless Indian national with a chequered past and an American who was part of her country's diplomatic set-up?

The 'foreign hand' theory was a favourite theme song in the 1970s. As Prime Minister, Indira Gandhi had raised the bogey of the 'foreign hand' on 3 March 1976, when the Emergency was in force and freedom of the press and human rights had both been grossly curtailed. Speaking at Calcutta, Indira Gandhi had warned her foreign critics not to interfere in India's affairs. 'As the Prime Minister, I can say the more they try to suppress us or oppose us, the stronger and more united we will be,' she told a motley gathering. 'We don't care for their criticism, whether it came from the Socialist International or any other organization.'

Without naming 'certain foreign powers', she had remarked, 'They always run down India, belittle its achievements, whether [it's] the launch of Aryabhata [India's first satellite] or the Pokhran nuclear test. Now they have got an excuse to criticize us afresh as Emergency has been proclaimed.'[16]

Indira Gandhi perhaps had her own insecurities and apprehensions. Her biographers Pupul Jayakar and Katherine Frank have elaborately documented how the assassination of Sheikh Mujibur Rahman in August 1975 had numbed and terrified her. A few months before the assassination of Bangladesh's founder and President, she had been briefed by the then R&AW chief R.N. Kao that the Bangla artillery was conspiring against him. She had sent Kao to Dhaka to brief Rahman, but 'Bangabandhu' was confident that he wouldn't be assassinated by his own people.

On 15 August Indira Gandhi was about to leave for the Red Fort to deliver her address to the nation when she heard about the massacre in Dhaka. Apart from Rahman, the others who had died in the brutal attack included his wife, three sons, two daughters-in-law and two nephews.

'Rahul [Gandhi] is about the same age as Mujib's son [nine-year-old Russell, named after Bertrand Russell]. It could be him tomorrow. They would like to destroy and kill my family,' Indira had told Jayakar that day.

Out of power between March 1977 and January 1980, Indira—who had been told by Kao that she faced a 'real threat' from foreign hands—feared for her life and did not even appoint a new cook during this period, apprehensive that she might be poisoned.

When she returned to power in 1980, the shrill cry over a 'foreign hand' and international conspiracy became even more strident as

---

16 Rasheed Kidwai, 'Amid Slugfest Over Rafale, the Invisible "Foreign Hand" Makes a Comeback in Indian Politics', News18, 1 October 2018, https://www.news18.com/news/opinion/opinion-amid-slugfest-over-rafale-the-invisible-foreign-hand-makes-a-comeback-in-indian-politics-1894089.html

Was It a CIA Operation?

Punjab separatism gained momentum. In October 1984, Indira was assassinated by her personal security guards.

The foreign-hand theory made a comeback in the Rajiv Gandhi era, when the young Prime Minister battled Bofors payoff charges. Rajiv would often talk about an 'invisible' foreign hand out to impede India's development.

After Rajiv Gandhi's assassination, the Justice (Retired) M.C. Jain Commission, which probed the conspiracy angle, wrote extensively about the foreign hand assisting the Liberation Tigers of Tamil Eelam (LTTE), the Sri Lanka-based Tamil militant outfit that killed Rajiv. Jain had sought a multi-agency probe into Rajiv's assassination to unearth the actual conspiracy behind the assassination.

At the height of the Anna Hazare agitation in 2011–12 in New Delhi, the Sonia Gandhi–led Congress claimed there were powers out there trying to destabilize the Manmohan Singh government. Foreign NGOs working in India have constantly faced the charge of stoking rights-based popular agitations.

The 'foreign hand', with its chequered history, remained a question unanswered in the Rustom Nagarwala story. But what was surprising and out of character for a probe commission, i.e., the Reddy Commission, was that it didn't probe this angle—Nagarwala's American connection—when it investigated the controversy that had tossed up the name of a former Prime Minister and other well-known figures of the time.

Nagarwala's girlfriend Jeanette Spears was an American citizen who worked in the US embassy in Delhi, and the couple would roam around in the capital city and outside at a time when Nagarwala was virtually jobless. So deep was their love that the two had even purchased 'burial grounds' in the US so they wouldn't be separated even in death.

Some of Nagarwala's friends who appeared before the Reddy Commission told the probe panel about his visits to the embassy.

One of them, Dadi Mistry, even spoke about the 'tinned food' and American stuff that he used to bring home. Another friend recalled that the couple visited them in Bombay while on a sightseeing tour across India. A happy couple, some would say. Nagarwala, who had no means to make a decent living in India, followed his girlfriend to Japan after she was transferred there. They even visited each other in India and Ceylon, where she was posted later.

It's possible that Nagarwala and Spears were committed lovers, but given their individual backgrounds—and the wider geopolitical backdrop of the Cold War—doubts were bound to be raised about their relationship, for obvious reasons. Nagarwala was once in India's armed forces and Spears worked in the field of diplomacy. Also, as documents would suggest, Nagarwala had foreign bank accounts on which he would issue cheques.

Justice Reddy was, however, dismissive of suggestions that the commission should have looked into the foreigner angle. In his report, he referred to what Nagarwala's friend Pudumjee had told the commission: 'He [Pudumjee] had given a good deal of information about the relationship between Mr Nagarwala and Miss Jeanette Spears of the US embassy, all of which is not very relevant. Nothing has been suggested that that relationship had any sinister significance, except for the fact that there seemed to be a deep friendship between the two. Miss Spears, even when she was posted out of India, would visit him and even now is said to be in touch with the family by sending them cards, etc.'

Meeting with 'One Miller'

There was evidence before the commission that Nagarwala had met the personal assistant of Chester Bowles, America's ambassador to India between 1963 and 1969. Justice Reddy was dismissive of this meeting too.

Was It a CIA Operation?

The commission had accessed a note from Bhawani Mal, deputy director of the IB, which mentioned that 'Nagarwala had met one Miller, who was on the personal staff of Chester Bowles, former American ambassador'. The note was prepared when Markandey Singh, SP (CID), had met Mal.

In the note sent on 30 June 1971, Mal, who would later become the chief of Delhi Police, said, 'Miller's name had featured in Nagarwala's papers seized by Delhi Police, and this was duly noted by us in our scrutiny report. The AD(U) has been asked to report whether Miller had also come to our notice. In due course, Nagarwala may have to be interrogated in detail about his contacts with Miller.'

The 'AD(U)' mentioned in the note probably referred to an officer of the rank of an assistant director in the IB, who kept an eye on the activities of foreigners posted in embassies and missions in India.

After Nagarwala's arrest in May 1971, Delhi Police's CID official Jagdish Prasad had visited Tihar and met Nagarwala at the office of the jail's superintendent. In his report, Prasad recalled what Nagarwala had told him. 'Regarding Mr Miller of the US embassy, Nagarwala stated that Mr Miller was the personal assistant of the then US ambassador. He had gone to the embassy in December to see the ambassador in person for passing on some vital information regarding the war in Vietnam,' Prasad's report said.

Prasad then quoted Nagarwala as saying, 'Since the ambassador was not available, I met Mr Miller and passed on the information to him. I had earlier passed this very information to Prime Minister Indira Gandhi in person and also to Mr Haksar. I never met Mr Miller after that.'

The commission would later criticize the official for his unauthorized and illegal visit to the jail.

Prasad had also asked Nagarwala about several names 'found in his possession', such as Kenneth K. Wolwer, Dr Karston Kettel, Mikio Gotoh, Rev. A.L.J. Hotal and Masaru Hoshimo. Details of these people, however, were not part of the files accessed by the authors at the National Archives of India.

Newspaper Raises a Query

In 1988, a three-part series published in *Hindustan Times* alleged that the investigators of the Reddy Commission were 'stopped from probing Nagarwala's American connection' on the plea that 'this was out of the scope of the commission's terms of reference', and that this was done by the then Prime Minister Morarji Desai.

In the article, titled 'The Unexplored CIA Trail in the Nagarwala Case', the newspaper maintained that the investigation team had found evidence suggesting 'Nagarwala's close links with the Americans and the possibility of him being a CIA agent'. Quoting intelligence sources, the report said the investigators had kept the inquiry commission in the 'dark' but Prime Minister Desai 'posted'.

When the newspaper contacted Justice Reddy, he said, 'All this is news to me. I was not told that Nagarwala had bank accounts in the US.'

When Desai, who had by then retired from active politics and shifted to Bombay, was asked about Nagarwala's US bank account, he said, 'I don't remember.'

The commission, in its report, said the IB and R&AW were, at some time or the other, asked to make inquiries into the case, but did not find anything 'new'. A former additional secretary of the R&AW, on the condition of confidentiality, informed the commission that the external intelligence agency had made inquiries regarding Nagarwala's connections with any 'outside intelligence agency' and found that 'he had not come to their notice'. The IB and R&AW had both declined to divulge their sources. The commission remarked that 'these investigation agencies have not been of much assistance'.

Foreign Transactions

C.V. Narasimhan, who was the CBI director then, forwarded certain documents to the commission that were related to the seizure of some papers forwarded by the home ministry to the National Archives that can be accessed by the public (VI/11022/4/80/Part 99). These papers show foreign bank transactions of Nagarwala.

Narasimhan had also written to the commission's director (investigation), K.P. Tiwari, on 12 October 1977, informing him that a source had 'handed over some bundle of papers'. The contents of the bundle had been scrutinized and the papers that 'appeared to be relevant to the present inquiry' were being forwarded to the commission, Narasimhan wrote. These documents included two letters written by the undisclosed source to Indira Gandhi's social secretary Usha Bhagat, a number of telephone numbers listed in Nagarwala's diaries and 'some foreign bank accounts', among other things. The list of documents presented before the Reddy Commission showed the names of several persons, 'mostly foreigners from whom Nagarwala had received letters', Narasimhan added.

Nagarwala's banking transactions show that he had issued ten cheques in favour of other persons on an account at the First National City Bank, New York. Between 5 September 1966 and 1 November 1967, he had issued cheques of amounts ranging between $26.18 and $700, totalling $2,826.10. The transactions also showed that Nagarwala had made a mail transfer order of £178 to a bank account in the UK. The documents included two typed letters—one addressed to someone in Switzerland, indicating the transmission of a draft for $5,000, and the other seeking permission from the RBI to purchase foreign exchange equivalent to Rs 14,400 for medical treatment in India.

The *Hindustan Times* article mentioned another bank account with the First National City Bank, Nagoya, Japan, and questioned the lifestyle Nagarwala maintained without any known sources of income. It was also quite unnatural for an embassy staff to be seen moving around in Delhi and outside without inviting the attention of intelligence agencies.

Narasimhan had suggested to Tiwari that Indira Gandhi's officials be questioned. 'The telephone numbers should be identified', as also 'the significance of foreign banks and foreigners whom he [Nagarwala] corresponded with'. These documents are part of File No. VI/11022/4/80–Part 143.

While Indira Gandhi's officials P.N. Haksar, Usha Bhagat and B.N. Tandon were among those questioned, no investigation papers pertaining to foreign banks and foreigners were found in the Nagarwala documents available at the National Archives checked by the authors.

SECTION V

WRAPPING UP

CHAPTER 22

KEY FINDINGS: WAS IT A BOTCHED-UP PROBE?

It was October 1978. Over seven years had passed since that summer afternoon when the scam that shook the nation appeared to have unravelled on its own the very day it happened. Rustom Sohrab Nagarwala, the alleged conman who had pulled off the spectacular heist, had been caught, the stolen cash had been recovered and everything seemed to suggest that the police had done a clinical job in wrapping up the case.

Clinical? Not quite, if one were to go by the conclusions drawn by Justice Jaganmohan Reddy. He felt that the entire process, from Nagarwala's confession to his conviction, seemed to have been 'manipulated'.

In its report submitted to the Morarji Desai government on 23 October 1978, the commission strongly criticized Delhi Police for botching up the investigation. It felt that the police, considered somewhat professional in the 1970s, seemed in undue haste to wrap up the case once it had nabbed Nagarwala and recovered the stolen money. In the process, the commission felt, it had neglected different aspects of the investigation.

The police's approach led to allegations that they were trying to insulate the then Prime Minister Indira Gandhi from the probe, while contradictory and conflicting versions that police officials came up with before the commission about the chain of events made it clear that the investigators had not done their job properly. In Justice Reddy's opinion, case diaries and primary documents maintained by the investigators were riddled with flaws, starting with the registration of the First Information Report (FIR) at the Parliament Street police station. The case was later handed over to Delhi Police's Crime Branch.

'[The] unanswered questions could have been unravelled only by an uninhibited investigation, but that was not done at the time for the obvious reason that it will be oriented to ascertain whether the then Prime Minister was involved (or not). The principle of the police investigation that everyone whose name was involved … [is a] suspect until cleared has not been followed in this case,' the commission said in its report.

P.A. Rosha, who was DIG, Delhi Police, at the time of the investigation—and later joined the BSF and then became inspector-general of police (Haryana)—also felt that the probe could have been handled better. 'In retrospect, I would certainly say that a contested trial with examination of all concerned as witnesses would have been much better and would have gone a long way in allaying the misgivings in the public mind,' Rosha said in his written submission to the commission.

'At the same time,' he added, 'I also feel that the police did not withhold any facts or conceal them, nor could they prevent the accused from making a confession if he voluntarily chose to do so.'

This chapter takes a look at the different aspects of the probe as it summarizes the commission's key findings.

Key Findings: Was It a Botched-Up Probe?

Registration of the FIR

Chief cashier V.P. Malhotra had approached the police first, saying that he had been duped by someone after he received a call from the then Prime Minister Indira Gandhi and her principal secretary, P.N. Haksar. But the police did not entertain his complaint and made him wait for a long time at the police station. The ostensible reason was that the case could be weakened if Malhotra, the key witness, also became the complainant. Instead, another SBI employee was made the complainant.

The other view was that Malhotra was also an accused in the case and his complaint should not be the basis of the FIR. In fact, after a few days, the same police arrested Malhotra on the charge of breach of trust!

Malhotra claimed before the commission that he had dictated to a friend who wrote the complaint in Urdu. The use of Urdu in police cases in Delhi was not uncommon then. Malhotra said he had signed the document and given it to the police. But police officials denied having received any such complaint. The official view was that Rawail Singh, another bank employee, had submitted the written complaint.

During the cross-examination, however, Rawail Singh could not recall who wrote the complaint. His explanation was that the police could not read his original complaint, so it was rewritten by someone, and that he had merely appended his signature in Urdu.

Police officer Mohinder Kumar, who had registered the FIR (No. 815), said he had applied offences under the Indian Penal Code's Section 409 (breach of trust by a public servant) after consulting his seniors. However, the two seniors supposedly consulted by him denied his assertion.

According to the FIR document, the time of the registration was 4.35 p.m. But Rawail Singh claimed that it was around 8.30 p.m. when the police wrote down his complaint.

From the cross-examination of officials, the commission came to the conclusion that the FIR was registered after the investigation had already started and the police had virtually made a breakthrough in the case. By then they had traced the taxi in which Nagarwala had travelled from Panchsheel Marg after getting off the private Ambassador in which he and Malhotra had arrived, while a police team had visited the SBI branch from where the money had been withdrawn. Another taxi driver, Om Prakash, who had dropped Nagarwala at Connaught Place, had already been tracked down by the police team, which had also visited the Parsi dharamshala where Nagarwala stayed. Besides, the FIR had been drafted in consultation with the CBI and the Crime Branch of Delhi Police. But what the commission found unusual was the presence of a 'civilian' official at the police station when the case was being registered. Who was the official? The needle of suspicion pointed towards B.N. Tandon, the joint secretary in the Prime Minister's secretariat.

'The police treated the FIR as a mere formality and were careful enough to register it only after they had come to know fully as a result of their investigation the upshot of the Nagarwala episode. The FIR was drafted by the police itself after the money was recovered and it [the FIR] was given and registered at 8 or 8.30 p.m. in the night, though indicating that it was in fact given at about 4.20 p.m. and registered at 4.30 p.m.,' the commission said.

It was like putting 'the cart before the horse', Justice Reddy remarked. Had Nagarwala's retrial taken place, he added, the absence of Malhotra's FIR and the 'obtaining of another FIR after [the] investigation was completed', that too 'dictated to the first informant' (the complainant), would have 'cast grave doubts and suspicion' on the prosecution's case, which may have resulted in 'giving the benefit of the doubt to the accused [Nagarwala]'.

Key Findings: Was It a Botched-Up Probe?

Police Case Diary

According to Justice Reddy, the police in their case diaries did not record the true sequence of events. 'I regret to have come to the conclusion that the case diaries (of the police) were cooked up and do not have a record of what actually took place,' he said after reviewing the evidence.

The case diary mentioned that Malhotra had accompanied the police, led by D.K. Kashyap, the chief investigator in the case, from the time the case was reported to when the suitcases containing the stolen cash were seized from *The Statesman* employee N.B. Captain's Defence Colony residence.

The case diary claimed that Malhotra was taken to Shantipath, as he alone could have identified the taxi driver, Balbir Singh, who was hired from the taxi stand to take Nagarwala from the nearby Sardar Patel Road to the airport. Kashyap took Malhotra and Balbir to Defence Colony, where Nagarwala was dropped off. Malhotra was also shown in the records to be present at the house of Captain when the suitcases were confiscated. All along, right from the time the wireless message was flashed describing the details of the taxi in which Nagarwala had travelled, to the recovery of the cash, Malhotra was supposedly present with the police team.

Malhotra, while deposing before the commission, denied that he had accompanied the police team and said he had been at the police station all along, a contention that other witnesses too, including key police officials, supported in their statements. Among those who supported Malhotra's contention was Y. Rajpal.

The case diary stated that the cash was seized from the barsati-floor residence of Captain, and the details of the amount recovered from each suitcase were specifically mentioned in the seizure report. The suitcases were then sealed and locked. The seizure memo was signed by the two taxi drivers, Balbir and Om Prakash, and Captain's statement was appended to the report.

In his alleged statement to the police, Captain claimed that the notes recovered were in big bundles and had the chits or markings of the SBI, which were identified by Malhotra. However, Captain and his wife Nergiz told the commission that the suitcases were not opened in their house, nor was the money counted, and both expressed ignorance about the contents of the two suitcases. Captain even claimed that it was only the next day that he got to know from newspaper reports that the suitcases contained cash. He said he was 'shocked and surprised', and had immediately informed the manager of *The Statesman* and its editor, Kuldip Nayar. Captain also said that his wife was so upset that she had a 'miscarriage'.

Malhotra, too, claimed that he saw the cash at the police station. Inspector A.K. Bose, who was part of the raid team, asserted that Malhotra was not with them when they visited Shantipath, Defence Colony, New Rajinder Nagar or even Captain's house. Bose told the commission that Nagarwala wanted the police team to go in plain clothes so that the matter could be kept a secret from Captain and his wife. While coming down from the barsati floor, the team had peeped into the suitcases and seen the currency notes.

The commission objected to the seals being broken and then being resealed at the police station after the money had been shown to journalists at the press conference. 'The authenticity of the seizure memo is thus lost and if the seizure memo is to be accepted, the authenticity of the seal is lost,' it said.

When Was the Revolver Seized?

The case diary claimed that during interrogation, Nagarwala had revealed that he had hidden a revolver among his belongings kept at the dharamshala. Following this, the revolver was recovered.

But several witnesses, including the manager of the dharamshala, said that the weapon, along with cartridges, were found when the police searched Nagarwala's room *before* he returned to the dharamshala late on the evening of 24 May 1971.

The police's claim about the revolver, the commission felt, was 'invented perhaps to satisfy' some legal requirements. One was that the taxi driver Om Prakash had told the police that Nagarwala had shown him a revolver at Rajinder Nagar. Consequently, the gun had to be seized *after* the arrest.

Then, to make the seizure admissible under Section 27 of the Evidence Act, it had to be carried out *after* Nagarwala's arrest on the basis of his disclosure. If it were shown that the revolver had been seized before the arrest, any subsequent statement by Nagarwala related to the revolver after his arrest would have become inadmissible under the Evidence Act, the commission felt.

Currency Notes

Inspector Bose claimed that the serial numbers of all the currency notes seized from the two suitcases were noted down by the police in fifteen to twenty pages. But neither did the case diary make any mention of the list, nor was the list produced before the commission.

Mimicry

The police claimed that Nagarwala was made to mimic the Prime Minister's voice 'two to three times' after his arrest, but the case diary is silent on this.

Air Force Plane

Nagarwala, in his statement, had disclosed that an Indian Air Force plane was waiting for him and that he was to take the money to

Bangladesh. The police did not follow up on the claim and no investigation was done at the aerodrome.

Taxi Drivers' Arrest

The commission took exception to the alleged detention of the two taxi drivers, Balbir Singh and Om Prakash, on 24 May 1971. *The Indian Express* had reported on their arrest, but Rajpal had described it as a 'wrong report'.

'I am not so sure,' Justice Reddy said in his report, adding that 'we have it in evidence of Balbir Singh, taxi driver, that he and Om Prakash were also arrested and kept in a lock-up under orders of Rajpal'.

However, Justice Reddy would also note that Balbir Singh said that he 'came to know later' that they had been 'purposely locked up in order to keep a watch on Nagarwala and to ensure that he does not commit suicide'.

Complacent Cops

Once Nagarwala had been caught, the police seemed to have become complacent, which was evident from the fact that Paramjit, the Marina Taxi Service driver who had driven Nagarwala to Lt Col. Keshwala's house and later to Mrs Badhwar's house from Connaught Place, was not interrogated properly. He could have provided details about Nagarwala's visits to different places on 24 May, the day the money was withdrawn from the SBI branch. Instead, the police relied on Nagarwala's confession, which did not mention his visits to Keshwala and Mrs Badhwar.

Moreover, the police investigation was not yet complete when Nagarwala was produced in court. Neither had the investigators recorded the statement of Rawail Singh, the bank official, nor had they procured details about Nagarwala's proposed 25 May

Key Findings: Was It a Botched-Up Probe?

visit to Ranikhet, where he was supposed to meet O.P. Malhotra, a retired major.

Yet another glaring omission pertained to the identification of the woman who had tried to contact Nagarwala over the phone when the police team was searching his room at the Parsi dharamshala. The police were satisfied with Nagarwala's version that she was his girlfriend, who was to accompany him to Ranikhet. Nagarwala had told Bose she had no role to play in the offence.

Malhotra and the Taxi Number

Did Malhotra give the taxi number to the police to enable them to trace Balbir Singh's taxi that led to the recovery of the stolen cash? Justice Reddy had doubts about this too. In his view, Malhotra gave the number *after* the taxi had been traced.

Justice Reddy said a possible reason that Malhotra was mentioned as the person who gave the police the taxi number was the need for 'untainted evidence'. This is what Justice Reddy said: 'Police officers knew Malhotra well before the incident' and 'to get Nagarwala convicted', the police needed the 'untainted evidence of a witness'.

Had Malhotra been 'tainted' or 'presented in circumstances which would impress him with taint', his evidence against Nagarwala would not have held. The alternative for the police was to charge both Nagarwala and Malhotra with conspiracy to cheat the bank. 'If so, the story involving the Prime Minister would have [had] to be countered only by the Prime Minister herself,' Justice Reddy said, adding that Haksar then would have been her 'corroborating evidence'. It would have been then argued that Haksar was her secretary and the evidence would have been viewed from that 'angle'.

The third alternative, Justice Reddy said, was to have Malhotra as 'approver'. But there were 'infirmities' involved and 'the best course, therefore, in the circumstances' was to 'keep Malhotra untainted and unsullied to make his evidence credible'. That could then also be made to appear that he was, in fact, not criminally culpable.

The police had 'developed a vested interest in Malhotra's innocence'. Well known in police circles, his statement was, therefore, made to 'conform' to Nagarwala's confession, Justice Reddy felt.

Justice Reddy also doubted the presence of an honorary magistrate in Malhotra's room when the telephone call purportedly came from Prime Minister Indira Gandhi's office. The police, Justice Reddy said, wanted a credible witness to testify that the call did come.

Mystery over Rs 30,000

The recovery of Rs 30,000, concealed in a scooter tyre and tube, did not surprisingly find mention in either the seizure memo or the case diary, although many witnesses, including the policemen present at the Parsi dharamshala, were witness to the recovery of the cash from Nagarwala.

There were seven seizure memos—all true copies because the originals were destroyed in the fire at the Tis Hazari court—but none related to the Rs 30,000 seized from Nagarwala at the time of his arrest. The seizure list, with quotes from the police, was also reported in newspapers the next day, particularly in *Hindustan Times* and *The Statesman*. Even Rajpal wrote to the Ministry of Home Affairs on 25 May about the cash being seized from the 'tyre and tube'.

Interestingly, one of the seizure memos, dated 24 May 1971, mentioned that 'one tyre Firestone along with tube (National)' had been seized, but was silent on the contents of the tyre and the tube.

Nagarwala, during his preliminary interrogation, had said that the Rs 30,000 was his 'share' of the booty and not part of the bank's money. But his confessional statement was silent on this amount. Later, when a CID officer interrogated him at Tihar Jail in the office of the jail superintendent, he conceded that the amount was part of the money stolen from the SBI branch.

Key Findings: Was It a Botched-Up Probe?

When he appeared before the commission, Inspector Bose said that the Rs 30,000 recovered from the tyre and the tube, and the Rs 500 handed over by taxi driver Om Prakash, were added to the cash at the time the recovered money was being counted at the police station, bringing the total amount recovered to Rs 59,94,300. Subsequently, Captain handed over Rs 2,600 kept in two envelopes that Nagarwala had given to him at his Defence Colony residence.

In the absence of a seizure memo—and in the light of Nagarwala's initial claim—the commission raised doubts about whether the Rs 30,000 was part of the stolen money. The police, the commission felt, was particular enough to mention that the Rs 500 Balbir Singh had handed over was added to the amount recovered, but not particular enough to mention what they had done with the bigger amount.

Nagarwala had also claimed that he was carrying Rs 6,000 when he left the dharamshala. He later stated before the CID officer that he had given Captain Rs 3,500 and not Rs 2,600, as mentioned earlier.

If the police papers and Nagarwala were to be believed, that he had Rs 36,000 with him, it was natural for the commission to point out that the police should have investigated the source of that money. The records show that when Nagarwala was handed over to the jail authorities, the constable accompanying him had given Rs 100 to jail officials towards his prison expenses.

There were also contradictory versions about the taxi driver Om Prakash returning Rs 500 to the police. A generous Nagarwala, after his taxi ride, had given Om Prakash five hundred-rupee notes. It was said in the case diary that the driver had tossed the notes among the currency wads at the time the notes were being counted. But there were witnesses who maintained that Om Prakash had handed over the cash immediately after he was traced.

Judicial Botch-Up

Justice Reddy, a former Supreme Court judge, was of the view that the entire court proceedings—from the time Nagarwala was produced to when he was convicted and sentenced—was 'invested with a lack of judicial objectivity which is expected in proceedings in a court'. It is worth recalling here that one of independent India's speediest trials concluded in three days.

Ordinarily, confessions are recorded in public (in open court), and only in rare cases is a recording done in camera. In the Nagarwala case, it was held in-camera because the accused wanted it to be so. According to the suggested procedure, 'unless there are exceptional reasons to the contrary, confessions should be recorded in open court and during court hours [and] police officers investigating the case should not be present'.

While Nagarwala's confession was recorded in-camera, his statement was made available to the media the same evening, on 28 May 1971, which proved that there was nothing that merited an in-camera confession. 'There may be yet other reasons, but where the purpose of recording the confession in-camera is to make it public immediately no sooner [than] it was recorded, then there certainly is some other motivation for acceding to the request,' Justice Reddy observed.

Justice Reddy in his report dwelt upon the 'special attention' that magistrate K.P. Khanna gave to recording the confession, going out of his way by skipping lunch and also depriving Nagarwala of his. The action is 'indicative of the magistrate falling in line with the desire of the police to generate speed for obtaining conviction and sentence', Justice Reddy remarked.

The commission took exception to the way the case was transferred to a magistrate of a different jurisdiction—from Parliament Street to Chanakyapuri—and how, after recording

Key Findings: Was It a Botched-Up Probe? 239

the confession, Khanna proceeded in 'breakneck speed' to charge and convict Nagarwala. Justice Reddy said the magistrate ignored the fact that the statement of the accused was not a confession and that the 'plea of guilty was not to have been accepted without some evidence', as had been stated by the Supreme Court. The magistrate 'does not seem to have acted objectively', he remarked.

Another point the commission raised was that the magistrate who convicted Nagarwala tried to show that it was an ordinary case, but nonetheless admitted that it was a case that required a heavy sentence of at least five years.

Justice Reddy said that Khanna was conscious that 'the nature of the case was such that it should have been tried by a court of sessions', and that the crime deserved a higher sentence beyond two years, which could only be given by a sessions court. But the magistrate, he added, 'circumvented' the limit and achieved the twin objectives of convicting Nagarwala with lightning speed and handing down the maximum sentence within his powers on each of the two charges, by making the sentences 'run consecutively, with a heavy fine, which, if not paid, will add another year'.

The magistrate admitted that 'ordinarily sentences on different counts are only made to run concurrently. He also admitted that since the money was recovered, it deserved a lesser sentence. One expected him to make the sentences to run concurrently but he acted contrary to what he professed,' Justice Reddy said.

Nagarwala's appeal, Justice Reddy added, was not only an allegation against the police for having 'tortured' him and 'induced' him into making a 'confession' with the promise of freedom, 'but also against the magistrate' when he said the confession was dictated in writing by Satpal, Kashyap and other police officers.

'On the entire evidence before me, considered cumulatively, the association in the public mind, with the magistrates having been subject to pressure, is not unjustified,'

The retired judge pointed out that Nagarwala was produced in court for recording his confession, although the investigation was not yet complete, the statement of a key bank official, Rawail Singh, was not yet over and the police had not recorded the statement of O.P. Malhotra, whom Nagarwala was supposed to meet in Ranikhet. The police, the judge said, had also not received details about Nagarwala's background from Pune and Bombay.

Justice Reddy also took exception to the last-minute change of jurisdiction, from the Parliament Street police to the Chanakyapuri police, saying it was 'not without some design'. While the money transaction took place in Chanakyapuri, everything else related to the offence happened in the Parliament Street police station area.

'In fact, the police themselves started the proceedings and continued them throughout as if the jurisdiction was of the Parliament Street police station, and they could not have been wrong,' the commission's report said. The last-minute change in the jurisdiction meant that three magistrates would come into the picture in three days. Otherwise, the magistrate in charge of the Parliament Street police area, S.P. Karkare, would have tried the case.

The commission's report said questions had been raised in view of the 'ugly haste with which the case was disposed of'. Even Nagarwala's confession, upon which magistrate Khanna acted, is 'no confession at all', it said. 'It does not bring out the ingredients required under Section 419/420 IPC. It is an exculpatory statement, since he says that the whole thing was a hoax.'

When magistrate Khanna appeared before the commission, Justice Reddy asked him whether a person could be said to confess if he exculpates himself. Khanna, in his reply, admitted that it would 'not be a confession' in that case. The magistrate's plea was that 'since the accused pleaded guilty in my court, these things did not occur to me at that time', the commission said in its report.

Key Findings: Was It a Botched-Up Probe?

Khanna was on deputation from Uttar Pradesh to Delhi when he tried the Nagarwala case and gave the judgment. He was later reverted to his parent state, Uttar Pradesh. When he appeared before the commission, he was under suspension and was facing charges under the Prevention of Corruption Act.[17]

Nagarwala's Health

Apart from procedural issues, Delhi Police would come in for criticism for 'not taking precautions' even after being aware of Nagarwala's health condition.

Inspector Bose told the commission that when police officials were climbing the stairs to Captain's barsati floor, Nagarwala was 'panting and had to halt twice'. At the police station later that night, Nagarwala was served 'salt-free food' at his request. Nagarwala had also told the police team not to 'ill-treat' him as he had suffered a 'paralytic stroke and heart attack'.

District SP Rajpal, too, was aware of Nagarwala's health condition and senior police officers had considered this aspect when it was decided to seek judicial remand for the accused on 25 May.

DIG Rosha was, however, not aware of Nagarwala's ailments. Asked by the commission what he would have done had he known about Nagarwala's health issues, the IPS officer said, 'The very first thing would [have been] … to get him examined by a medical officer; and the second, where he should be kept [whether in the hospital] and whether he is fit to make a statement. That is the normal procedure.'

In his observations, Justice Reddy remarked, 'In spite of their knowledge', which is corroborated by Nagarwala in his bail application that he was suffering from a heart ailment, the police were

---

17 Justice Jaganmohan Reddy Commission Report, p. 132.

'reckless in not taking precautions'. Instead, Nagarwala was made to re-enact and demonstrate his morning telephone conversation with Malhotra, although, by their own admission, the police said that Nagarwala 'was tired and [had said] he would do [the telephonic conversation] the next day'.

'I must also comment upon the conduct of the police at the time when Nagarwala was arrested, namely that even after having taken note that he earlier had had a heart attack and was a heart patient, they did not send him for medical examination and did not inform the court or the jail authorities that he was a heart patient. This was a duty that was incumbent upon them and they failed to discharge [that duty]. It would also indicate callousness on their part,' Justice Reddy said in his report.

Did Nagarwala Know Malhotra?

The SBI maintained before the commission that Nagarwala did not have an account with the bank. Nagarwala, in his statement, had said that he had visited the branch on the fateful day to get change of a hundred-rupee note and was advised to meet Malhotra by the staff. During the interrogation he had also said that he used to go to the bank to encash drafts sent by retired Major O.P. Malhotra almost every month. Malhotra had submitted details of the drafts that he had given to Nagarwala. The retired army official Malhotra had an account with Punjab National Bank and not with the SBI.

The commission pointed out that if cheques or drafts were to be realized at Punjab National Bank or at any branch of the SBI or any other bank, it could be done 'if any officer or employee is well known' to the customer. Considering Nagarwala's frequent visits, 'it would not be too much to assume' that Nagarwala used to visit the bank to encash drafts or cheques. 'There is, therefore, corroboration of Nagarwala's replies during his interrogation that he used to go to the State Bank of India each month for encashing the drafts, and if that is so it will not be too much to infer that he would have been visiting Malhotra, the chief cashier, to get the cheques or drafts encashed without difficulty.'

The commission remarked, 'If Nagarwala was a regular visitor to the bank and had been meeting Malhotra, which Malhotra may now deny as Nagarwala is no longer alive, Nagarwala would have noticed him receiving telephone calls or heard about his receiving telephone calls from VIPs and his taking money to them, which according to Rajpal Malhotra had admitted that he was doing.'

Otherwise, Justice Reddy observed, 'one fails to understand how Nagarwala could get an idea that by merely telephoning as a VIP Malhotra would take money out of the bank, take it to him in the hope of obtaining a cheque subsequently.'

Nagarwala's Death Was Natural

The former Supreme Court judge said he was 'clear in my mind, and it would be wrong for anyone to suggest that Nagarwala was done to death or killed and did not die a natural death'. But he was scathing about the 'carelessness with which he was handled merely because he was an undertrial prisoner whose case had become sensational'. Nagarwala, Justice Reddy added, was 'passed on from one hospital to the other, each wanting to avoid any responsibility'.

Readers will recall that between 10 January 1972, when he suddenly developed chest pain in Tihar, and 2 March 1972, the day he died, Nagarwala was moved back and forth between the jail hospital, Irwin Hospital, Maulana Azad Medical College and GB Pant Hospital. In fact, barely a week before he died, one of the doctors who had treated Nagarwala recommended that he no longer needed to remain in the CCU.

All this prompted Justice Reddy to remark that when human beings were ill, they should not only be shown 'greater care and sympathy', but also the 'same attention ... as in the case of a person who is free and who is entitled to receive such treatment'.

Kashyap's Death an Accident

About another death too—that of police officer D.K. Kashyap—Justice Reddy was certain that no foul play was involved. Kashyap, the chief investigator in the Nagarwala case, died when a recklessly driven tonga smashed into his car on 20 November 1971.

Justice Reddy had no doubt that it was an accident. None of the occupants of the car—Kashyap's wife, sister-in-law or the driver—nor any of the independent witnesses to the incident had 'even a grain of suspicion as to the manner in which Shri Kashyap's death took place', he said in his report.

Kashyap's death was due to an accident, 'beyond a shadow of a doubt', however much extraneous considerations might induce people to believe that this was also an incident in which persons connected with the Nagarwala case were done away with.

The former judge was clear that all the doubts raised by Kashyap's father—which perhaps gave rise to doubts of others who have written on this aspect—had been 'satisfactorily answered'.

In his book *India after Nehru*, Kuldip Nayar wrote that 'the fact that Nagarwala was arrested on 24th May and sentenced within five days gave rise to ugly rumours that there was more to it than met the eye. Subsequently, the death of police officer Kashyap, who investigated the case, also of a heart attack, increased suspicions. Another police official working on the case died in a road accident.'

Justice Reddy said, 'Evidently Shri Kuldip Nayar did not check the facts. No police officer other than Kashyap died in a road accident, nor was any other police officer involved in Nagarwala's case other than Kashyap, alleged to have died in an accident; nor did any such officer working on the case die of heart attack. When it was put to Kuldip Nayar, he frankly admitted that "it was pointed out to him subsequently that it was an accident and not a heart attack".'

The former judge added, 'Suggestions have even gone to the extent of referring to the murder of an uncle of Nagarwala—Shri Rustomji Shapurji Nagarwala, a retired commissioner of police—on 12 September 1973 at Hyderabad as supporting the general design to do away with all persons connected with Nagarwala. There is, however, no indication whatever as to how the late commissioner of police, though related, had any manner of connection with the case and how anyone murdering him would benefit therefrom. It would appear that anyone connected with Nagarwala, however remote the connection may be, and whether he was in any way concerned with the incident or not, could not be expected even to die a natural death! Such was the incredibility which had been aroused in the case; so it is not surprising that when a relation of the late Nagarwala was murdered, though about two years afterwards, the suspicion would be raised even in respect of a death [with] no connection [with] or relevance [to] the incident.'

Whose Voice Was It?

Nagarwala could mimic voices. Even on 24 May, when he had gone to N.B. Captain's Defence Colony home with two suitcases full of cash, he had sprung a surprise on Captain's wife, Nergiz.

Captain wasn't at home then and Nagarwala, imitating his voice, had asked Nergiz to open the door. 'Hello sweetheart, how could you come home so early?' Nergiz had asked while opening the door, only to find Nagarwala standing outside.

Even Dadi Mistry, with whom Nagarwala had stayed before shifting to the Parsi dharamshala, had been taken in more than once.

Nagarwala, who had met his boss J.N. Marshall at dinner parties, had twice called up Mistry's office and spoken to him in Marshall's voice, after giving the impression that they were long-distance calls. Both times he had 'mimicked a female voice', as if a telephone operator was putting through a long-distance call from Bombay.

In Tihar, many of Nagarwala's fellow inmates had laughed at his efforts to imitate the voice of Indira Gandhi. But the jail's deputy superintendent, N.S. Thakur, with whom Nagarwala had spoken on the intercom, felt that it was a 'truthful' reproduction of her voice. A prisoner, Harnarain Aggarwal, too, was convinced that Nagarwala could mimic the voice of the then Prime Minister.

Some police officials, barring Rajpal, were also impressed by Nagarwala's ability to imitate the voices of Indira Gandhi and Haksar. Inspector Hari Dev, who was the SHO of the Chanakyapuri police station when the bank incident happened, told journalists that Nagarwala was a trained 'ventriloquist'. The peon-cum-clerk at the dharamshala, Nandan Roy, whose evidence was not accepted by the commission, claimed that he had heard Nagarwala changing his voice to that of women and children. Even his roommate, Dinyar Kolaji, who recalled hearing Nagarwala singing in the bathroom, said the former army man not only had a 'good voice', but 'could change his voice' too.

But there were many who doubted Nagarwala's abilities. Veteran Jana Sangh leader L.K. Advani, detained in Tihar for violating prohibitory orders at the same time Nagarwala was lodged there, told the commission that he found Nagarwala's mimicry 'nowhere near a female voice, not to mention Smt. Gandhi's voice'. Advani's party colleague, Kanwar Lal Gupta, had endorsed the view of the future deputy Prime Minister.

Nagarwala's mother Goolbai, sister Armaity, childhood friends Pudumjee, Gustap Rashid, Rustom Dalal and Ardeshir, and even Dr Mody, a prominent cardiologist in Pune who knew Nagarwala well, told the commission that Nagarwala could not mimic the voices of others. Nagarwala, they maintained before the Reddy Commission, had facial paralysis, and although that was not immediately obvious, his speech had been affected.

'[W]hile the evidence shows that Nagarwala could probably mimic a male voice, I would very much rely on and accept Pudumjee's evidence that Nagarwala could not mimic even a male voice,' Justice Reddy said in his observations.

What about Nagarwala's ability to imitate a woman's voice? Justice Reddy was clear about that too. 'There is no evidence of Nagarwala mimicking a female voice, except that of Malhotra, who, on his own showing, was under the spell of Smt. Indira Gandhi and was prepared to believe any kind of voice as that of hers, to show that he could also mimic the voice of a female [person],' Justice Reddy said in his report.

CHAPTER 23

JUSTICE REDDY'S CONCLUSIONS

We have finally come to the end of this narrative, an account mainly linear, except for a few chapters where we have tried to provide a backdrop to one of the most intriguing incidents in independent India, but largely forgotten now. To the best of our knowledge, everything that needed to be said about the Rustom Nagarwala case has been said in the preceding chapters. Now it's time to wrap up, a sort of epilogue that attempts to distil the key findings of the Justice Reddy Commission that probed the scandal. This is, after all, the story of not only one man who was tried and convicted, but an account where a whole system is on trial, so to speak, in the readers' consciousness. We pick up from where we had left off in the previous chapter and move on to some of Justice Reddy's main conclusions. Some of the passages that follow are repetitions of what has been said earlier in this book, but they are unavoidable, for the simple reason that this final chapter is essentially a recap.

One of Justice Jaganmohan Reddy's key conclusions was that neither Indira Gandhi nor her secretary P.N. Haksar had telephoned SBI cashier V.P. Malhotra, asking him to hand over Rs 60 lakh to a courier. The commission was also of the view that Nagarwala could not mimic anyone or 'at any rate could not mimic the voice of a female [person], much less [that] of Smt. Indira Gandhi'. But Malhotra did receive a telephone call on that fateful day, 24 May 1971, which hints at the possibility that someone else had mimicked the Prime Minister's voice and Haksar's too.

Another conclusion Justice Reddy arrived at was that Indira Gandhi did not personally know Malhotra to 'such an extent that she could trust him with any secret work or entrust with him such a large sum of unaccounted money'.

However, Justice Reddy said, there was sufficient evidence to show that Nagarwala had 'great regard' for Indira Gandhi and that the letter he wrote to her from jail showed a 'familiarity with which no stranger would write'. But the former Supreme Court judge put in a caveat too. 'It may be,' he said, 'that Nagarwala was giving out that he was a friend of Smt. Indira Gandhi.'

Did Nagarwala and Malhotra know each other from before 24 May 1971? According to the commission, they did.

Damning Indictment

The commission came down hard on law-enforcement agencies and also the judiciary in the way they had handled the probe and the trial. According to Justice Reddy, the police investigation was confined to the recovery of money, and what followed was manipulation of facts because the police felt that Indira Gandhi was 'somehow' involved in the whole affair. 'The attitude of the police may be described as that of a person sweeping everything under the carpet and feeling that they have done the cleaning,' Justice Reddy observed in his report.

He said the manner in which the police had investigated the case, and some of the unacceptable statements in their investigations, had only 'contributed to the mystery' instead of clearing it.

He said Nagarwala's confession was induced, not voluntary, and that the police had rushed the investigation with 'ugly haste and managed to extract a confession from Nagarwala on a questionable plea of guilty'. As for the magistrate who had convicted Nagarwala, Justice Reddy's observation was that he had circumvented trial by a court of sessions by handing down consecutive sentences.

The report pointed out that the trial magistrate had made no attempt to go behind Nagarwala's confession, examining neither Malhotra nor other witnesses to find out if the version given by Nagarwala was corroborated. The magistrate, Justice Reddy said, 'seems to have ignored all norms of caution by merely concentrating on the conviction and sentence with ugly haste, which is an anathema to judicial notions. This not only resulted in miscarriage of justice as pointed out by the appellate court in respect of Nagarwala, but in my view also resulted in the failure to bring out facts which would have thrown light on the allegations of involvement of others besides Nagarwala and Malhotra.' It was a damning indictment of the judicial process by someone who belonged to the fraternity.

Unaccounted Money

In another significant conclusion, Justice Reddy did not rule out the possibility that unaccounted money had been kept in the SBI branch. He refused to believe the statements of either the police, Nagarwala or Malhotra in the entire episode, except for the fact that Rs 60 lakh had been taken out of the bank in contravention of rules. To him, their statements were 'unreliable'.

Investigations by the panel had revealed that the bank's safe vault 'contained unaccounted boxes', while registers the police seized from the SBI branch were not produced before the commission. From the suppression of these documents, the commission said, it could be inferred that had these documents been produced, 'they would not have shown [a] Rs 60 lakh entry'.

Malhotra had admitted and repeatedly insisted that he used to carry money to VIPs—not large sums, though—and obtain cheques from them. It was evident, too, that he was acquainted with senior police officials, including those who would be directly involved with investigating the Nagarwala incident from the very day it happened, 24 May 1971.

Justice Reddy said the police investigation of the case was incomplete, not only in respect of questions about the involvement of the Prime Minister, but also in the ordinary aspect of Malhotra's breach of trust in parting with Rs 60 lakh from the bank's vault.

A proper investigation would have 'thrown light on the question whether the money belonged to the bank or whether it was kept in the bank's custody by someone, the possibility of keeping such money not being ruled out. The failure to investigate this aspect has affected the chance of finding out the truth on this important aspect,' the commission said.

Rap on the Government

The commission in its report said the then Union home secretary, Govind Narain, had directed the inspector-general of police, Delhi, to investigate if there was a conspiracy to 'tarnish the image of the Prime Minister'. The report also said the bureaucrat had told the commission that Indira Gandhi was kept informed of the progress in the case. The commission then proceeded to point out the apparent contradiction between what Indira Gandhi had said when she appeared before the panel and what Narain had said, before pulling up the Indira Gandhi government for not doing enough to clear the air on the mystery.

It is 'curious, therefore, to note that Indira Gandhi' had told the commission that she took 'no interest' in the case and that she had made no inquiry about it as it was 'a matter of little importance compared to the international issue of Bangladesh, which engaged her full attention', the report said. Her government, the commission noted, did not consider it proper to institute an inquiry 'to settle the dust of doubt and controversy which was being raised all the time and which came to thicken all the more as time passed'.

The commission added: 'The Intelligence Bureau and the Research and Analysis Wing were hardly likely to inquire into this with the kind of directions they had received or envisaged by their own closeness to the then Prime Minister to be helpful in any inquiry about the possible involvement of the then Prime Minister. The result is that facts have become more difficult to ascertain and in view of the absence of any evidence which has not been forthcoming, there still remain unanswered questions.'

Nagarwala's Motive

Justice Reddy was not prepared to accept that Nagarwala had got a 'sudden' idea to pull a 'hoax' on the bank. He also rejected Nagarwala's statement that he had 'left clues to lead the police to him so that they could discover the money'. If Nagarwala was to catch an Indian Air Force plane, as he had stated, the police should have investigated the airport angle, the former judge said. That would have answered many questions.

Justice Reddy remarked that the 'theory of hoax' put forward by Nagarwala 'cannot be believed, and if believed, will itself be considered to be a hoax, in view of several facts unearthed. Though these may not be sufficient to enable me to give a positive finding as to what actually took place, yet they raise several doubts. But alas! These questions were left untouched as if the respective authorities were afraid of finding out what had happened,' he commented.

The former judge expressed his inability to approximate what in reality 'actually took place, particularly when we are confronted with unanswered questions after so long a lapse of time'.

'Incontrovertible Facts'

However, Justice Reddy went on to assert four 'incontrovertible facts'—all pertaining to banking operations—which, he said, 'demolish the story that was put out by the authorities'.

The 'facts' were:

1. Suppression of original accounts written on 24 May 1971, and the writing of fresh accounts, which lead to the inference that if the original books were produced, they would not have shown the original entry of Rs 60 lakh in those books.

2. The failure of the bank to report the matter to higher officials 'leads to the inference that such transaction may not be unusual'.

3. The bank did have unaccounted boxes in its vault room. The commission cited the example of S.K. Taparia, deputy secretary and treasurer of the bank, storing and handling his personal boxes in the strongroom, and said it revealed 'gross irregularity and transgression of the rules'. That an official could do all these things rebuts 'the regularity of the bank's strict adherence to the procedures for the custody of safe deposit articles', the commission said, adding that the possibility that such things 'can take place is not completely ruled out'.

4. For Malhotra to say that 'the Prime Minister of a country could issue a cheque on government account without knowing on what account that would be given is to merely hazard a defence of a position which he could not defend. While rejecting his plea that he did all this under a spell, one can only say that he is not telling the truth.'

Whose Money Was It?

In Justice Reddy's view, there wasn't enough evidence to conclude that the money taken out of the bank belonged to the then Prime Minister. Even though the amount was not entered in the registers and the three others directly connected with the withdrawal—bank employees H.R. Khanna, R.P. Batra and Rawail Singh—had kept quiet, it may not be 'sufficient' to conclude without further evidence that the money was Indira Gandhi's or that it was paid on her instructions, Justice Reddy noted.

He suggested that if an inference were to be drawn that the three were willing to oblige people they knew, or believed that the Prime Minister had the power to direct a nationalized bank to pay out money without following rules, the question would arise as to why the Prime Minister would ring up a chief cashier.

Justice Reddy concluded with a phrase similar to what Winston Churchill had used in the context of the Nazi–Soviet pact at the beginning of the Second World War, saying that the investigations had further deepened the enigma wrapped up in the heart of the mystery. In 1939, Churchill had sought to describe Russia's intentions as 'a riddle, wrapped in a mystery, inside an enigma'.

Closure of the Case

The commission submitted two typed copies of its 820-page report, including 168 pages of appendices, to the Ministry of Home Affairs on 23 October 1978, eight days before its term was to expire.

A committee of joint secretaries—V.R. Gupta (finance), S.K. Lall (personnel), N.S. Mehta (law) and V.R. Laxminarayan (CBI)—was constituted to examine the report and suggest actions the government could take.

A.K. Varma, deputy secretary of home affairs, noted in the file that Prime Minister Morarji Desai had taken an 'informal decision' to refer the 'matter' (the report) to Union Industries Minister George Fernandes, the Janata Party's man Friday and a bitter critic of the Indira Gandhi regime, for his comments.

Fernandes, apparently, did not find anything major that could have helped the Janata Party corner Indira Gandhi, and suggested that 'it would be useful and desirable to highlight the memorandum of action taken', and to highlight the 'constraints' under which the commission had functioned.

The committee of joint secretaries went through the report and recommended that:

- The findings be accepted.
- A case of breach of trust against chief cashier Ved Prakash Malhotra be reopened after due legal process.
- Action be taken against the SBI for the lapses and dereliction of duty.
- The Delhi administration take administrative action for shortcomings in the investigations (the police).
- The disposal of the case by local courts be referred to the Delhi High Court.
- Instructions be given to jail authorities regarding (medical) treatment of inmates.
- The Delhi administration take action against officials responsible for not looking after Nagarwala while he was in custody.

On 19 April 1979, the Union Cabinet, chaired by Desai, considered the recommendations of the joint secretaries and the commission's report. The documents were placed in Parliament the next day. The Cabinet, at its meeting, also took note of the 'reported destruction' of certain papers, including SBI records, in the fire at the Tis Hazari court in 1974.

On 18 May 1979, Deputy Secretary Varma recorded in official notes that 'a fairly thorough investigation at a sufficiently high level' had been conducted of the fire at the Tis Hazari and, in 'all probability this [the fire] had been caused by the callousness and negligence of the staff' in charge of the record room.

Most of the files destroyed in the blaze 'related to old cases … which were due for weeding out', Varma noted. 'Nevertheless, a few files concerning the Nagarwala case also appear to have been destroyed in the fire.'

The Delhi administration wanted a fresh investigation as 'the possibility of deliberate arson/mischief [could not] be ruled out', as Verma had commented. However, the home ministry did not subscribe to the view, saying that earlier investigations had been 'thorough and objective', so there was no need to reopen the case.

About the case against V.P. Malhotra, the noting in the file was that since Delhi Police had earlier investigated the 'breach of trust' case (which had fallen through in court), the CBI should investigate the new case. This was noted in the file on 25 June 1979.

The CBI, however, said Delhi Police should reinvestigate the case, 'since except one officer, all police officers directly connected with the investigation' were no longer with Delhi Police. (Kashyap had died in a road accident; Bose had left the police and joined a private organization; and Rajpal, who had by then become a DIG, had been moved out of Delhi. The only officer connected with the probe who was still in Delhi was inspector Hari Dev.)

Delhi Police responded by saying it was too 'short-staffed' to reinvestigate the case, and wanted additional manpower. This was noted by Varma in the file on 24 August 1979.

By then, the political scenario had changed. Charan Singh had walked out of the Janata Party along with Fernandes, Biju Patnaik and Raj Narain, to become Prime Minister with the support of

Indira Gandhi's Congress on 28 July. Charan Singh's Janata Party (Secular) government would, however, last only twenty-three days, as Indira Gandhi withdrew support to his government. Charan Singh resigned, but continued as caretaker Prime Minister until January 1980.

One more meeting of officials was held on 24 October 1979, to clear the confusion about whether the entire Nagarwala case or only the Malhotra case would be reopened.

On 14 January 1980, Indira Gandhi was back in the saddle as Prime Minister, with her party routing the factitious Janata family in the national elections held in the first week of the New Year. The Congress won 353 seats; Desai's Janata Party, which included the erstwhile Jana Sangh group, secured 31 seats; and Charan Singh's Janata Party (Secular) got 41 seats. Neither of the Janata factions had the required strength to be recognized as the Opposition party in the Lok Sabha.

On 11 February 1980, the Cabinet secretary suggested that the 'opinion of the new government' be taken on the case, according to an official file noting. (The file noting did not mention the name of N.K. Mukarji, who was the Cabinet secretary then.)

A subsequent noting in the file included the suggestion of Delhi Police's legal adviser, who said that Malhotra could not be 'rearrested' as the SBI records had been destroyed. On 3 March, it was noted that an additional district magistrate had been asked to hold an inquiry into the affairs at Tihar Jail.

The last noting in the file was: 'It has been stated that the records pertaining to Nagarwala were delivered to the CBI for presenting to the Reddy Commission and some of the essential papers pertaining to the inquiry, in question, are not traceable as the file F 7 (72) ASUT itself is not traceable.'

The case was officially closed on 15 January 1981.

BIBLIOGRAPHY

Abbas, Khawaja Ahmad, *That Woman: Her Seven Years in Power*, Indian Book
Company, New Delhi, 1973.

Chandra, Bipan, *In the Name of Democracy: JP Movement and the Emergency*, Penguin Books, New Delhi, 2017.

Desai, Morarji, *The Story of My Life*, Pergamon Press, Oxford, 1979.

Dev, Dharam Yash, *The Nagarwala Mystery: The Sixty Lakhs State Bank Robbery Story*, Pradip Prakashan, Lucknow, 1977.

Gandhi, Indira, and Norman, Dorothy, *Indira Gandhi: Letters to an American Friend 1950–1984*, Harcourt Brace Jovanovich, UK, 1986.

Gandhi, Maneka, *Sanjay Gandhi*, Vakils, Feffer and Simons Ltd, Bombay, 1980.

Gauba, K.L., *The Mystery of Nagarwala Case*, Hind Pocket Books, New Delhi, 1977.

Ghosh, D.N., *No Regrets*, Rupa Publications India, New Delhi, 2015.

Bhagat, Usha, *Indiraji through My Eyes*, Penguin Books India, Delhi, 2005.

'Indiraji through My Eyes', *Hindustan Times*, 31 August 2005, https://www.hindustantimes.com/books/indiraji-through-my-eyes/story-aYVfI6mcba3rpxws6aFcVO.html

Jayakar, Pupul, *Indira Gandhi: A Biography*, Penguin Books India, Delhi, 1992.

Kapoor, Virendra, 'Vital Papers Missing from Nagarwala Files', *The Motherland*, New Delhi, 13 July 1971.

Kapoor, Virendra, 'Statement Made before the P. Jaganmohan Reddy Commission of Inquiry, Regarding Nagarwala Case', commission report, Government of India, 1978.

Kidwai, Rasheed, *24 Akbar Road: A Short History of the People behind the Fall and Rise of the Congress*, Hachette India, New Delhi, 2011 and 2013.

Kidwai, Rasheed, *Ballot: Ten Episodes That Have Shaped India's Democracy*, Hachette India, New Delhi, 2022, pp. 6-7.

Kidwai, Rasheed, 'Amid Slugfest Over Rafale, the Invisible "Foreign Hand" Makes a Comeback in Indian Politics', News18, 1 October 2018, https://www.news18.com/news/opinion/opinion-amid-slugfest-over-rafale-theinvisible-foreign-hand-makes-a-comeback-in-indian-politics-1894089.html

Kripalani, J.B., 'Those Sixty Lakh Rupees', *The Motherland*, New Delhi, 24 June 1971.

Ananth, V. Krishna (ed.), 'Why 1967 General Election Was a Watershed in Indian Politics and the Lessons It Left Behind', *DNA*, 28 February 2017, https://www.dnaindia.com/analysis/column-1967-poll-that-changed-india-2330738

Malhotra, Inder, *India: Trapped in Uncertainty*, UBS Publishers' Distributors, New Delhi, 1991.

Malhotra, Inder, *Indira Gandhi: A Personal and Political Biography*, Hay House Inc., New Delhi, 2004.

Malkhani, K.R., 'Mrs Gandhi in a Dock; L'affaire Nagarwala', *The Motherland*, New Delhi, 2 June 1971.

Manmohan, 'Nagarwala Primed to Defame Indira?', *Hindustan Times*, New Delhi edition, 10-11 November 1986.

Manmohan, 'Reddy Still Wonders, while Desai Does Not Remember', *Hindustan Times*, New Delhi edition, 12 November 1986.

Manmohan, 'Unexplored CIA Trail in Nagarwala Case', *Hindustan Times*, New Delhi edition, 13 November 1986.

Nayar, Kuldip, *India after Nehru*, Vikas Publishing House, New Delhi, 1975.

Reddy, P. Jaganmohan, 'P. Jaganmohan Reddy Commission of Inquiry, Regarding Nagarwala Case: Report', Government of India, October 1978.

Reddy, P. Jaganmohan, *The Revolution I Have Lived through*, Printwell, Jaipur, 1993.

Seton, Marie, *Panditji: A Portrait of Jawaharlal Nehru*, Dobson Books Ltd, London, 1967.

Smith, R.V., 'The Parsi Link with Delhi', *The Hindu*, 6 January 2020, https://www.thehindu.com/society/history-and-culture/how-the-parsi-communitys-association-with-delhi-dates-back-to-akbars-time/article30492344.ece

Snehi, B.K., '60 Lakhs Fraud', *The Illustrated Weekly of India*, New Delhi, 9 April 1972.

Tandon, B.N., *PMO Diary-1: Prelude to the Emergency*, Konark Publication, New Delhi, 2006.

'Was Sanjay Gandhi's Flight to Mauritius on the Night of the Alleged Theft (May 24) Just a Coincidence?', *Blitz*, Bombay, 4 March 1977.

'Inquiry Reports on 13 Communal Riots Since 1961 "Not Available", CIC Asks MHA for Status', *The Economic Times*, 30 December

2018, https://economictimes.indiatimes.com/news/politics-and-nation/inquiry-reports-on-13-communal-riots-since-1961-not-available-cic-asks-mha-for-status/articleshow/67310258.cms

Karsten, Lucy, 'Taking the Piss: A Brief History of Athletes Drinking Their Own Urine', *The Guardian*, 22 August 2015, https://www.theguardian.com/sport/2015/aug/22/taking-the-piss-a-brief-history-of-athletes-drinkingtheir-own-urine

'The Nagarwala Case: Is the Truth Buried?', *India Today*, 1 May 2015, https://www.indiatoday.in/magazine/cover-story/story/19770430-the-nagarwala-case-is-the-truth-buried-823665-2014-08-06

Vaidya, Abhay, 'Sanjay Gandhi's Maruti Venture Was Point of Discord between Indira, Haksar', *Hindustan Times*, 27 May 2017, https://www.hindustantimes.com/pune-news/sanjay-gandhi-s-maruti-venture-was-point-of-discord-between-indira-haksar/story-eKF1BIn44S91tBwdndrJuO.html

National Archives Records, Government of India, New Delhi (maintained as file). Authors have accessed and have noted down the file details for all references made in the manuscript, such as

(a) Case diary of Delhi Police

(b) Sworn affidavits of the persons who gave evidence before the Reddy Commission

(c) Letters and documents provided by the CBI and individuals

(d) The home ministry file dealing with the Reddy Commission

(e) Trial court orders related to the case that are part of the Archives record

ABOUT THE AUTHORS

Prakash Patra is a New Delhi–based journalist. He began his career as a crime reporter with *National Herald* in 1980 and has worked with *The Pioneer*, *Hindustan Times* and *The Telegraph* in various senior positions. Political reporting is his forte and he has extensively covered major political happenings for close to three decades. He has been a member of the Press Council of India, secretary general of the Press Association of India and president of the Press Club of India. He has written scripts for two films, one of which has won a national award.

Rasheed Kidwai is a journalist, an author, a columnist and a talking head. He is a visiting fellow with the Observer Research Foundation (ORF), and a former associate editor of *The Telegraph*. Kidwai tracks government, politics, community affairs and Hindi cinema. He is the author of *Sonia: A Biography*, *24 Akbar Road*, *Ballot*, *Neta Abhineta: Bollywood Star Power in Indian Politics*, *The House of Scindias*, *My Life in Indian Politics* (co-authored with Mohsina Kidwai) and *Bharat Ke Pradhanmantri*.

HarperCollins *Publishers* India

At HarperCollins India, we believe in telling the best stories and finding the widest readership for our books in every format possible. We started publishing in 1992; a great deal has changed since then, but what has remained constant is the passion with which our authors write their books, the love with which readers receive them, and the sheer joy and excitement that we as publishers feel in being a part of the publishing process.

Over the years, we've had the pleasure of publishing some of the finest writing from the subcontinent and around the world, including several award-winning titles and some of the biggest bestsellers in India's publishing history. But nothing has meant more to us than the fact that millions of people have read the books we published, and that somewhere, a book of ours might have made a difference.

As we look to the future, we go back to that one word— a word which has been a driving force for us all these years.

Read.